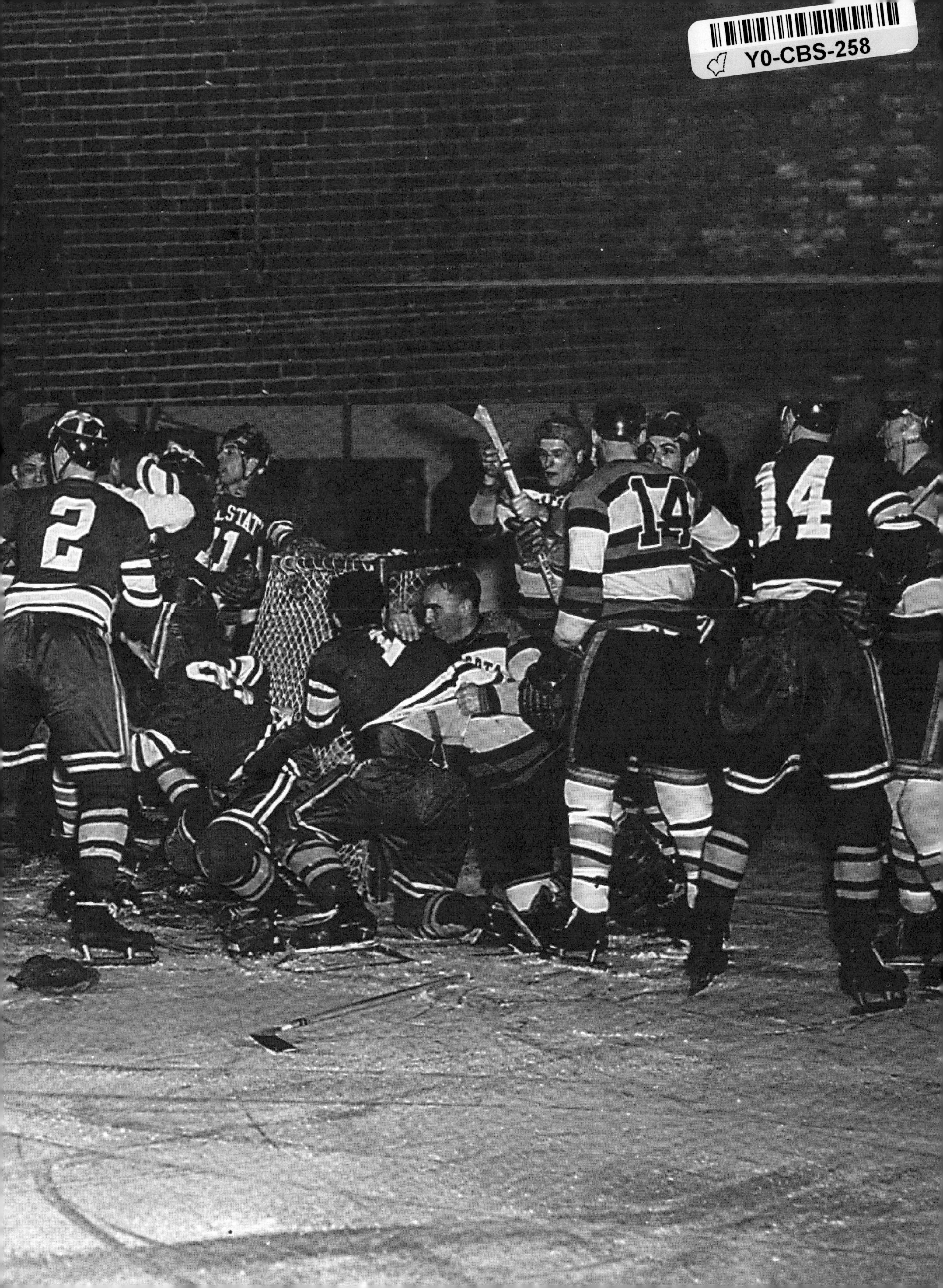
2
14
14

© 1997 Mike Prisuta
Visions Sports Management Group, Inc.

All rights reserved.
No part of this book may be reproduced in any form or by any electronic or mechanical means,
including information storage and retrieval systems, without written permission in writing
from the author and publisher, except by a reviewer who may quote brief passages in a review.

All photography, except where noted, is exclusive property of Michigan State University

Visions Sports Management Group, Inc.
P.O. Box 338, East Lansing, Michigan 48826-0338

Jacket and interior design by: Camron Gnass

Printed by Walsworth in the United States of America
First Printing: October 1997

ISBN: 0-9658933-1-6

Thank You

The publisher would like to thank the
following for their support of

AWE INSPIRING
The Storied History of Spartan Hockey

Century Cellunet

Citizen's Bank

The College Store

Harley Hotchkiss

Joe Louis Arena

The Kellogg Center

Michigan Hockey Magazine

MSU Alumni Association

MSU Blue Line Club

MSU Bookstore

MSU Federal Credit Union

Spartan Country

Spartan Sports Den

Student Book Store

Dedicated to my parents, Bronko and Margaret Prisuta, who gave three children the freedom to attend any university they could qualify for academically (even out-of-state schools) and the financial backing to make it happen; to my sister, Nancy K. Murphy; and to my brother, Robert Prisuta (a fellow Spartan).

Acknowledgements

The first step in trying to determine whether this project was feasible was making a trip to the Michigan State University Sports Information Department, to find out if the necessary pictures, statistics, rosters, press releases, etc., were available. Thankfully, Michigan State is, among other things, a leader in the sports information and publicity field, and possessed a wealth of background material and file photographs essential to a work such as this. Sincere thanks are thus owed to the entire MSU Sports Information Department for being so thorough and complete in record keeping, and for cooperation above and beyond the call offered to a reporter who would drop in unannounced periodically to conduct research. Although just about everyone who works in the Spartan Sports Information Department was inconvenienced at some point throughout this lengthy process, a discouraging word was never heard.

Special thanks are reserved for Sports Information Director John Lewandowski, sports information intern Nate Ewell, and Assistant Sports Information Director John Farina, a professional colleague and a friend since my days as an undergrad at The State News.

A debt of gratitude to Halama Brothers Electric in Monaca, Pa., must also be acknowledged. Without their repeated use of HBE's office space and supplies, computers and laser printers, and without the patience and direction of HBE President Michael C. Halama in getting these themes and ideas from the theory stage onto the printed page, "Awe Inspiring: The Storied History of Spartan Hockey" never would have gotten off the ground.

Without the creativity, resourcefulness, and inspired leadership of publisher Visions Sports Management, meanwhile, this work might well have been just another sports book in an already glutted market. Instead, thanks to Visions' people, publishing, and promotional skills, we believe we've come up with something special.

Editor Stephanie Waite and photographer Sylvester Washington Jr. are also deserving of recognition for their contributions, as is the management and editorial staff at the Beaver County Times in Beaver, Pa., for providing the opportunity to get the work started via a three-month leave of absence from my responsibilities at the newspaper.

Finally, heartfelt appreciation must be extended to those who have served the MSU hockey program over the years. We're not just talking about those who played or coached or the many who were interviewed while this book was being pieced together, either, but anyone and everyone—regardless of the era or the capacity in which they served. This is their story most of all.

Mike Prisuta
August 12, 1997

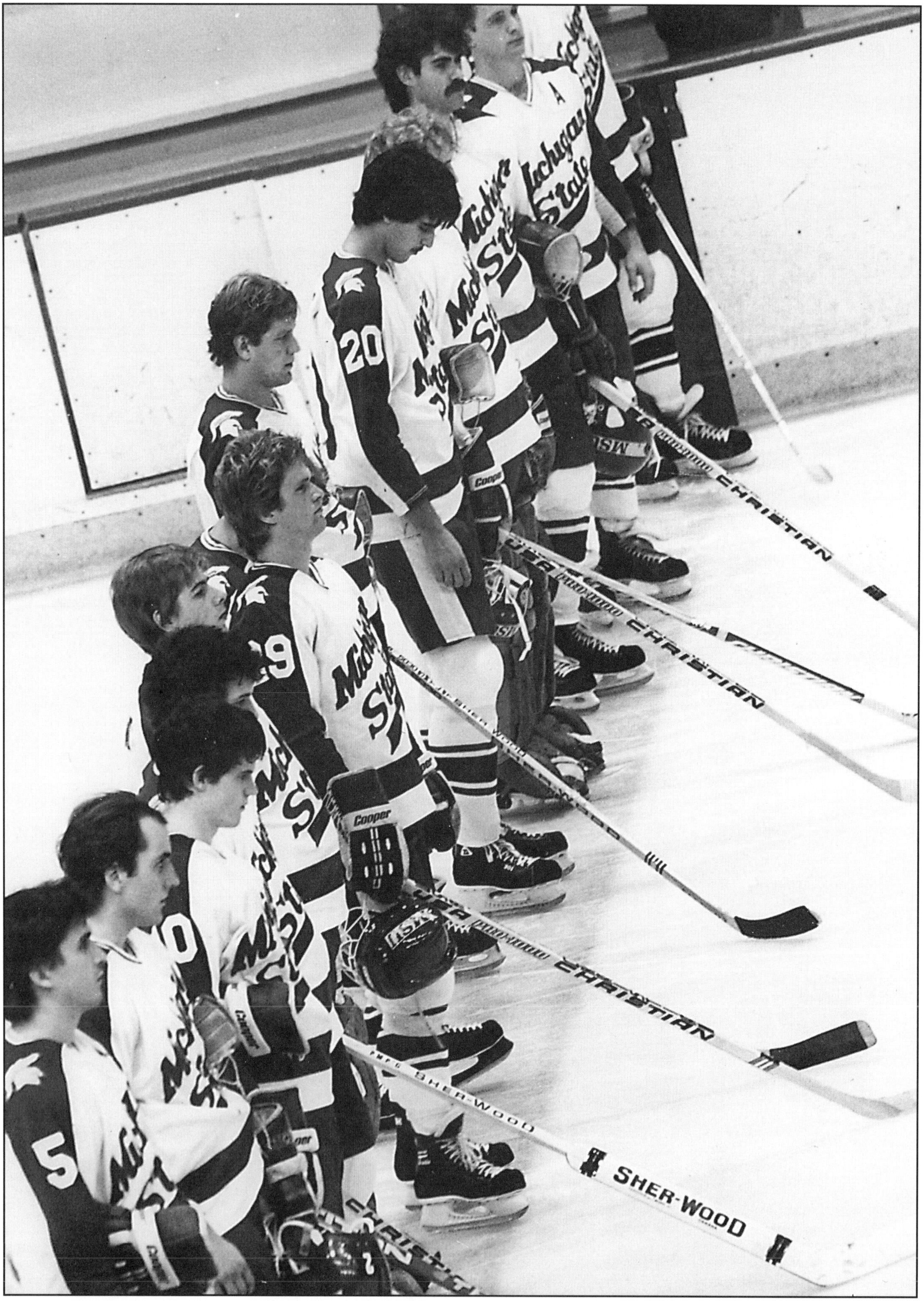
20
CHRISTIAN
Cooper
5
SHER-WOOD

Table of Contents

Foreword-Amo Bessone...viii

Foreword-Ron Mason..ix

Introduction..x

Chapter One- "It Was Pretty Simple, if You Wanted to Play, You Played"..........................2

Chapter Two- "We'll be Lucky to Win a Single Game" 8

Chapter Three- "They Made Believers Out of Everybody"........................20

Chapter Four- "I Had a Driving Passion to Score Goals and to be the Best"..........28

Chapter Five- "He Was the Architect for the Excellent Program and Facilities We Have Here Today" 36

Chapter Six- "One Hell of a Place to Coach" 46

Chapter Seven- "We Won Everything but What We Wanted to Win"............58

Chapter Eight- "As Good Once as They Ever Were"................................70

Chapter Nine- "It Was My Dream to Wear the Green and White" 84

Chapter Ten- "There Are No In-Betweens"..96

Chapter Eleven- "A Sport of High Recognition and Interest"....................106

Chapter Twelve- "We Took It to the Limit"..120

Chapter Thirteen- "The Enthusiasm of a Scientist" 128

Chapter Fourteen- "It Rekindles the Great Memories That You Have of Being There"........138

Appendix-..149

Foreword

- by -
Amo Bessone

I was asked to write a few thoughts about Spartan hockey but to limit my thoughts to just a few is almost impossible. Whenever I think of the Green and White, Michigan State University, East Lansing, etc., so many tremendous memories are brought to life.

But if I must limit my thoughts, I have to think about what really matters, not just with Spartan hockey, but in life. People. People have always been the most important thing to me. Spartan hockey allowed me to meet and become friends with so many great people. Fellow coaches, my players, university officials, fans, and even referees!! It is the people that have made Spartan hockey great as well as the entire sport of college hockey.

Whether it was a post-game party at the house with a visiting coach, sharing a joke with a player, or helping the MSU Blue Line Club get started, it was always those relationships with people that mattered most to me. Our Final Four appearances were great, but the people who made it possible were greater.

There is no question in my mind that I have been blessed. I was blessed to have gotten the opportunity to coach at such a great school as Michigan State University. I was blessed to have such a wonderful family. And I have been blessed to have been associated with so many great people. "Awe Inspiring" is the story of people. Enjoy the story.

Amo Bessone
August 1997

Coaching Record of Amo Bessone
28 Seasons at MSU
367-427-20   .463

Final Four Appearances:

1959	Second Place	
1966	National Champions	
1967	Third Place	

All-Americans:

1959	Joe Selinger G		1971	Don Thompson F
1962	John Chandik G		1972	Jim Watt G
1964	Carl Lackey D		1973	Bob Boyd D
1965	Doug Roberts F		1974	Norm Barnes D
1966	Doug Volmar F			Steve Colp F
1969	Rick Duffett G		1975	Tom Ross F
			1976	Tom Ross F

Foreword

- by -

Ron Mason

When I first met Mike Prisuta, I knew he was a sports addict and especially a tremendous hockey enthusiast. When he aptly named Joe Louis Arena, Munn Arena East in the 1980's, I knew that he was on the right track.

Even though Mike has moved to Pittsburgh, PA., I have talked with him on many occasions, and he makes special trips to see our team play, and always has been a great Spartan believer and has a wealth of hockey knowledge both at the college and professional level.

I respect his writing ability, and certainly his portrayal of the history of Spartan Hockey that takes you behind the bench, on the street, in the locker room, and in the stands, recounting all the excitement and in some cases agony of a major college hockey program.

I think you will enjoy reading this book, as there have been many unique situations over the years, surrounding our program.

Ron Mason
August 1997

Coaching record of Ron Mason

18 seasons at MSU

486-233-44   .666

Final Four Appearances:	1984	Fourth place
	1986	National Champions
	1987	Second Place
	1988	Third Place
	1992	Third Place

All-Americans:	1982	Ron Scott G	1989	Kip Miller F
	1983	Ron Scott G		Bobby Reynolds F
	1985	Dan McFall D	1990	Kip Miller F
		Kelly Miller F	1991	Jason Woolley D
		Craig Simpson F	1992	Joby Messier D
	1986	Mike Donnelly F		Dwayne Norris F
	1987	Mitch Messier F	1993	Bryan Smolinski F

Introduction

"The game was for more than just us"

Exactly when the initial inspiration for this project first surfaced is uncertain, but the precise moment I knew it had to be done occurred sometime on the afternoon of July 10, 1993, at Munn Arena.

That's when Nelson DeBenedet told me about "The Fight."

The occasion was the 1993 MSU Hockey Alumni Reunion, which featured a round of golf at Timber Ridge Golf Course on Friday and then a couple of alumni games on Saturday at Munn, followed by a banquet that evening at the University Club. As a former hockey beat writer and columnist for The State News living in suburban Pittsburgh, I had welcomed the opportunity to return to campus that weekend to renew some old acquaintances and in all likelihood forge some new ones.

That's where DeBenedet came in.

Since he was a former Spartan icer (1967-69) and a former member of the Pittsburgh Penguins the team I had followed passionately while growing up and as an undergrad at MSU, and one of the teams I cover as part of my professional responsibilities these days at the Beaver County (Pa.) Times I made a point of seeking DeBenedet out. I wanted to hear what he had to say about two of my favorite subjects, Michigan State and the Pens.

When he told me about "The Fight," I laughed so hard I almost fell out of the Munn Arena bleachers.

It seems the Spartans, DeBenedet explained, had a defenseman back in the 1960s named Doug French, who was definitely on the wild side. And one night during a game against Minnesota, French got into several run-ins with the Golden Gophers' Dick Paradise, a player DeBenedet said also had a reputation as something of a free spirit. Now, two players such as this dropping the gloves and squaring off wasn't all that unusual at the time, DeBenedet pointed out, but the story of what transpired after the game was one for the ages.

This was back when the Spartans played in Demonstration Hall, and had to dress (along with the visiting team) across the street in Jenison Field House. Most nights, this led to nothing more than a little inconvenience for both squads. But this time, Paradise decided to take things as far as possible.

When the game ended and the two teams made their way back across the street to Jenison, he was waiting there for French, who as luck would have it was the last of the Spartans to leave Dem Hall. The two began brawling again, DeBenedet recalled laughing almost hysterically himself in the retelling and didn't stop until several minutes later, when MSU coach Amo Bessone and others came sprinting out of the locker room to break up the fracas.

The way French tells it is even better.

"I got my ass kicked," he recalled. "We had fought during the game, and then going back to Jenison after ... right by one of those side doors, he popped out from behind one of the bushes.

"He had on a white topcoat. He looked like a ghost coming at me. A big, strong kid he was, too.

Geez, he kicked my duff."

Apparently, this type of thing is part of the Spartan Hockey experience. Still, during my 41/2 years on campus as a student and nearly another 10 of following the program after graduation, I had never before heard the story. I began to wonder almost immediately what other entertaining tales were out there that others had to tell.

There were plenty.

There was the night Sandy McAndrew got more than he bargained for in Ann Arbor.

"My sophomore year, 1964-65," McAndrew said. "I hit Mel Wakabayashi, and as I hit him I fell and my stick just went loose in my arms. We slid into the boards, and they didn't have any screens on top of the boards. Well, as I hit the boards and started to get up, a fan leaned over, picked up my stick and broke the stick over my helmet. Of course, I went flat on my back as if I were dead.

"Amo came running across the ice. The fan just kind of stood there and shook for a few seconds, then ran out of the building. Amo went after him.

"So then on Monday, he calls me into the office and says, "How ya' doin'?' I said, "I've had a headache for a couple of days, but I'm doing all right.' And he said, "Well, do you want to press charges?'

"Not being aware of what "pressing charges' was all about, I said, "Well, all I have is a headache, and it'll probably go away today.' And he said, "Well, our school would rather that you not press charges.' I said that was all right with me.

"I think the guy that did that ended up getting a 10-year ban on going to hockey games. And you know, I probably could have gotten some money out of that. But back then we never thought that way. I still don't think that way, but that was quite a unique episode."

This, too, is part of the Spartan Hockey experience.

So is a frigid trip to Grand Forks, N.D., on which the Spartans played games against the Fighting Sioux in sub-zero temperatures in an "indoor" rink in February of 1967. This was back when the Fighting Sioux were still providing ice the old fashioned way (by letting atmospheric conditions create it rather than by employing an ice-manufacturing system built into the arena's floor) and thus couldn't heat their building even on nights when the temperature dipped to 28 below and then to 7 below zero. The Spartans tried to cope by wearing long underwear and stocking caps. They nearly froze, anyway.

"I've played outside when the wind was blowing and skated with the snow in my face, but this is the worst yet," MSU All-American Doug Volmar complained.

"I was just simply miserable," reported goalie Gaye Cooley. "My feet and hands felt like they were frozen. My glove was so stiff I couldn't keep hold of the puck."

"I'll never come back here again until they get heat," Bessone vowed.

This, too, is part of the Spartan Hockey experience.

So is a glorious stretch in the 1980s that saw Michigan State humble arch-rival Michigan so easily and so often it became almost routine.

"It's not as big a thrill as it once was," coach Ron Mason said of playing the Wolverines in January of 1985. "Five or six years ago, this was the game we pointed to. It was a chance to do something positive for our recruiting, get some good local press and at least be able to say we were headed in the right direction after the occasional win against them.

"Now, they're looking at it that way. It's getting harder and harder for us to play Michigan because we've had so much success against them."

Success continued to come easily that January weekend, as an 11-2, 9-4 home-and-home sweep upped MSU's record to 15-1-1 in its last 17 games against UM.

This, too, is part of the Spartan Hockey experience.

So is an in-house confrontation that preceded a national-championship celebration in Providence, R.I., in 1986.

"At our off-day practice at the Final Four, we were so relaxed it was unbelievable," said Dee Rizzo, a forward-defenseman role-player on the '86 champs. "Our feeling is we're going to win it all tomorrow night. It doesn't matter who we're going to play, Harvard, the New York Islanders, it doesn't matter. We're ready to go.

"We're so loose (defenseman) Tom Tilley grabs the Sparty head (the oversized appendage worn by MSU's skating Spartan mascot) and starts skating around. He was waving the 'S' flag and falling down and we were just laughing our asses off.

"Then we started warming up and (forward) Brian McReynolds starts yelling at a couple of the guys over breakout passes. We were so loose and we figured, "Hey, it's not like we're going to learn anything today,' and maybe we weren't concentrating and some of our passes were going astray. And unfortunately for Mac, who was just a great hockey player, he took like three in his skates and he got pissed off and he started yelling.

"I sort of yelled back at Mac. I basically said, "Mac, what's your problem? We're one day away from the biggest game of our lives. Will you just relax and quit yelling at people?'

"Than Mac started yelling at me. And then Mase (Mason) comes over and wants to know what the hell's going on and pretty soon I was almost in tears, tying to explain to him that everything was all right."

It was soon enough. The Spartans beat Harvard, and the championship was commemorated by a photo of one player in Green thrusting a finger into the air while another is hoisting him off the ice. It's a picture that's been featured in the MSU Hockey Media Guide, one that hangs in the hockey office at Munn and one that over the years has become as famous and as beloved to Spartan Hockey as that shot of Levi Jackson bolting 88 yards to beat No. 1-ranked Ohio State in 1974 is to MSU football, or the reproduction of Shawn Respert kissing the block 'S' at center court on the Breslin Center floor has to MSU basketball. It's also a picture so emotional and compelling that it was featured prominently on the cover of this project.

The player telling the world "We're No. 1" is Dee Rizzo.

The player lifting Rizzo to the heavens is Brian McReynolds.

This, too, is part of the Spartan Hockey experience.

So is Joby Messier proving during the 1995-96 season that while Spartan captains may be replaced from time to time, they never truly abdicate.

Messier, a nasty-as-he-had-to-be defenseman from 1988-89 to 1991-92, was in East Lansing on leave from his professional career while rehabilitating an injury. And he was appalled by what he saw on Saturday, Feb. 10 at Munn Arena.

Fresh from absorbing a 7-1 thumping at Western Michigan, the Spartans needed to bounce back at home to keep their Central Collegiate Hockey Association championship hopes on course and to avoid letting the Broncos crowd back into the picture. And when junior forward Tony Tuzzolino scored to give State a 3-1 third-period lead, it appeared MSU would do so. Tuzzolino, however, let emotion get the best of him. In celebrating what at this point was one of the biggest goals of the season, Tuzzolino dropped his stick and began shaking his gloved hands (as if to suggest "My stick's so hot even I can't handle it"). It was a dose of hot dog that Mason usually has a hard time swallowing from opponents, let alone from one of his players.

Messier let Tuzzolino know the act was unacceptable a few days later by entering the Spartan locker room and attaching Tuzzolino's gloves to his stick with so much athletic tape that the gloves were no longer visible. Messier also left a note: "Maybe the next time you won't make such an ass of yourself."

This, too, is part of the Spartan Hockey experience.

So is raw emotion so profound it can reduce an about -to-graduate student athlete to tears.

"There was this couple, Keith and Mary Groty, and they had a son who was 9-years-old," said John Sturges, a flashy forward on the spectacular and explosive MSU teams from 1972-73 through 1975-76. "And one day, Keith came up to me after practice and said, "Can I talk to you for a minute?' I said "yeah, yeah, yeah ...'

"I didn't know who he was. But he talked about his kid having terminal cancer, and how I was his son's favorite hockey player and would I mind, if I had the chance, coming to visit him? I was like "uh ... OK ... sure ...'

"This kid ended up being an inspiration to the whole team. I would go visit him and the team would go visit him, we'd bring him signed hockey sticks, we gave him a jersey ... this kid was really strong. But he ended up dying.

"Then, my senior year, at the hockey banquet, this Keith and Mary Groty got up and presented me with a little award. It was a little mug with an inscription on it. And when they spoke, they spoke not only of me but of the entire team and what we had done for their son. There wasn't a dry eye in the place.

"I show my kids that sometimes now. There was an article written about it and I keep it in that little cup. That made me grow up. That made me realize the game was for more than just us."

The Spartan Hockey experience is indeed for more than just the players, coaches and administrators at Michigan State. It is for all of us, for Spartans everywhere, whether they be undergraduates, alumni or simply those who have chosen to adopt Michigan State into their hearts.

Hopefully, this project will bring you a little closer to it.

Enjoy!

And Go Green!

Mike Prisuta
MSU Class of 1984

In Memorium

The publisher and author would like to recognize the hard work, dedication, and love of Spartan hockey from a person who truly embodied the Spartan Spirit.

Connie McAuliffe

AWE INSPIRING

The Storied History of Spartan Hockey

It was pretty simple, if you wanted to play, you played...

CHAPTER 1

Chapter 1

Knute Rockne was a fan of Spartan hockey.

On second thought, perhaps "fan" isn't exactly accurate after all. Rockne, it must be said for the record, wasn't a regular follower of the team, either before or after becoming a "Pigskin Messiah" in South Bend, Ind. And the Spartans weren't even known as the Spartans when they first began to dabble in this hockey nonsense way back in the 1920s. They were referred to as the "Aggies" at the time, and they weren't officially sponsored by the Michigan Agricultural College.

Still, on at least one occasion, The Rock was there.

"One time at Notre Dame they had an outdoor rink back then one of our players got his foot cut right through the skate," recalled Carl Moore, a member of the first MAC team in 1922 and the squad's captain in 1926. "Well, somebody came over between periods and helped to bandage it up. We didn't know who it was at the time, but we found out later it was Knute Rockne.

"Everybody was interested in hockey back then. Even Knute Rockne was there to watch a game."

Must have been the novelty of the thing.

The records show that what is now Michigan State University first put a team on the ice on Jan. 11, 1922. The game was played against the University of Michigan, in Ann Arbor. Michigan won, 5-1.

Oh, the indignity of humble beginnings.

But this, at least, was a beginning, and one

The 1922 team, the ones that started it all way back when. M.A.C.'s puck pioneers included, top row, from left: Carl Moore, John Noblet, unidentified, and Russell Boyle. Front row, from left: Leighman Crosby, Clifford Hauptli, Harry Burris, Frank Doherty, unidentified, Fred MacDonald, and George Delisle.

not entirely unlike the starts that spawned the football and basketball programs that would eventually put the nation's pioneer land-grant institution on the athletic map. Although football was first played in 1896, it wasn't until the 1930s under Charlie Bachman, and then again after the arrival of coach Clarence L. "Biggie" Munn in 1947, that the Spartans established themselves nationally, paving the way for the school's admittance into the Big Ten Conference in 1953 in the process. As for basketball, that was first played by the Aggies in 1899, but it wasn't until the 1920s that the program would uncover a coach who would discover success and longevity. Benjamin F. VanAlstyne took over in 1926-27 and stayed at the basketball helm through 1942-43.

So it was neither surprising nor unprecedented that hockey started out at something less than a championship level.

Hockey's problem, alas, was staying power.

Only three games were played in 1922, six the following season including the first victory in school history, a 6-0 home shutout of the Lansing Independents on Feb. 11, 1923 and none in 1924. Just one game was staged in 1925, when the school officially changed its name to Michigan State College, while from 1926 through 1930 schedules that contained at least four games but never more than seven were completed.

There never was all that much to get excit-

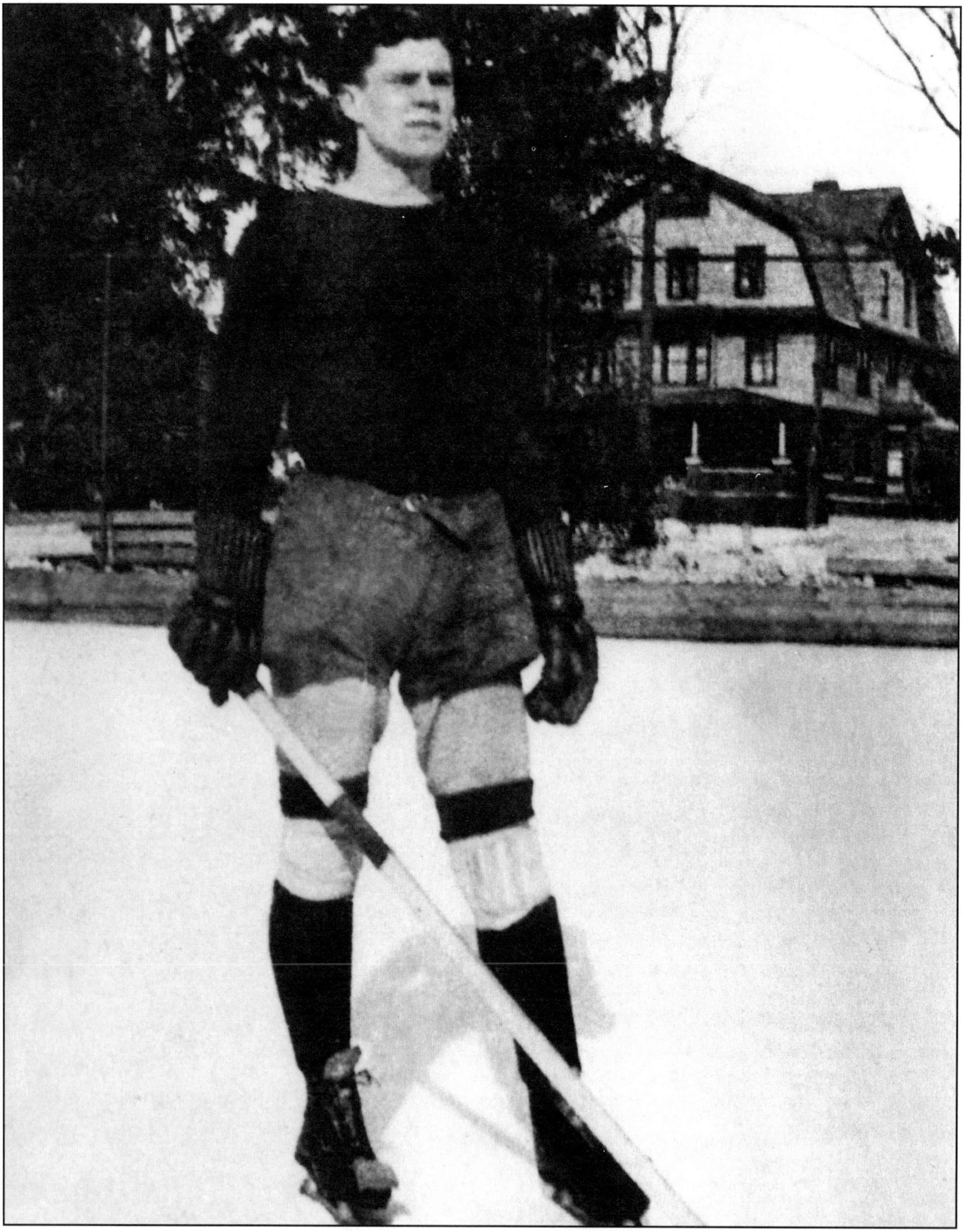

ed about. Such a pedestrian pace, however, would soon prove quite appealing when compared to the alternative. For after the entire 1931 schedule was canceled because of weather conditions (playing outside, it had to be cold enough to maintain ice but not so cold that no one cared to venture outdoors to play or watch) and the 1932 campaign was well on the way to suffering a similar fate, the sport was dropped entirely. It didn't resurface again until 1950.

That 19-year hiatus must have been hell on recruiting, but we digress.

Back in 1922, when that first official game was played (according to Fred W. Stabley's "Spartan Saga," a pair of informal games had been staged in 1906 against Lansing High School), hockey itself was in its embryo stages in the United States (the Boston Bruins wouldn't become the first American-based team to compete for the Stanley Cup until 1924-25). Not surprisingly then, what passed for hockey on a frozen river in the Roaring '20s only moderately resembled the game that's played before packed houses at Joe Louis and Munn arenas today.

"I was from Sault Ste. Marie (Mich.), and we had enough fellas down here that we were able to organize it," Moore said, recounting how that first team came into being. "It was pretty simple, if you wanted to play, you played."

Bureaucracy, red tape, Title IX, volumes of NCAA regulations and other modern concerns weren't a problem.

"We only had about 3,000 students back then," Moore pointed out. "We decided we wanted to have a team and that was it. All of us were from the U.S. I don't think there were any Canadians. We rode over on the old Interurban (a series of heavy-weight, electric streetcars that in the pre-

Carl Moore, a member of the Michigan Agricultural College's first hockey team in 1922 and the squad's first captain in 1926, strikes a simple pose on a simple outdoor rink.

Depression days linked Michigan cities such as Lansing, Jackson and Ann Arbor) down to Ann Arbor, played the game, they brought us something to eat and then we went back on the Interurban.

"We didn't have the blue lines. We didn't have the red line. And you had to skate onsides at all times. If the puck went back, the whole team had to come back behind the puck. You could pass the puck ahead as long as the man you were passing to was equal to you, then he'd have to go get it. That made it twice as much work.

"We didn't hit like they do today. I just don't see this charging. If I had anything to do with it, I'd kick 'em out the first time they banged somebody into the boards; that's wrong. But one thing I remember is you could give a guy the (butt) end of your stick in the ribs and nobody would notice.

"The standard boards were three or three-and-a-half feet. I think Olympic hockey was using one-foot boards at the time. We never used slap shots. Once in a while to clear the zone maybe, but not to shoot. And at the time we were playing quarters. Basketball was the same at that time, four quarters. And you could only substitute once in a quarter, which meant that if you were any good you didn't come out, except maybe once a game. You could go back in once if you came out.

"I don't remember the timing, what it amounted to (in minutes). After a while we went to thirds (three periods). That was called 'Canadian style,' because that's what Canada was playing at the time.

"We were not recognized, even as a minor sport. We never got letters or anything, but (the school) did back us as a team. We had a trainer who used to work on us and take care of us. The equipment, almost everything was cast off. We had old, green jerseys that buttoned between your legs. That was the old football jersey. And we had these old shorts. They gave us jockstraps and metal cups. There were no other pads. Sometimes, somebody would wear, I think it was an old, fiber football pad, but that was it. We didn't even wear a cap or a hat or anything, let alone the helmets they wear now. We'd have socks, but we didn't wear underwear until it got too damn cold out. They furnished us with some once it got colder. We did have the very best gloves that were made (although the goalie in 1926, George Delisle, who was also a third baseman at MSC, opted for a baseball glove for his catching hand). You had to have your own skates, too, but they sharpened them for you."

Initially, they played not on the banks of the Red Cedar, but on the Red Cedar itself (Notre Dame was far from the only institution relying on outdoor ice at the time). As the 1920s roared on, games were eventually moved to tennis courts near Morrill Hall, and finally to courts adjacent to Demonstration Hall.

"Every time we played, even that first year on the river, after we played the ice would be flooded to take the wrinkles out," Moore said. "They would pay a couple of us players 40 cents an hour to take care of it. We'd stay a couple of hours and get 80 cents a piece.

"That was a lot of dough in those days."

The first opponents were Michigan, Notre Dame and the Lansing Independents. Playing without a coach in 1922 and 1923, the 20-or-so hockey-playing Aggies went a combined 2-7 (the two wins were over the Lansing Independents; the team was a disappointing 0-7 against the Fighting Irish and Wolverines).

Finally, in 1925, a leader emerged.

John H. Kobs.

Also the basketball coach at MSC in 1924-25 and 1925-26 (he went a combined 11-26 for a .297 winning percentage) and the freshman football coach for a stretch, Kobs wasn't exactly the Toe Blake or Ron Mason of his day. Baseball was Kobs' game, and the home field where Steve Garvey, Mike Marshall, Kirk Gibson and so many others starred is quite appropriately named in Kobs' honor.

Under Kobs' direction, Michigan State won 557 games and lost 364 for a winning percentage of .605 over 39 seasons. He suffered through just four losing campaigns in his nearly four-decade stint at MSU, and he led his 1954 team to the Big Ten and NCAA District No. 4 playoff championships, and

Although none of his former hockey players made it into the NHL, John H. Kobs helped M.S.U's Robin Roberts become a baseball Whiz Kid in Philadelphia.

to a third-place finish at the College World Series in Omaha, Neb. The Philadelphia Phillies' Robin Roberts, Dick Radatz of the Boston Red Sox and the Los Angeles Dodgers' Ron Perranoski are among those who played baseball for Kobs and went on to play in the major leagues.

As far as hockey was concerned, however, Kobs had much in common with his players. He was trying something new because it was appealing, physically demanding and competitive, just as they were. Still, John H. Kobs was a coach in every sense of the word.

"He was great," Moore gushed. "I can't ever remember seeing John with skates on, but he knew athletics and he knew how to get you in shape. With John, you were either in shape or you didn't play.

"With Kobs, we'd practice every day for an hour or so. It was scrimmaging more than anything; scrimmaging, always scrimmaging. He didn't call signals or any of that. I don't know if Kobs ever played hockey, but he was from Minnesota (actually, Kobs was a native of Cavalier, N.D., but he attended high school in Lake City, Minn., and graduated from Hamline University in St. Paul, Minn.) so I guess he knew enough about it. He helped with everything when we'd scrimmage.

"And after we'd scrimmage, he'd line us all up at one end the whole bunch and then he'd blow that whistle. And we were all supposed to start at the same time and see who could get to the other end first. And when you got to the other end, he'd

John H. Kobs, M.S.C.'s first hockey coach.

blow that whistle again. And if you were the first one going in the first direction, he'd expect you to be the first one again coming back.

"With Kobs, you wanted to be the first one coming back. He was a swell fella."

The team didn't improve drastically under Kobs, but it improved nonetheless. The 1928 squad went 3-3 (.500 at last), with the victories coming in a pair of hard-fought, 1-0 decisions over an outfit known as the Battle Creek Independents (by now MSC was branching out), and with a 2-1 triumph over Michigan (how sweet it was). That season was followed up by a 3-3-1 run in 1929. Two of the wins that year came over a congregation listed only as "Detroit" in the MSU Hockey media guide (bet it wasn't the Red Wings); the other was over a group representing the Battle Creek Civic Club. The tie was a double-overtime, scoreless affair with Battle Creek-Ralph's Sports Shop (and you thought playing Ferris State in Big Rapids, Mich., lacked glamour). In 1930 the record dipped to 1-4 (MSC fell to 0-1-1 all-time against Ralph's in the process).

And that was it until the 1950.

Moore, meanwhile, had to wait even longer than that to get his letterman's jacket. Much longer. Four-plus decades longer.

That didn't happen until the 1993-94 season, but for Moore it was worth the wait. During a ceremony at Munn Arena he received not only a letterman's jacket, but an MSU jersey adorned with the No. 1 at the appropriate spots and his name stitched across the back, and a large photo of the 1926 team. It was a fitting tribute for the man who had been the school's first official captain and one of its hockey trailblazers.

"We didn't think it was all that big a deal starting out," said Moore, who dropped the first puck in Munn Arena history at another ceremony commemorating the facility's official opening in 1974. "Hockey was popular in the Soo back then. We just wanted to play."

By 1926, the name had been officially changed to Michigan State College and the squad had grown. Pictured are, from left: Harold Rich, unidentified, Clifford Hauptli, Russell Van Meter, Carl Moore, Robin Hancock, Sim Keller, Harry Burris, Frank Hodge, unidentified, George Delisle, and coach John H. Kobs.

We'll be lucky to win a single game...

CHAPTER
2

Chapter 2

They began again in 1950. Play was actually supposed to resume at Michigan State in the fall of 1949, but delays in the completion of the ice plant at Demonstration Hall forced some adjustments to be made in the schedule. In the grand scheme of things, however, when the season started really didn't matter; getting a team organized and eventually onto the ice did.

"They wanted to get into the Big Ten conference," said Harold Paulsen, Michigan State's first coach when hockey moved indoors, "and they thought it was pretty important to have a hockey team to get into the Big Ten."

University president John Hannah, thus, was determined to get one. That's why plans had been enacted to turn Dem Hall into a hockey arena. And that's why Paulsen, a three-time All-American and a member of Minnesota's fabled, undefeated 1939-40 AAU championship team (legendary Gopher coach John Mariucci was also on that squad) had been hired on Aug. 1, 1948, to coax the fledgling program into existence and beyond.

There was, however, one major problem in the early going.

"They were more concerned about football, basketball and track," Paulsen said. "They wanted a hockey team all right, but they didn't want to put any money into it.

"We really had a hard time getting started at all."

One of the hang-ups was the recruiting budget; Paulsen didn't have one. And even if he would

Although coach Harold Paulsen had no use for fighting, brawls broke out occasionally, anyway. This one, against Paulsen's alma mater, Minnesota, delighted the crowd at Dem Hall during the 1950-51 season.

have been blessed with an abundance of funds, "You just couldn't get hockey players to come there," he said. "In that area of Michigan, hockey wasn't very popular. Detroit had some high school hockey, but that was about the only place, there and in the Upper Peninsula. So prospects were pretty skeptical about coming to Michigan State. And I really couldn't blame them, either."

Before Michigan State could worry about players, however, there were some other concerns that had to be addressed. Paramount among those was what any players Paulsen would manage to recruit would be playing with.

"One of the first things we did was find out what equipment from the early teams was still salvageable," said Sam Breck, Michigan State's first hockey manager. "All of that had been stored someplace in Jenison Field House (the longtime home of Michigan State basketball). We had to go looking for it. When we found it, all that was there were gloves and sticks, and the gloves were stiff as boards. We hauled them out and did what we could to oil and lubricate them."

In starting over, it seems no job was too small. And at first, there was always another job to do. Other equipment had to be ordered, except for skates. The school wasn't providing those at the time, which made Paulsen's nearly impossible recruiting job just a little bit tougher.

Another one of Breck's tasks was to make a

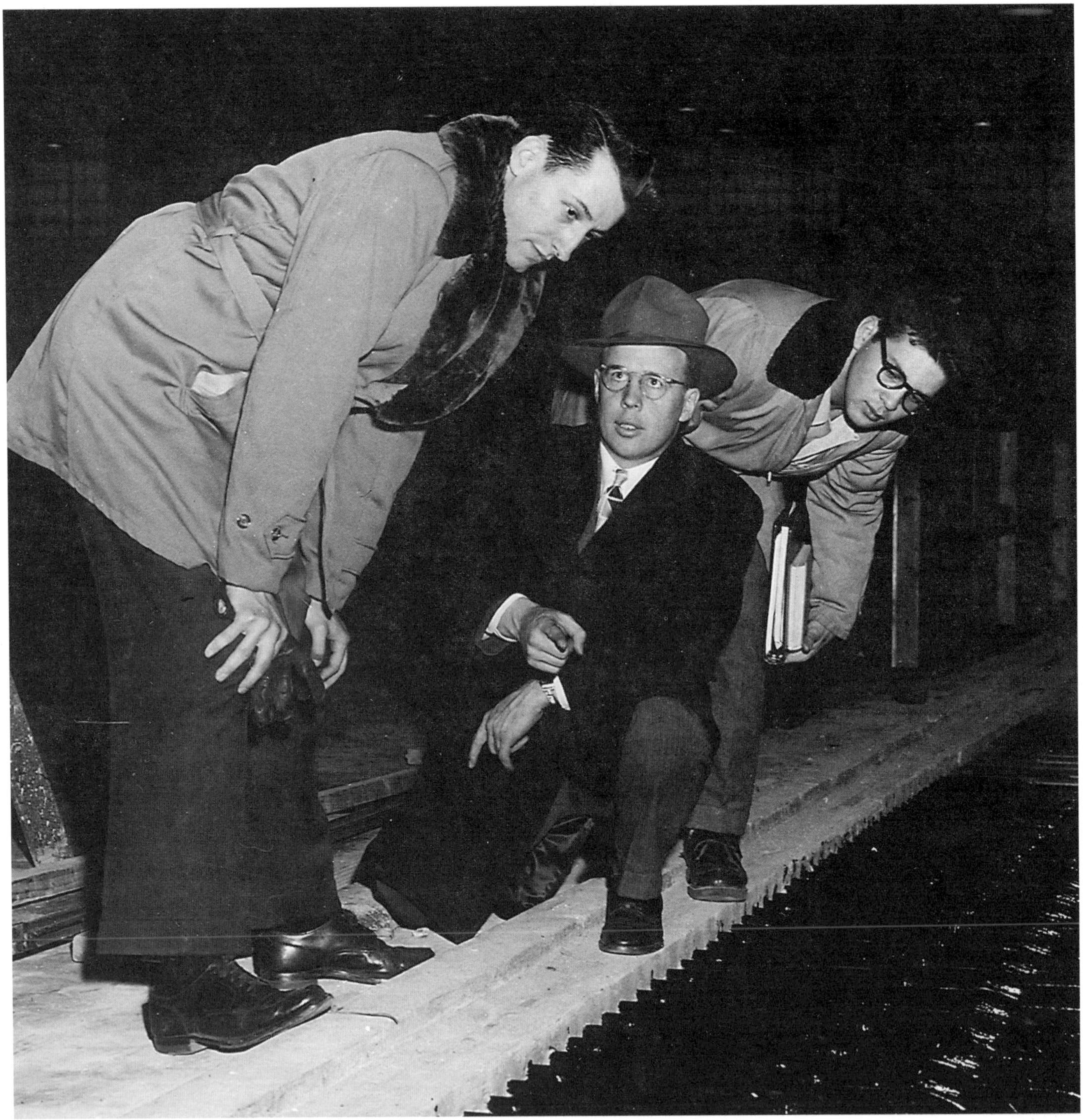

trip down to the Olympia in Detroit, where he measured the nets and the boards at the NHL Red Wings' home and then sketched plans so the welding shop at Michigan State could construct the necessities required to play the game. Breck also investigated how the ice was resurfaced at the time, for this was long before the Zamboni machine became a regular part of any hockey operation. What Michigan State ended up with to prepare the ice for play before games and between periods was a pair of carts supported by automobile tires (painted green, of course) that released hot water through a mop-like device made of towels. These were employed after a couple of volunteers made an initial scraping of the ice with shovels.

"They did a very credible job," Breck said.

Credible enough that the new MSC Ice Arena in Dem Hall was "rated as one of the finest ice plants in the country," according to a booklet prepared before the 1950 season by then-Sports Information Director Fred W. Stabley. It was also one of only a couple that could manufacture ice any time it liked, and boasted a playing surface that measured 200 x 87 feet (NHL regulation today is 200 x 85).

Before hockey moved in, Dem Hall had been used for "basketball, military drill, displays, riding shows and other varied activities" through its first 25 years. It was also the home of the Michigan State ROTC. unit. Once 12 miles of piping was installed, an ice surface could be ready for use by either hockey players or figure skaters in eight hours.

So at least the Spartans had a new 4,000-seat home. All they needed now was a team. Paulsen put one together by advertising in the student newspaper, The State News, by holding open tryouts and by trying to convince anyone he knew

Before he could coach Michigan State's first indoor team, Harold Paulsen (center) had to first make sure Demonstration Hall's new refrigeration unit was working properly.

back in Minnesota (which, along with Massachusetts, was about the only amateur hockey hotbed in the United States at the time) to give Michigan State a chance.

A native of Roseau, Minn., Paulsen signed a contract with the NHL's Chicago Blackhawks upon leaving the University of Minnesota in 1941. He never made it to Chicago, however, enlisting instead in the U.S. Navy after the outbreak of World War II. Once he left the Navy, Paulsen returned to Minnesota and worked as an athletic director, health director and coach at the high school level, and began working toward a master's degree in education at the University of Minnesota (which he completed in 1947). When Michigan State Athletic Director Ralph Young called, Paulsen sensed an opportunity to get into big-time hockey and signed on. He was 29 years old at the time.

Paulsen was also a disciple of the "show 'em" school of coaching. He would regularly strap on the skates and take the ice with his players during workouts, a habit that's a common practice now but was very rare in the late 1940s and early 1950s.

"I did that quite a bit because I always enjoyed skating," said Paulsen, who was famous for his skating while at Minnesota and left the school as the Gophers' all-time leading scorer. "I really believed in skating. You have to be a skater if you're going to be much of a hockey player. We felt that even the goalie had to be a pretty good skater." Small in stature but quick and graceful on skates, Paulsen patiently went about trying to form a team out of the collection of 18 wannabes initial tryouts and recruiting produced. A quiet, gentle man and a gentleman, Paulsen never used profanity and abhorred fighting. One of Breck's vivid early memories of Paulsen is the coach bringing his young son, Harold James, who suffered from polio and wore braces on his legs, to practice and gently guiding him around the ice.

"That was rather touching," Breck said.

Paulsen's team, unfortunately, was rather comical, just as Paulsen expected it to be.

Faced with a first-year schedule that included established programs from Michigan Tech,

Michigan, Minnesota, North Dakota and Western Ontario, Paulsen outlined MSC's opening season as follows: "There isn't a weak team on our card, and we are young and inexperienced. Against that type of competition, we'll be lucky to win a single game.

teammates, a group that included Straffordville, Ontario, native Harley Hotchkiss (the majority owner of the Calgary Flames today, but at the time merely a junior center). None of them had any college hockey experience.

View-obstructing pillars were an almost unavoidable part of the hockey experience at Dem Hall, unless you were fortunate enough to grab a standing room spot at ice level as a few curious observers discover at an early 1950's practice.

However, we do hope to make it interesting for some of our opponents before the season is over."

Eight of Paulsen's original 18 players were from Michigan (Benton Harbor, Cadillac, Dearborn, Detroit, Grosse Pointe and Hancock). Others came from places such as Arlington, Mass.; Margate, N.J.; Greenwich, Conn.; Montreal, Quebec; Fort Dodge, Iowa and Cleveland, Ohio. Junior defenseman James Doyle, who played his high school hockey in Thief River Falls, Minn., where Paulsen had coached, stood out enough in preseason workouts to be selected as captain by his

And as it turned out, they weren't a lucky bunch.

MSC went 0-14 that first season. It started with a 6-2 loss at home to Michigan Tech. It ended with a 17-1 defeat at the hands of Michigan. In between the Spartans surrendered 15, 14, 13, 12 (twice), 11 and 10 (twice) goals on various nights. The most they ever scored was five, in a 9-5 loss to Western Ontario, which tied the opener against Tech for the closest differential (four goals) of the opening campaign.

Ouch.

"It was pretty sad because we just didn't have the talent," Paulsen explained. "They had very little experience, they hadn't been good high school players we really didn't have any that had been outstanding we always had a problem getting a good goalie and we just didn't have any that could play defense exceptionally well. It was really a struggle.

"We had some fellas from the east that thought they were pretty good hockey players, but actually they weren't. They would get kind of upset, but they just weren't great hockey players.

"One of my high school teams in Minnesota could have defeated that first Michigan State team pretty easily."

These Spartans struggled even in competition for use of the ice at Dem Hall. Due to the popularity and quality of figure skating at the time, and because ice shows could generate revenue while hockey could not (tickets cost $1 on game nights; the charge was 75 cents for students and employees holding season booklets), hockey often had to work its practice schedule around figure skating practices and events.

Not that all of the above made MSC's first season on ice a total loss.

"We had real nice jerseys," Paulsen said. "We were a good looking team, but ..."

Nine players returned among the 20 who suited up for the 1950-51 season. One of the newcomers was sophomore forward Richard Lord, a native of Montreal and, according to the university's pre-season booklet "one of the few Negro ice hockey players to be found anywhere." State broke into the victory column on the season's first weekend with a 9-5, 12-3 sweep of the Ontario Agricultural College and finished 6-11. Surprisingly, it turned out to be Paulsen's final season.

"We were getting better," he said. "We were just getting started, but we had started from so far back, from scratch, that it really took a long time to get going. The players had trouble skating, to say nothing of playing the game. And you can't make a hockey player in a year or two or three. It takes

quite a while. But the school actually thought we should be progressing faster in hockey than we were."

And so it was mutually agreed upon that Paulsen should resign. He continued to teach primary health education courses and the history of physical education at Michigan State, and he started work on a doctorate. Hannah had been pushing staff members to do that, since the Big Ten would also consider how many among the faculty had Ph.D's when evaluating Michigan State's application for conference membership. But as for hockey, that just wasn't going to work out any more for Paulsen.

By this time Paulsen had once again been informed by football coach Biggie Munn (a fellow Minnesota native) that he would continue trying to hoard as many of the athletic dollars as possible for his football program. And the university was more than happy to honor most of Munn's requests, so this was as good a time for Paulsen to get out as any. There were no hard feelings upon the changing of the guard.

Paulsen earned his doctorate in physical education from the University of Michigan (where he had been attending Saturday classes despite what he called the "terrible, terrible rivalry between the two schools") in 1956. He then left to become athletic director and chairman of physical education at Slippery Rock State Teachers College in Pennsylvania, and eventually wound up back in Minnesota, teaching physical education at Mankato State. He retired in 1987.

"I got to know Biggie Munn real well because he was a Minnesota man and I knew a lot about him," Paulsen said. "He was a pretty good friend of mine and he liked hockey. But he had a lot of work to do to and he needed as much as he could for football because he was trying to turn a fairly weak program into a strong one. He ended up building a good football program there, which is what the school wanted and what the Big Ten wanted."

Although that kept hockey buried on the back burner, "I really enjoyed my time in East

Lansing," Paulsen said. "Things were really happening there at the time. And I always believed so much in the Big Ten. I was so happy when Michigan State was finally able to get in (in 1953). I thought that was just great."

Paulsen's replacement was an outgoing, enthusiastic, former Illinois star and a former professional hockey and baseball player at the minor-league level named Amo Bessone. No one at the time could have imagined he'd stay for 28 seasons. One of the reasons Bessone, who had been the head

coach at Michigan Tech, even came to Michigan State in the first place was he was simply trying to get a good night's sleep.

"They had an indoor rink that manufactured ice, and at the time that was a big thing," Bessone said of Michigan State. "At Tech we played inside, but we still had to depend on the weather. We'd have to open the doors and windows of our building and let the rink freeze the night before, and then not let the fans in until just before game time.

"The State job was better for me because I wasn't going to have to get up at 2 or 3 a.m. and go

Coach Amo Bessone chats with his 1952-53 captains, Dick Lord (No. 13) and Richard Northey (No. 4).

flood the ice rink. Plus, they were going into the Big Ten the next year. That was a pretty big thing, too."

So at least the Spartans had that going for them, which was nice. Yet while the indoor, man-made ice was a true perk, the MSC Ice Arena at Dem Hall was already becoming infamous for its quirks.

One involved the locker rooms: Dem Hall didn't have any. Players from both teams had to dress in Jenison Field House, then walk across the street to a small area where they could put on their skates. When the games ended, both team would then walk back across the street to Jenison to shower and change.

"That was actually an advantage for us," said John Sturges, a Spartan during the team's final two seasons at Dem Hall in the mid-1970s. "The other teams just weren't used to it. You'd see them walking from Jenison to Dem Hall and they'd all have dress shoes on, because they had to wear coats and ties on the road, and their shin pads on and their suit coats wrapped around their shoulder pads ... They looked like dorks.

"We had some warmups that Michigan State had given us, coats and hooded shirts that matched our uniforms. We looked more professional. And the other team was always thinking, "This is nuts.' It gave us an edge."

Another inconvenience in the early days was bathroom facilities for the teams; there weren't any. If a player really had to go, he had no choice but to remove his skates and use the men's room that had been provided for the fans. For a while that wasn't a problem, since there weren't many fans to contend with. But once the Spartans started drawing and the between-periods lines started to grow, the players were forced to improvise.

"One time one of our kids, Gordie King (who played in the early to mid-1950s) had to go real bad," Bessone said, "and he couldn't get into the john. So he used a waste basket. And our manager forgot to clean out the waste basket (or, perhaps the manager merely chose not to do so), and it was in one of the rooms that the ROTC. used. Holy

Christ, did that colonel or whatever he was raise hell when he found out.

"But the next day they put johns in."

As for the ice itself, that was always one of the best sheets anyone ever played on. But getting on it remained a tricky proposition, even early in Bessone's tenure. The rink manager was still giving figure skating priority too often to suit Bessone, who sometimes had to try and get his practices in at 9, 10 or 11 in the morning, which conflicted with players' class schedules. Finally, Bessone complained to his athletic director, Young.

And Young, who had been unaware of the scheduling conflicts, at long last put an end to them.

"He said, 'Our athletic teams are scheduled to practice from 3 to 6 p.m. From now on, the hockey team will practice at 3 p.m.'" Bessone said.
One of the first real characters in Spartan hockey history (but most definitely not the last) was MSC's first goalie, 5-foot-7, 140-pound sophomore Delmar Reid. "He was very inexperienced and very gutsy," Breck said. "Reid lost quite a few teeth getting hit in the mouth with the puck (goalies didn't wear masks then), but he didn't mind because his teeth were bad to begin with and he needed the dental work. He was absolutely fearless."
Innovative, too.

"He got in trouble over Thanksgiving weekend that second season. He was married and he lived in married housing in the Quonset huts (which used to be located between Case Hall and where the Breslin Student Events Center stands now). Well, that year he decided to cook a duck for Thanksgiving dinner for himself and his wife, Serita, so he took a duck from the Red Cedar River. The police found the bones outside his Quonset hut and hauled him in for taking a duck out of season.

"Paulsen chewed him out about that, too. "Now, we don't want you getting into any kind of trouble ...'"

One of the fringe benefits early on was the occasional chance to mingle with NHL players. That happened one time when, on a return trip from Michigan Tech, the train the Spartans were on stopped in Chicago and picked up the Montreal

Canadiens. And as it turned out, Maurice Richard, Butch Bouchard and the rest of the Flying Frenchmen were more than happy to share laughs and insight with their wide-eyed, hockey-playing counterparts from the college ranks. And in 1954, the Spartans began playing a series of season-opening exhibition games against the Detroit Red Wings.

"That was our budget," Bessone said. "The Red Wings would come up and play us in Dem Hall, we'd pack the place and we'd give the Red Wings $500. I had a pretty good relationship with (Detroit General Manager) Jack Adams. He was a good guy.

"Those games were a lot of fun. We'd play even-Steven the first period, and then naturally they'd show their superiority. Then, in the second period, we'd swap goalies. They'd get our guy and we'd get (eventual NHL Hall-of-Famer) Terry Sawchuk. And Sawchuk used to always be talking to our defense; 'Now listen you guys, just don't get in my way,' and, 'Don't let 'em in too close to shoot. I've got $5 on this game with these guys. If they score on me they get $5 ...' He'd play two periods and then they'd put the trainer in.

"We used to give 'em $500 and then feed 'em a big dinner after the game. Then one year Adams said, 'Amo, these guys all want to get back to Detroit. Make it $600 and you don't have to feed us.' It was still a hell of a bargain for us. But eventually, the Big Ten stepped in and said we couldn't play pro teams any more."

Senior defenseman and captain Robert Jasson accepts The Michigan Press Trophy from Bill Burke of The State Journal prior to a game against Minnesota in 1958, an unmistakable sign that Michigan State hockey was finally on the rise.

In addition to fun and funds, MSC's relationship with the Red Wings provided equipment .

"We used to bum whatever we could off of them," Bessone said. "They'd give us all their used stuff; sticks, gloves, even skates. The skates were pretty well used, too. But some of our kids didn't have money to buy skates, and we weren't supplying them."

Another thing the Spartans weren't supplying as the program grew was a good view. Seating at Dem Hall was limited to both end zones and one side of the ice. And only a few seats in the first few rows of each section offered an unobstructed glance at the action. The vast majority of the sightlines were impaired either by sharp angles or by one of the arena's numerous support pillars.

"We were the only rink that guaranteed you a lousy seat," Bessone said.

The program grew gradually, anyway.

On Feb. 6, 1954, goalie Ed Schiller made 73 saves (a Spartan record) in a 5-4 loss to Denver. In 1954-55, a couple of future Olympians Weldie Olson and Gene Grazia provided highlights for a last-place team in the Western Intercollegiate Hockey Conference (the forerunner of the Western Collegiate Hockey Association). In 1956-57 the Spartans beat Minnesota, which featured a heady forward by the name of Herb Brooks, three times. The victories were Michigan State's first over the Golden Gophers in a series that started with an 0-28-1 streak. And in

1957-58, State enjoyed its first breakthrough year on ice.

Michigan State beat Michigan for the first time since 1928, and three of four times overall. Michigan State beat Ohio State, 18-0 and 17-3, and in the latter contest, goalie Joe Selinger played for-ward and scored a goal. Alto Altobelli, who started that night in goal, moved to forward and scored a goal, and Bessone turned the coaching duties over to student manager Dave Green in the third period (is that rubbing it in, or what?). Michigan State also won the mythical Big Ten championship (contested

Goalie Joe Selinger (No. 1), defenseman Robert Armstrong (No. 3) and defenseman Butch Miller (No. 4) battle Michigan in front of a packed house at Dem Hall in the 1958-59 season.

Joe Selinger became Michigan State's first All-American in 1958-59. Selinger didn't need a boarded up net to do it, either, just solid support from defensemen such as Robert Armstrong.

for by Michigan, Michigan State, Minnesota and Ohio State) and produced its first winning season with a record of 12-11.

They even came home with a trophy, the Michigan Press Trophy, for winning six times in eight tries in games against Michigan and Michigan Tech. That had been awarded annually since 1950 by The State Journal in Lansing, the Ann Arbor Gazette and The Mining Gazette in Houghton to the winner of the annual series between the three schools and had belonged to Michigan ever since. The significance of the Spartans taking the Press Trophy away from the Wolverines wasn't lost on Munn, who had stepped down as the football coach and become Michigan State's athletic director shortly after winning the 1954 Rose Bowl.

"I am proud of the Michigan Press Trophy

Amo and his team won," Biggie said. "The progress that the hockey team has made this year has made me very happy."

By the time the 1958-59 season rolled around, Michigan State was on the verge of something spectacular. Selinger, who would earn All-America honors that year (the first Spartan to do so) was back for his third campaign between the pipes, and 15 other returning letterwinners would suit up again. By now the roster was littered with Canadians, featuring 19 in all. Among them were brothers Bruno and Ed Pollesel of Copper Cliff, Ontario (a suburb of Sudbury that would supply more talent in the years ahead), and defenseman Elwood "Butch" Miller of Regina, Saskatchewan (the first but hardly the last Miller to distinguish himself at Michigan State). The preseason press booklet claimed the team "could very easily take up where it left off last year."

Gordie Howe and the Red Wings won the exhibition opener, 10-3, but Adams was impressed none the less. "Every year I come up here they get bigger and better," he said of the Spartans. This year they wound up being better than ever. Although there was no conference title to win (the Western Intercollegiate Hockey Conference was dead and the Western Collegiate Hockey Association was scheduled to begin play the following season), Michigan State won six games in nine days in capturing a pair of tournaments out east (beating Northeastern, Boston College, Boston University, Brown, Princeton and Rensselaer Polytechnic Institute), handled the usual opponents in the midwest (Michigan, Michigan Tech, Minnesota, North Dakota), and finished 16-5-1 in the regular season. For the first time, Michigan State was rewarded with a trip to the NCAA Final Four, in Troy, N.Y.

By virtue of his All-America status, Selinger (who had a 2.67 goals against average and went 17-6-1 in 24 games) was the obvious headliner. Yet proof of just how good a team State had become could be found at the other end of the ice as well, as three different players wound up leading the squad in goals (Terry Moroney, 23), assists (Dick Hamilton, 26) and points (Joe Polano, 41).

"I wasn't that effective; what it was was good team play," Selinger maintained. "We had good forwards who would backcheck and good defensemen who would cover up. When you have that kind of combination, it makes it pretty easy.

"You have to have a team in front of you before you can make All-American. I know the guy who was the goaltender before I was, Eddie Schiller, was a pretty darn good goaltender. But hell, they couldn't win. When I was a freshman, Eddie was still there. He'd stop 40 or 50 shots a night, they'd just pour shots at him and he'd make a lot of saves but he had no support.

"If he would have had the support I had, he'd have made it. He just came along at the wrong time."

Selinger and the Spartans made it to the championship game by beating BC, a team they had beaten 6-0 in the regular season, 4-3 in the semifinals. That set up a fifth meeting with North Dakota to decide the national championship. The two teams had split their four regular-season games, with each winning once in the other's home arena. No wonder they ended up deadlocked at 3-3 following 60 minutes of regulation play in the title bout.

Michigan State, by virtue of its two third-period goals that forced the extra session, had the momentum. And early in the overtime, Bessone thought the Spartans had it won.

"I had a kid named (Bill) MacKenzie walking in on their goaltender all alone," Bessone said. "He was a good goal scorer and I said, 'Well, this is it. This kid will score.' He did everything right, too. He pulled the goalie out and everything else ... and he shot the puck over the top of the net."

Moments after that ... disaster.

"They took a long shot and Selinger, who was a hell of a goalie, dropped the puck. It fell right out of his hand," Bessone said. "They had a kid standing right there (Reg Morelli) and he just tapped it in."

At 4:18 of overtime, Michigan State's dream died.

"It was exciting," Selinger said. "It would have been more exciting if we had won because State had never done that before."

"We should have won it all that year," Bessone insisted. "I felt like we had the best team there. And I thought we had it won in overtime, then they came right back and scored. But that's the way the game goes, you know? A lucky break here, a lucky break there ..."

At least the stakes had been raised in these games of chance at Michigan State in the 1950s, a decade that opened with the Spartans fielding a team that would be lucky to win a single game, and closed one win shy of winning it all.

They made believers out
of everybody...

CHAPTER
3

Chapter 3

Amo Bessone prepared for his 15th season behind the MSU bench in the fall of 1965 with credentials that were something less than impressive on the surface.

There had been just four winning seasons in the previous 14.

One of those, however, had been recorded the year before, in 1964-65, when State went 17-12-0 overall and 8-8 in the Western Collegiate Hockey Association. And the top line from that team Mike Jacobson, Tom Mikkola and Sandy McAndrew, a threesome that had accounted for 65 of the Spartans' 165 goals was back intact. All told, 13 lettermen were returning. And defenseman Bob Brawley, who also played linebacker for Duffy Daugherty, was scheduled to report once the football season was completed.

And so there was genuine optimism in the air around Demonstration Hall prior to the outset of the

Goalie Gaye Cooley had his quirks, but came up huge in the clutch in the 1966 title run.

1965-66 season, more than at any time since the Spartans had made it all the way to the NCAA title game in 1959.

"We had a lot of guys that could put the puck in the net," Jacobson said.

The most accomplished among those was Doug Volmar, a 6-foot, 190-pound junior winger from Cleveland Heights, Ohio, who could also play defense. He would go on to score a team-leading 26 goals and register a team-leading 28 assists for a team-leading 54 points in 29 games in 1965-66, and finish his three-year Spartan career (freshmen still weren't eligible to play varsity hockey) with 74 goals, 49 assists and 123 points. Volmar was also destined to earn All-America honors in '65-66, and would eventually play in three seasons with the Detroit Red Wings.

Of course, no one knew any of that back in the fall of 1965. What was known at the time was Volmar could really shoot the puck.

"He probably had the hardest wrist shot of anybody I've ever seen in hockey," Bessone said of Volmar, who started out as a figure skater back in Cleveland Heights and didn't take up hockey until the age of 14, after he became too big for figure skating. "Gordie Howe said the same thing when (Volmar) was playing with the Red Wings."

A gifted athlete, Volmar would also letter on the tennis team in the spring of 1966. His ability on the court wasn't really a surprise, considering Volmar had first learned how to shoot a puck by

practicing with a tennis ball in his family's basement while growing up.

"He hits a tennis ball the same way he shoots a puck," Bessone said. "It looks as if it will explode."

The team looked as if it might, too, mostly because of Volmar.

"Mostly we had a bunch of unique players that year that were slightly above average," Jacobson said. "But Volmar, I guess, was our king.

"He had a cannon."

Unfortunately, Volmar and the rest of those slightly above average Spartans also had a unique problem on their hands when it came time to open practice. There was no ice to practice on. A mechanical failure had temporarily robbed Dem Hall, the facility that had first lured Bessone to Michigan State because it produced ice indoors, of its ice-making capabilities. At the crucial juncture when they should have been preparing for the season ahead, Bessone's Spartans instead were literally out in the cold.
They did what they could when they could while the repairs were being effected.

They played soccer, they put in hours of roadwork, they played floor hockey with their equipment on (except for the skates, of course) ...

"I can remember going over to the football stadium and running an awful lot of stairs," defenseman Don Heaphy said.
"I guess that was the beginning of off-ice training for us," Jacobson added.

They even traveled down to the University of Michigan twice in search of ice (bet that hurt), in a desperate attempt to somehow get ready for the campaign ahead. Alas, when the season was ready to begin, MSU was anything but ready.

The 1966 NCAA Champions, front row, from left: Gaye Cooley, Matthew Mulcahy, Don Heaphy, Gerry Fisher, Mike Coppo, Tom Purdo, and Larry Roche. Second row, from left: Trainer Clyde Stretch, Sandy McAndrew, Tom Mikkola, Mike Jacobson, Dainis Vedejs, Ron Roth, Doug Volmar, Tom Crowley, Wayne Duffett, and coach Amo Bessone. Third row, from left: Team Manager William Smith, Richard Bois, Bill Faunt, Doug French, Nino Cristofolli, Robert Fallat, John Schuster, and manager Ralph Faust.

"We flew out to Colorado College for the season-opening (weekend) series on a Tuesday, just to get some ice time," McAndrew said. "That was a nice trip. We were there Wednesday, Thursday, Friday and Saturday. That was a really fun trip."

It just wasn't a very productive one. For in those days, players didn't train year-round, as they do today. And in those days, as is the case today, conditioning via roadwork or a stationary bike or what have you "is a lot different than conditioning on the ice," Bessone said. "If you don't get that skating time in, your legs give out."

Denied of the chance to gasp while performing countless stops and starts (a standing ritual at most Bessone practices), robbed of an opportunity to get their timing down on the power play and the breakout, the Spartans bombed out early.

The season opened with 4-0 and 4-3 (in overtime) losses at Colorado College, a team that would go on to win two of its next 16 WCHA games. Even worse, the out-of-shape Spartans got banged up in the early going. Hard.

"It took us almost half a year to recuperate," Bessone said.

Spartan pride took a few beatings, as well. The sweep at the hands of Colorado College was followed up by a 5-3 loss to St. Lawrence and a 6-3 loss to Clarkson. When they finally opened the home portion of their schedule, the Spartans beat North Dakota, 11-5, then promptly lost to the Fighting Sioux (5-3) and Denver (8-6), which dropped MSU's record to 2-6 after eight games.

At the midpoint, following a 5-1 loss to Minnesota at Dem Hall, the Spartans were even worse. They had lost five of seven home games, they had yet to win more than two in a row anywhere (and they had accomplished that modest feat just once) and they were an uninspiring 4-9 overall. In the second half, however, they suddenly became a different team.

Gaye Cooley, a sophomore, eventually took over in goal after backing up and then splitting time with Jerry Fisher. Brawley got acclimated and started throwing his nearly 200 pounds around on a regular basis. Jacobson, who had been limited by injuries, started to get healthy and get more involved. Volmar and winger Mike Coppo continued filling up the net, and others started contributing timely goals as well, providing much-needed balance to the attack. The once-shaky defense came together. And with their skating legs finally under them, the Spartans became a team that could stick and move with the best of them.

"We clicked at midseason," Bessone said. "And everybody that beat us early, we beat 'em the second time around."

Everybody except St. Lawrence, at any rate. A 6-5 overtime win over Minnesota-Duluth at home got the Spartans started, and the wave they continued to ride in the season's second half didn't fade until Michigan State had won seven of eight. The only loss in that stretch was a 6-5 OT decision in Minnesota, and an 8-7, 4-2 sweep of Michigan more than made up for that. Although the Spartans dropped three of their last four (including a 1-0 overtime loss in Ann Arbor in the regular-season finale), the Michigan State team that began preparing for the postseason hardly resembled the one that first began working out in the preseason. Despite a 12-13 finish overall and a sixth-place standing in the WCHA, these Spartans had grown close and confident during the months in between.

"The chemistry was very, very good," Heaphy said. "When we saw that it looked like we had some momentum going towards the end, we started to feel pretty good about ourselves going into the playoffs. I can remember us having a lot of team meetings, with just the guys, just to pull together.

"We had a lot of leaders on that team. I don't think you can really point to one person who was saying 'let's do this,' or 'let's do that.' It was pretty much all of us. The attitude was, 'Let's get together and help each other.' There was never any criticizing. It was always a positive-type thing."

When they weren't practicing, playing or meeting among themselves, the Spartans could normally be found at one of the "hockey houses" various team members were renting. They partied together just as hard as they played together.

"That was a great bunch of guys. We all got

along," Jacobson said. "The chemistry was the key to it."

Cooley was another. Although he would finish with an impressive 3.10 goals-against average in 18 games overall, he was nearly as unbeatable down the stretch (holding four of the Spartans' final six opponents to one goal) as he was unusual off the ice.

"He was a real nut-job," said defenseman Doug French. "If you said 'black,' he'd say 'white.' He liked to party, too. But he was a real tough kid, a real competitor. When things got down, he was a real scrapper. He didn't take shit from anybody.

"At the beginning of the season, Gaye was inexperienced, and Jerry Fisher wasn't a real good goaltender, but he was all we had. Finally, Gaye came around once he got squared away in school. He had a rough time in school at first because he just didn't want to read or study or do anything. He was that kind of guy."

Cooley was also the kind of guy who would try anything once. On that first road trip to Colorado, for example, he got caught breaking into the hotel kitchen in the wee hours of the morning .

"I don't know if he was trying to steal food or what, but he told them he was a hotel, restaurant and institutional management major, and that he had just wanted to see how a really nice hotel was run," French remembered. "The next day they ended up giving him a tour of the kitchen and all the facilities."

Known as a "wrong-handed goalie" because he wore his catching glove on his right hand, Cooley often set himself apart from the crowd.

"I always thought he was OK because at least he wasn't under-handed," McAndrew said. "But he was different. He was also a very good goaltender.

"He knew how to play the angles and he had an attitude. He told me once when he played goal his attitude was, 'You're not going to score anything on me.' It had nothing to do with the team in front of him, you just weren't going to score on him. And if you got one, you weren't going to get another. That's the way he thought."

That's the way Cooley played in 1965-66 when it mattered most.

"He was on fire at the end," Jacobson said. "I think we all were."

"One of the things about our team that year was, we always thought we could win, but we didn't know if we could win and there was never any pressure to win," McAndrew said. "We'd just go out and play. Then, if we won, we'd say, 'Well, we thought we could.'

"We never really actually knew what we were doing while we were doing it, and we never thought we were hot shit as a team. We were just playing and having fun."

The Spartans were hot enough to win at Michigan, 3-2, in the first round of the playoffs, as Cooley kicked out 31 of 33 shots. There was, however, little time or reason for a celebration. For all the Spartans' fourth victory in five meetings with the Wolverines had earned them was a date with defending-NCAA champion Michigan Tech.

Momentum or not, this didn't figure to be easy, even if it was to be played at Dem Hall.

Tech had gone 23-5-1, whipping Michigan State 8-4 and 4-2 at Tech in the process. And those wins had been recorded in the season's second half, after the Spartans had gotten their act together. Still, Bessone thought there had been some extenuating circumstances.

"We lost twice at their place, but it was 31 below zero outside and 10 below inside at game time (Tech still didn't manufacture ice indoors at the time)," Bessone said. "Also, they had a small arena and relied on an excellent short-passing game. I felt we could beat them on our larger ice surface."

State did, 4-3.

"We just outskated and outshot them," Bessone said. "Our kids were in the right frame of mind, and I think Tech was a little cocky."

And so, for the first time since 1959, it was on to the Final Four for the Spartans.

"We never should have been there, eh?" Heaphy said sarcastically. "There had been this big story done in Time magazine, a number of pages, done on Michigan Tech and how great they were and what a great record they had and so on and so forth. But the final sentence was something like, 'However, they were beaten out by Michigan State.' I think it was Time magazine that did the article, Time, or Newsweek, whatever ... We loved that."

The Tech victory allowed MSU to arrive in Minneapolis for the Final Four boasting an above-.500 record (14-13) for just the second time that season (State had also been 11-10 at one point). Obviously, that didn't inspire a lot of fear in the other three competing teams (Boston University, Denver and Clarkson). At the pre-tourney banquet, the coaches at those institutions got up one by one and spoke of all they had accomplished so far, and all they still aspired to achieve. Finally, it was Bessone's turn.

His message? "We don't have much of a record, but we've worked hard and we've made it here and we'll do our best. Not much is expected from us, but we'll make a tournament out of it."

MSU made the tourney a short one for Boston University, beating BU, 2-1, in the semifinals. French netted his first goal as a collegian in opening the scoring in the second period, Volmar added another midway through the third and that was that. Cooley wound up coming within 23 seconds of posting his first career shutout and just the second in NCAA Tournament history.

Now, all that stood between the Spartans and their first national championship was Clarkson, which had beaten MSU at Clarkson, 6-3, in the fourth game of the season.

As had been their habit throughout the season's second half, the Spartans once again extracted some sweet revenge. Leading 2-1 after two, hard-fought periods, Michigan State exploded for four goals in the third and won going away. Coppo started the onslaught just 17 seconds in, his second of the game and 21st of the season. Winger Bob Fallat made it 4-1 State at 3:38 and Volmar and center Willie Faunt added more icing late.

It ended at 6-1, a margin as lopsided as the

run that got the Spartans as far as the University of Minnesota's Williams Arena for the Final Four had been improbable. Brawley's first goal of the season, which gave State a 2-1 lead at 14:31 of the second, stood up as the game-winner. Cooley, the tournament MVP, wound up being beaten only while MSU skated two-men down in the opening 20 minutes.

Bessone and MSU accepted the championship trophy with a final overall record of 16-13.

Len Ceglarski and Clarkson settled for second at 23-3.

"This definitely has to be the greatest thrill of my life," Bessone said to the press. "It was a great team effort and the kids deserved it. They fought and scratched all the way. We had our troubles early in the season ... but I figured we had potential all along. I know one thing, our kids worked very hard for this and they're very deserving of the championship.

"They made believers out of everybody."

And in such a convincing fashion that Bessone's only concern late in the championship game was the status of his son, Johnny.

"He had gotten hit with a puck right before the game ended, so I didn't stay on the ice for the celebration," Bessone explained. "I had to run down to the locker room to see how he was doing. He was only 10 years old.

"When I got there, they were stitching him up. He had been peeking over the boards when he got hit. I had just got through telling him to get back in the stands.

"That was the only injury we had."

Johnny Bessone was stitched up by Bob May, who had coached North Dakota to an NCAA Championship Game victory over Michigan State in 1959, and had since moved on to Minneapolis to practice dentistry.

"I wasn't worried about the stitches. I was worried about my son's teeth," Bessone said. "But I found out his teeth were fine. Then we had a little fun.

"We always used to eat at this one restaurant for our pre-game meals and stuff up there, the DiNapoli Cafe, and man, did they throw us a party after the game. I was in a sweatsuit because I had been doused under the shower after the game, but it was still a lot of fun."

The fun continued that evening at the team hotel.

"We were partying in somebody's room and somehow a mattress caught on fire," French said. "We didn't know what to do when that happened, so we just threw it out the window. We thought we might get in a bit of a jam-up for that, but Amo was in there with us, so we thought 'what the hell ... ' "

The merriment lasted well into the night and the next day.

"It was a pretty sickly-looking group coming off the plane in Lansing," Faunt said.

And a relatively lonely one, too. Unlike the

A cartoon in the Minneapolis Star set the stage for the 1966 championship battle.

1986 national championship, which inspired a wild celebration on campus, a raucous crowd which greeted the team when it finally arrived back at Munn Arena, an impromptu pep rally and a parade, the '66 triumph barely caused a stir back in mid-Michigan. Even the Lansing State Journal was rather restrained in delivering the news, devoting much more coverage to the ongoing state high school basketball tournament in its March 20, 1966, editions than the Spartans' first hockey national championship.

"We didn't come home as conquering heroes; we just came home," Jacobson said. "I think there were maybe 10 people at the airport ... All we did was party like hell."

They had earned it.

"That," Faunt said years later, "was the team that built Munn Arena."

Years later, some of the 1966 Spartans insist they receive more accolades for winning that national championship now than they did back then. Part of the reason for that is the rebirth of MSU hockey and the national title captured in '86 by Ron Mason's Spartans. Another is hockey simply wasn't the big deal around campus in 1966 that it is today, although winning it all clearly elevated the program's status that spring.

"After that, for the first time, you'd be walking down the street and you'd see (MSU football players) Ron Goovert or Don Bierowicz or Bob Viney or Don Japinga and they'd recognize you, or you'd hear people whispering 'Hey, Michigan State hockey,' " French said. "That really made you feel good."

There were other advantages as well.

"I was having trouble in that 'American Thought and Language,' " French said. "So I men-

Doug Volmar's powerful slapshot helped the Spartans to their first-ever hockey National Championship.

tioned it and I was told, 'Don't worry, just sign up for this section and this professor.' So I did that and I walked in and the guy says, 'This is your name?' I said 'yes.' Then he said, 'And this is your student number?' I said 'yes' again, and then he said, 'OK, have a nice semester.'

"That's one way I kept eligible. There were a few other classes with other guys doing the same thing. It made all the difference in the world."

Enough that even 20 years later, the team was still being formally honored by the university. And for those who returned to campus, donned a jersey one more time and marched out onto the field at Spartan Stadium at halftime of the MSU-Iowa football game in the fall of 1986 (along with the '86 champions), "all those feelings came rushing back," McAndrew said.

"That was the neatest feeling I've ever had. That was the best athletic feeling I've ever had, that's for sure."

"That season was something special, something satisfying," added Mikkola. "Most other seasons, you just played, you just won or lost. Unless you made it to the Final Four, it was just another hockey season.

"But you remember winning the title. You've got that plaque of the naked hockey player, a guy wearing just skates and a stick; I don't know why he's not dressed. Do they do that for basketball? Anyway, that's what they gave you. And you remember the championship. You remember that you won it.

"You did it. We did it."

Once they had, there was no longer a need for this improbable championship team to make a believer out of anyone.

I had a driving passion to score
goals and to be the best...

CHAPTER
4

Chapter 4

For a select few stardom at Michigan State, no matter how pronounced, was merely a prelude to bigger and better things. Gene Grazia and Weldie Olson were members of the gold-medal winning U.S. Olympic Team in 1960. Kelly Miller was paid $1.8 million in 1993-94 to play hockey for the National Hockey League's Washington Capitals. Joe Murphy, who made $2.8 million with the St. Louis Blues in 1996-97, and Craig Simpson have lifted the Stanley Cup above their heads in Edmonton. Danton Cole was a member of the NHL-champion New Jersey Devils in 1995 (he even brought the Cup to Rick's Cafe American, a noted hockey hangout just across Grand River Avenue from campus in East Lansing to cele-brate). And Harley Hotchkiss, a forward on MSU's first indoor team in 1950, today is the majority owner of the Calgary Flames.

But of all the players on all the teams through all the years, only one stands above the rest based solely on what he accomplished as a Spartan, even though he stood just 5-foot-7 and weighed only about 165 pounds.

Even though he never skated as much as a shift in the NHL.

His name is Tom Ross, and as an undergrad first in Demonstration Hall and then at Munn Arena, he was as graceful and amazing as they come.

The statistics-Ross is first in MSU history in career goals (138), assists (186) and points (324)-say Ross was the best the Spartans ever had. That's only natural, seeing as how the statistics also say that Ross is the most prolific scorer in NCAA Division I history. The top five all-time at the conclusion of the 1996-97 season were Ross, Michigan Tech's Mike Zuke (310 points), Spartan Steve Colp (300), Minnesota's John Mayasich (298) and Nelson Emerson of Bowling Green (294). Only Phil Latreille, who played at Division II Middlebury College in Vermont from 1957-61, scored more points than Ross (Latreille had 346) in college hockey history.

And while the statistics alone don't tell the whole story, the Spartans surely have never been blessed enough to dress a player that was any better.

Or even as great, at least at State.

"Oh, geez ... I don't know about that," Ross protested. "I guess I can't say that because all of the eras were different. If you just look at the statistics and stuff, sure, you're going to come to that con-clusion.

Tom Ross was so good he was once featured on the back of a Wheaties box; in this day and age he'd grace the front.

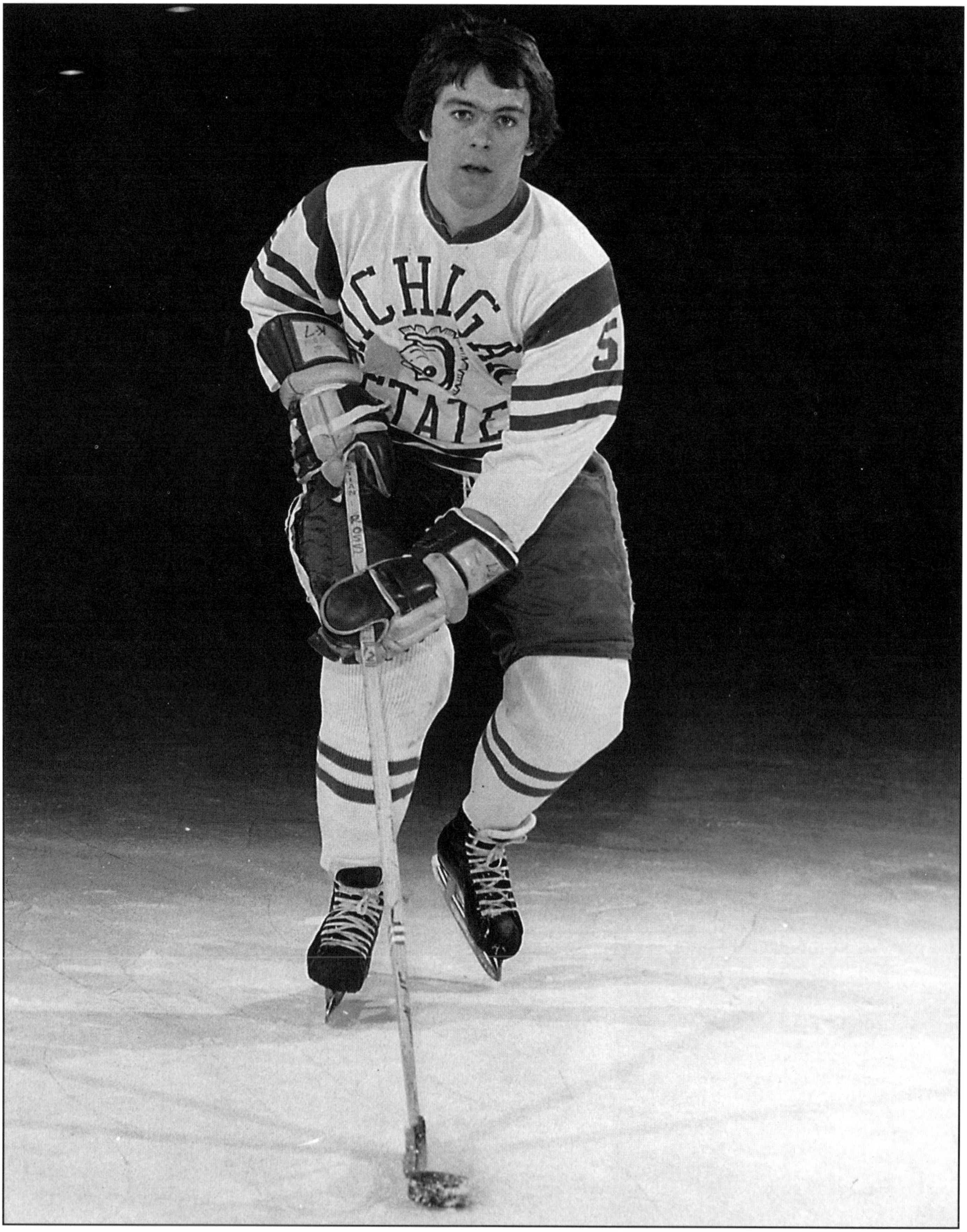

"But there are an awful lot of good players, if you look in the National Hockey League, from Michigan State. And some of them now come in there and play for two years, or three, or one, and then they're gone. If they had stayed for four years, if they had started out with four other guys and stayed for four years like I did, they might have done better."

Better than 324 career points? Theoretically, a player such as the Philadelphia Flyers' Rod Brind' Amour might have. As a freshman in 1988-89, Brind' Amour put up an eye-popping 59 points. But even at that, Brind' Amour would have had to average 88.3 points over his final three years to catch Ross. And only eight times in MSU history has a player scored 88 or more points. Three times, that player was Tommy Ross.

Murphy, another one-year wonder, might have had a shot to do it, too. But had he stayed for the duration of his eligibility Murphy, who produced 61 points as a freshman for the 1985-86 National Champions, would have had to average 87.6 points over his final three seasons to put his name up there with Ross.

Even a talent such as Kip Miller, the Spartans' only Hobey Baker Award winner (the Heisman Trophy of college hockey, which has been awarded annually since 1981), couldn't stack up to Ross, statistically speaking. And Kip Miller, third all-time at MSU with 261 points and the author of one of school's two 100-point campaigns (Ross is the other) played for four seasons, just as Ross did.

Unreachable? The numbers Ross put up are almost obscene. Twelve goals and 22 assists for 34 points in 36 games as a freshman; 37 goals and 51 assists for 88 points in 38 games as a sophomore; 38 goals and 59 assists for 97 points in 40 games as

The most prolific scorer in NCAA Division I history, Michigan State's Tom Ross.

a junior; and finally, 51 goals and 54 assists for 105 points in 41 games as a senior. Although Mike Donnelly (59 goals in 1985-86) and Pat Murray (60 assists in 1989-90) have eclipsed two of Roscoe's records, Ross' senior point total still stands as the MSU all-time, single-season, high-water mark.

His most remarkable accomplishment, however, might be this: From Dec. 19, 1973 until Dec. 12, 1975, Ross registered at least one point in 79 consecutive games.

Wow.

"I guess one thing I had was determination," Ross said. "When I was out there, I knew it was my job to score goals and set up goals, at whatever the cost might be. I don't know how many penalty minutes I had, but I hardly had any penalties (47, for 94 minutes in 155 games). The reason why was my dad always told me, 'Tommy, you can't score a goal when you're in the penalty box.' So I never used to take a lot of penalties.

"I can remember playing games where people would just literally take their sticks and two-hand you and they wouldn't call penalties. But I'd just take it and continue to play because if I wanted to score a goal, I couldn't take a retaliatory penalty. And I wanted to score goals. I had a driving passion to score goals and to be the best. And my guide to being the best was numbers, how many goals I had, how many assists, how many points."

As it turns out, Spartans fans everywhere owe a debt of gratitude to both of Ross' parents.

His father was the one that got the hockey career started. He was the one who would flood the yard behind the house at 1936 Carlysle in the Detroit suburb of Dearborn each winter, just as they do in Canada.

"He'd be out there for hours putting this rink in, and he'd get up in the middle of the night just to put more water on it," Ross recalled. "But the rink wasn't very smooth because the contour of the ground was bumpy. And there were trees in the yard, fences you had to go around, all kinds of things that you had to dodge. There were always a lot of quick starts and quick stops, things like that."

It was there, apparently, that Ross first

"I had a driving passion to score goals and to be the best..."

began to craft what years later Amo Bessone called "a deceiving shift in his skating.

"He's very clever on his skates," Bessone noted while Ross was starring for the Spartans. "He probably picked that up coming up through the ranks, because he was always smaller than most of the players.

"It's probably something he developed on his own."

At times, yes. At times, Ross was working on keeping his head up and not running smack into the trees with his brother Doug (who played for present Spartans mentor Ron Mason at Lake Superior and Bowling Green, and who went on to serve as the head coach at Alabama-Huntsville). At times, an enthusiastic portion of that one particular neighborhood in Dearborn was there.

"I always used to try to get the guys to come over and play, get games going, get everything organized," Ross said. "The neighbors behind us did the same thing, so it was a fairly long rink. I can remember just going back and forth, doing shooting drills, stickhandling ... by myself a lot of the time. I can remember getting home from school and going right out onto the rink, getting called in for dinner and then going right back out there again.

"As we continued on, I didn't really play any other high school sports. I was kinda small for football. I tried football, but that didn't pan out. And basketball conflicted with hockey, and I liked hockey. I could swim; I wasn't a bad swimmer, but that conflicted with hockey, too. And track ... I didn't have the long legs for running. Hockey just fit perfectly for me.

"And my grandparents were from Winnipeg. I had some Canadian extraction in there somewhere, so ..."

So hockey it was. Ross didn't play at Edsel Ford High School in Dearborn, but he was good enough to suit up for the prestigious Detroit Junior Red Wings. Still, when it came time to land a college scholarship, Ross wasn't exactly overwhelmed with offers. He was 5-foot-nothing. He wore size 6 skates. There had been some correspondence with Michigan State through the mail, and a few phone conversations with assistant coach Alex Terpay, "but those were mostly to my parents," Ross said.

Mason, for one, remembers scouting Ross while recruiting during his days at Bowling Green. He remembers being less than impressed by what he saw, too.

"I don't think a lot of people every thought Tommy Ross would turn out to be the player he was," said Mason, who never offered Ross a scholarship.

A couple of weeks before he was scheduled to graduate from Edsel Ford, Ross still didn't know where he was headed.

"Finally, Alex called and told my mom they'd like me to come," Ross said. "She said, 'He'd like to come, but the only way he's coming is with a scholarship.' So they said 'OK,' and that's how I ended up there. Michigan State was the only school I ever talked to.

"Two weeks after that I got a call from the (major junior) Toronto Marlboros, but my mom told them I had already signed up to go to Michigan State."

So there you have it. Dad got him started in hockey. Mom got him into Michigan State expense free. Ross did the rest. As part of a freshman class that also included Colp, Brendon Moroney, Daryl Rice and John Sturges, Ross became the catalyst of the best MSU teams that never made it to the NCAA Tournament. These were teams that won at least 22 games for four straight seasons, teams that never won a Western Collegiate Hockey Association championship, but never finished with a losing conference record, and teams that lit up scoreboards and filled up the stands, first in Demonstration Hall, and then in beautiful, new Munn Arena. Teams that brought you to the edge of your seat. Teams that were truly something to see.

"It was wide open, absolutely," said Sturges, who played on Ross' wing for four seasons. "You didn't want to be a goalie on our team. But we had a lot of talent."

Ross quickly established himself as the most talented of the bunch, which the Spartans suspected he might even before he played his first game. Although he was listed at just 5-6 and 155 pounds in MSU's 1972-73 Hockey Media Guide, Ross was written up as follows: "His experience is about the best among the new players ... A center who figures to develop into a standout performer ... Comes to State from the Detroit Junior Wings ... He's a powerful skater, has good moves and a lot of hockey sense."

Even so, Ross got off to something of a slow start.

"I don't think I scored a goal until Christmas," Ross said. "Or maybe it was when we were in Cleveland for a tournament. I forget where we were even at when it happened. But I know the first half of the season I didn't do too well. The second half I did fairly well."

For the record, Ross scored his first career goal on Dec. 19, 1972, in an 8-3 victory over Brown University at the Cleveland Invitational.

Soon after that the numbers began to pile up.

"I never really thought about it too much. It just kind of happened," Ross said. "It was coming together at the end of my freshman year and it just kind of continued on out.

"Amo had us practice a lot of the specialty-team work all the time. We practiced penalty killing and the power play for a long time each day. I think that really helped with our confidence and puckhandling. And he didn't really start to switch guys around too much where he'd say, 'OK, you guys are lousy. We're going with five new guys.' Even though we went through some bad spells, he'd stick with us. That helped build our confidence. And when we got into game situations, we knew we could score.

"We also did a lot of shooting drills in practice. You have to give Amo credit. I don't know how much we worked on some of the other things, but we worked on shooting all the time. And really, when you think about it,

when you get in close and you have to score, you have to score. We had a lot of players who, once they got in close, that was it. All the guys on the team really had a good touch around the net. I think all the shooting drills and specialty work really paid off in the long run."

It did for Colp, who stands second behind only Ross on MSU's career points list with 300. And for Rice, who is fifth all-time in scoring with 225 points. Ross, however, was always a cut above, even on these high-flying, free-wheeling teams.

Tom Ross and fellow All-American Steve Colp helped comprise one of college hockey's most exciting and explosive attacks in the early-to-mid 1970's.

"Tommy was a pretty phenomenal hockey player," Sturges said. "And we had a power play that was second to none. I can remember seeing an article a few years ago about Northern Michigan, which had what some people thought was the best power play in college hockey (in 1991, when NMU beat Boston University for the national championship). And it quoted (Wisconsin coach) Jeff Sauer, who was coaching at Colorado College when we played. And he said, 'Well, there was one that was better, the Colp-Rice-Ross-Sturges power play at Michigan State.

"I played the point, you had Rice, Ross and Colp up front and the fifth guy was Norm Barnes (from 1972-73 through 1973-74) and then Pat Betterly (in the 1974-75 and 1975-76 seasons). And we were really able to move the puck around, especially Tommy. The kid could handle the puck unbelievably well. And if he got it, nine times out of 10 you knew he'd put the puck in the net."

The way Ross saw it, he was just doing what he was supposed to.

"A goalie never really beats you," he once explained. "A goalie takes up a very small space in the crease when you think about it. He can't cover the entire net. So you can either shoot it where he isn't, or try to fake him and make him commit early and leave another part of the net open."

Often, he made it look just that easy. Ross was especially devastating over his final two seasons. In 1974-75 and 1975-76, Ross was a two-time All-American, a two-time national scoring champion and a two-time MSU MVP. He probably could have added "U.S. Olympian" in there somewhere, too, but as it turned out Ross was too much of a Spartan at heart to leave East Lansing for a season.

"Tommy was asked to play for the Olympic team in 1976," Sturges said. "He wanted to graduate with our class."

So he stayed at State. And instead of going to the Olympics, Ross went back and forth to class on the same rickety bicycle he'd been riding around campus for three years. And he went to Mac's Bar to drink beer and hang out with his teammates. And he continued going about the business of rewriting

the MSU record book and trying to help carry the Spartans to a national championship.

Ross almost pulled it off, too. The '75-76 season ended one game shy of the Final Four, with a 7-6, triple-overtime loss to Minnesota.

Minnesota went on to win the national championship.

Ross had to settle for going down in history.

"He probably had the greatest career of any athlete ever at Michigan State," Bessone said. "Tommy could do it all."

He could at Michigan State, at least. But that apparently wasn't enough to convince NHL types Ross deserved a chance to play with the big boys. The Colorado Rockies, St. Louis Blues and Detroit Red Wings all owned Ross' rights at one time or another, but none of those organizations (none of which were burning up the league at the time, by the way), felt obliged to give Ross more than a job in the minors.

He spent his first year after graduation in Port Huron (St. Louis' International Hockey League affiliate), but lost half a season to torn knee ligaments. Then it was on to Kalamazoo, a Detroit farm club in the IHL, where he scored 82, 116 and 103 points and was on two Turner Cup-champion teams over the course of the next three seasons. And still Detroit wouldn't give Ross so much as a cup of coffee.

"Tommy Ross could have played in the NHL, but they never gave him a break because they thought he was too small," Bessone said. "I used to tell (former Detroit General Manager Ted) Lindsay, 'Christ, he's as big as you were. This kid can really go.' He'd lead Kalamazoo in scoring, go to training camp and lead the team in scoring and they still never gave him a shot. Finally, he quit after his fourth year and went over to Europe to play. That was a disappointment.

"Now he plays in these old-timers games. And he can still really go."

Several factors played a hand in Ross never quite making his way to the NHL. One was that he never had an agent pushing and pleading his case. Another was even the MSU Hockey Media guide inadvertently slighted him on one occasion, listing him at 5-5, 155 one season after he had "grown" to 5-7, 165. Another was the climate in the NHL in the mid-to-late 1970s. Everyone was looking for goons and thugs to counter what was happening in Philadelphia, where the Broad Street Bullies were terrorizing and clubbing their way to back-to-back Stanley Cup championships. Still another, and in Ross' eyes a most significant one, was a five-week trip to Europe Ross made with the U.S. National Team in March of 1975.

"The coach was Bob Johnson and there was a lot of politics involved," Ross remembered. "They had a lot of Minnesota players over there playing (Johnson, the former coach at Wisconsin, was a native of Minneapolis), and I was playing on the third or fourth line. I played against these same guys in college all year long and I was better than they were, but I was on the third or fourth line. And every second period, our line sat. I'd play a period, three or four shifts, then sit a period, then play three or four more shifts ...

"I got kind of frustrated with that and I didn't play real well. And I think there were a lot of people (scouts) watching those games."
Maybe Ross reaching pro hockey's highest level-as so many Spartans have since-just wasn't meant to be.

"The guy I used to talk about all the time was Paul Woods," Ross said. "He played for Detroit for years. I would look at the statistics and say, 'What did he do last year? OK, he got three goals and five assists. He had eight points in 72 games.' Then I'd be in contact with Ted Lindsay and he'd say, 'Look at this Paul Woods. He comes in and lifts weights, he does this, he does that. Boy, is he ever good.' He'd be all gung-ho and say, 'We're going to rip up his contract and give him a new one because he's working so hard.' And I'd say, 'Well, that's fine. But if I played 72 games and had eight points or 10 points or 15 points, I'd give the money back and quit.' That was the attitude I had.

"But I certainly wasn't going to go up there and beat anyone up, and that's what they were all looking for at the time. It just happened to be the era, the timing. Now, if you came out of college with statistics like I had, you'd probably be fine."

You'd probably be a millionaire, too. Calgary's Theoren Fleury, for example, was granted a chance to play in the late 1980s even though he's listed at just 5-6, 160. And Fleury has twice scored 40 or more goals in a season, twice registered 100 or more points in a season and in the 1996-97 season earned a base salary of $2.375 million.

Ross never even sniffed money such as that. Once he gave up on ever realizing his NHL dream, he settled for playing in Holland for a season, then in Italy for three more before hanging up his blades. He's a family man now, and plays only in alumni, old-timers or social outings.

"I think I probably could have played in the NHL. I don't know how long I would have lasted and I don't know how well I would have done, but I know I deserved more of an opportunity," he said. "Even though I performed well everywhere, it just wasn't going to happen.

"Europe was a great experience. And when it was time to quit, when my wife thought it was time to settle down, it wasn't tough at all. You kind of start a new phase in your life. We were starting a family. And up until then, I had never had any Friday or Saturday nights free before. After a while, you're saying, 'Hey, this is kind of neat. I can go out with the gang on Friday night, I can go snow skiing, I can try different things ...'"

Ross plays hockey now on his terms, although not all that much else has changed. Sturges still has to occasionally get Ross out of a few tight spots when the Spartan alumni get together, and Ross still stands out among the rest.

"I'd like to think I still have it," Ross said, laughing. "It's not the passion it was once before, but I still enjoy it. The skating, the stickhandling, the shooting ..."

Throw 'scoring' in there somewhere, too. For at Michigan State, nobody ever did any of that any better than Tommy Ross.

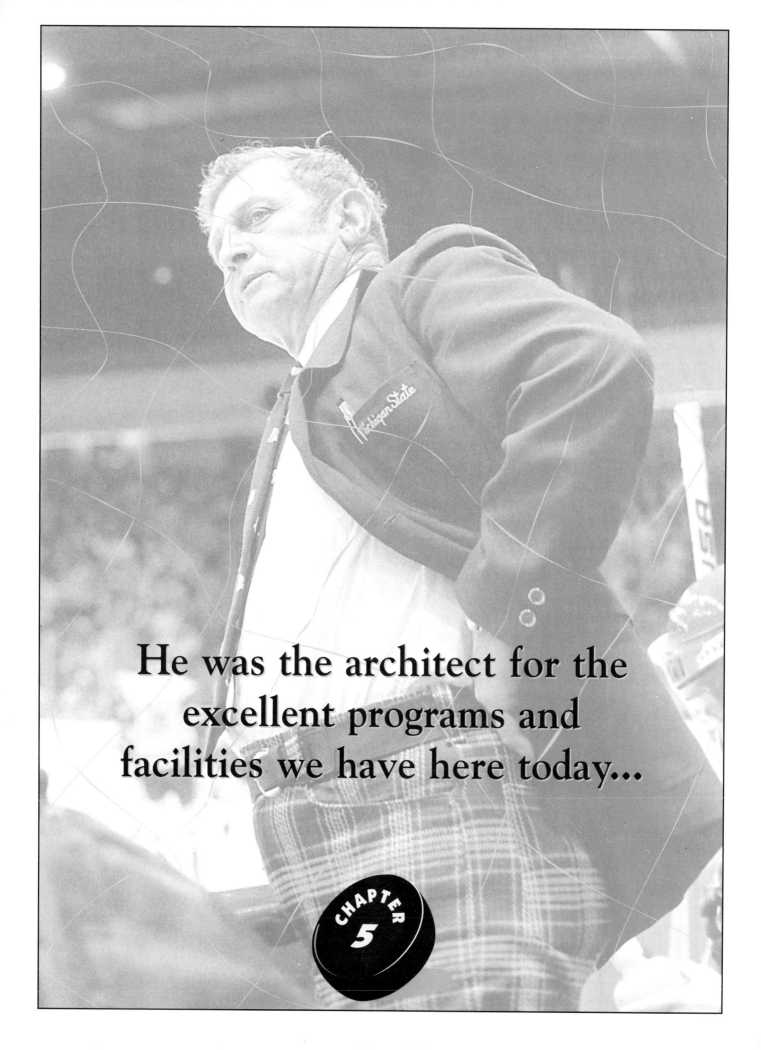

He was the architect for the excellent programs and facilities we have here today...

Chapter 5

His career record at Michigan State stands at 367-427-20, a winning percentage of .463 that suggests mediocrity more than the stuff of which legends are made. But in this case, the numbers don't begin to tell the entire story. For former Spartan mentor Amo Bessone is indeed a legendary figure, not just in East Lansing, Michigan, but all across the parts of America that passionately follow hockey (Bessone was a charter member of the MSU Hall of Fame and was inducted into the U.S. Hockey Hall of Fame in October of 1992), and not just because of his blue-collar charm. For Bessone, all the honors and accolades, career .463 winning percentage or not, there have been many over the years-were richly deserved.

"Amo Bessone, Hall of Famer" ought to say it all. But if his meritorious service to the game and to his beloved

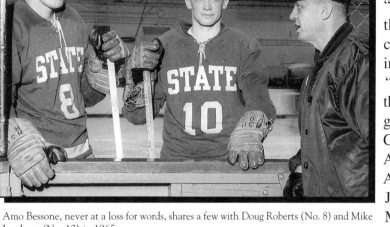

Amo Bessone, never at a loss for words, shares a few with Doug Roberts (No. 8) and Mike Jacobson (No. 10) in 1965.

MSU must still be justified by a number, the figure should have nothing to do with wins, ties or losses.

The number 28, the number of years Bessone served as the head hockey coach at Michigan State, defines the man as well as any.

"If I had it to do all over again, I wouldn't change a thing," Bessone said.

Well, maybe one or two. With another break, bounce or perhaps another timely goal here or there, Bessone's national championship count might well stand at three or four (in 1959, 1967 and 1976 he and his Spartans were oh-so-close) rather than one (1966). But then again, winning was never something that consumed Bessone. Certainly, he wanted to win as much as the next guy, and

Bessone competed like hell whenever the chance to win was at hand. But to Bessone and a few of the coaches of his time, guiding the sport through times of incredible growth was always a higher calling.

"Amo was sort of an icon there at Michigan State," said Herb Brooks, who played at Minnesota from 1957-59, coached the Golden Gophers from 1972 to 1979 (winning national championships in 1973-74, 1975-76 and 1978-79) and led Team USA's "Miracle On Ice" run to the gold medal in the 1980 Winter Olympics. "And he was one of the real leaders in college hockey during his tenure there.

"When I started, there were some real giants in the (Western Collegiate Hockey Association), Murray Armstrong at Denver, John MacInnes at Michigan Tech, Amo Bessone at Michigan State and Bob Johnson at Wisconsin. And throughout this whole thing, Amo still had time for everybody and for the growth of college hockey. To him the most important thing was finding ways to grow college hockey in the United States."

College hockey, meanwhile, had plenty of growing to do when Bessone first took over the Michigan State reins in the fall of 1951, especially in East Lansing. The sport was an extra-curricular activity back then, not a big business. The evolution of the game and its promotion were at least as important as who ultimately won and lost, if not more so. And a spirit of camaraderie among the competitors was always present, a spirit that in many cases today has gone the way of dinosaur

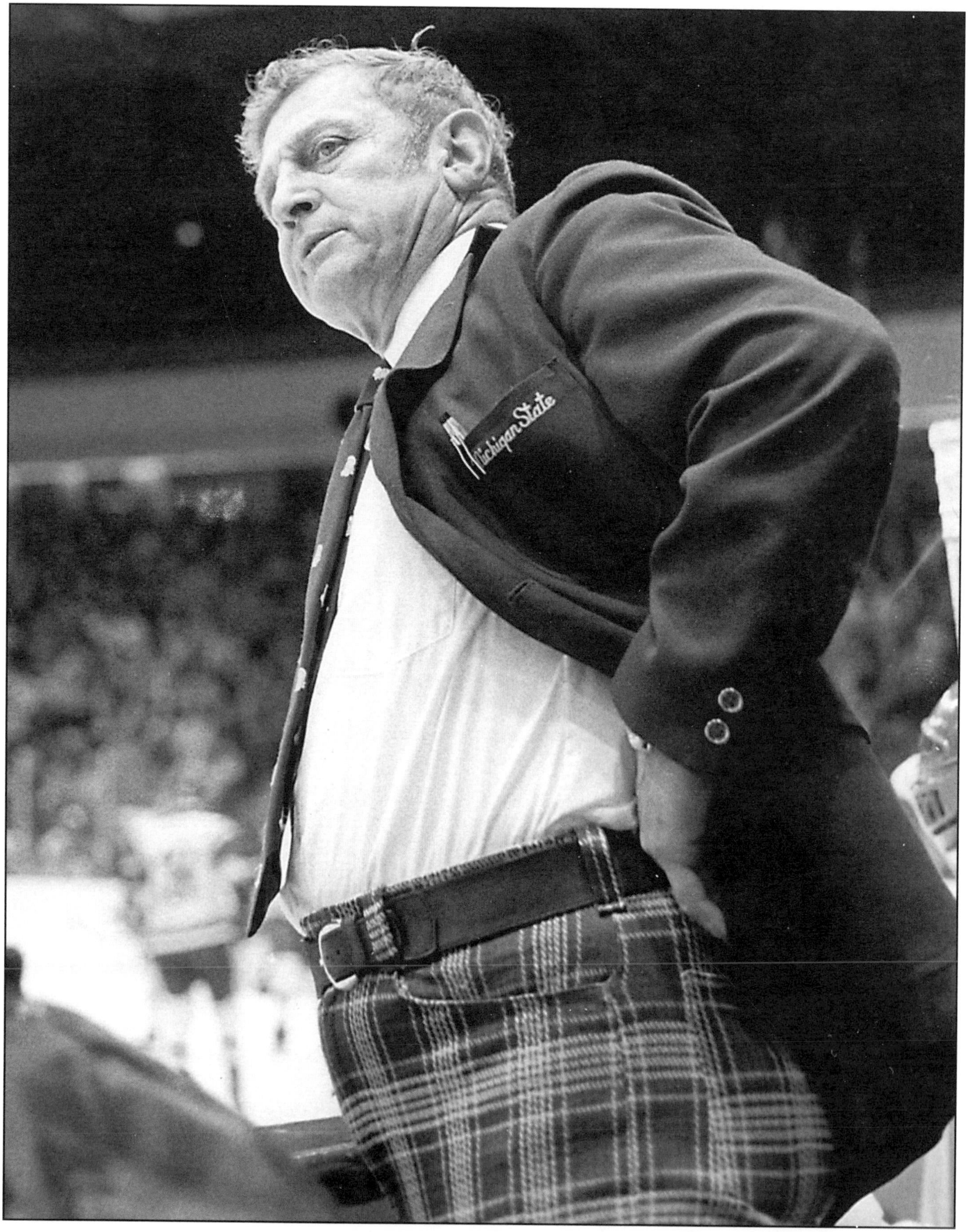
Michigan State

rinks such as Demonstration Hall and the long-outdated practice of recruiting basically over the telephone.

"Coaches got along better in those days," Bessone said, recalling the times when publicity, pressure and the constant distraction of dealing with a mass media were pretty much foreign concepts as far as hockey was concerned.

To illustrate his point, Bessone recounted the following anecdote, a personal favorite among the 1,000 or so Bessone anecdotes that have entertained Spartan hockey followers for decades:

"One time we played Colorado (College). So I picked up the Colorado coach, John Matchefts, at Jenison Field House and said, 'C'mon, we're going to my house.' And he said we had to go to the Holiday Inn first to pick up the two referees. So we were waiting for them at the bar, the referees had to take their showers first, and (MSU assistant football coach) Hank Bullough was in there, too. So Hank says, 'Hey Amo, come over here. I want you to meet somebody.' It was (Baltimore Colts head coach Don) Shula. The reason he was there was they were getting ready to sign (Spartan defensive lineman) Bubba Smith.

"So we get to talking and finally Shula says, 'Wait a minute, have I got this straight? You coach at Michigan State, and you coach at Colorado, and you guys played each other tonight and you're here to pick up the two referees and you're all going over to your house to have a party? Christ, that's the way sports should be.

"'If we ever did that in the pros, we'd be long gone.'"

Throughout Bessone's days at Michigan State, that type of thing was done all the time.

"Usually after the Saturday night game we'd always have a party at my house," he remembered. "We'd invite the other coach, his staff, their publicity man, the newspaper man, whoever travelled with them ... It was good. We'd have a big shindig at my house until about 3 a.m. I never saw a problem with it. I mean, why not? To me, if you can't have any friendship involved ... There's enough animosity and stuff like that going on (outside of athletics).

"Another time, I'm arguing with this referee, Dick Noblet, I mean I'm really giving him the business. And after the game the other coach, I forget who we were playing, is getting ready to come over and he says, 'Wait a minute, you mean that referee is coming, too? The way you two were going at it, I thought you were going to start throwing punches at one another.' I said, "He'll be here in a minute.'

"Next thing you know Dick comes in and the first thing he says is, 'Where's the beer?' He was a good kid, a good friend of mine. He played defense for me at Michigan Tech ...

"They don't do that much anymore. It's too business-like now."

The Spartan players also got regular tastes of Mrs. Mary Bessone's spaghetti, especially at the annual season-ending parties Bessone often said wouldn't break up "until the beer was gone."

It was a different program then, a different game, a different era.

"We used to have open tryouts the first few years. There'd be 150 kids on the ice. Some of 'em couldn't even skate," Bessone remembered. "One time when we were playing Colorado there were 18 people at Dem Hall. There was a figure skating exhibition or something going on after the game and 10 of the people in the stands had come in from Colorado for the figure skating thing. My first six or seven years at Michigan State, we were lucky to get 15 people."

Today hockey is a big-time operation. Almost everyone who plays is on scholarship, television brings the games to alumni all across North America and Munn Arena-the beautiful facility that was constructed because Bessone's program grew and grew to the point where it simply outgrew

The one, the only Amo Bessone.

ancient Dem Hall-is almost always packed to the rafters. One national championship? MSU would forever be in Bessone's debt even if that 1965-66 team had never caught lightning in a bottle and won it all.

No wonder they held a night for him after he retired (Sept. 17, 1979-Amo Bessone Night). No wonder former player Butch Miller presented Bessone with a new car, an Oldsmobile Cutlass Supreme, to commemorate the occasion. No wonder Athletic Director Joe Kearney spoke of Bessone in almost reverent tones when he told the throng that had assembled at the Kellogg Center to laud Bessone, "He was the architect for the excellent program and facilities we have here today."

He was a hell of a character, too.

Gruff, loud, rumpled, emotional, opinionated ... about the only thing Bessone wasn't was subtle (especially the time he punched one of his Providence Reds teammates in the face during an American Hockey League game because the guy was getting on Bessone's brother Pete, who happened to be playing for Cleveland that night). And his sense of humor was often as entertaining as any of the best of his 28 teams ever were.

Take another of the 1,000 or so Amo anecdotes, for example - Bessone's reaction to the Minnesota fans' habit of chanting "Oh, shit" in unison whenever things weren't going the Golden Gophers' way. Noticing a University of Minnesota professor seated near the MSU bench at one instance while this was going on, Bessone quipped, "Hey professor, you sure have a horseshit English department around here."

Although he actually considered attending Michigan, Amo Bessone wound up playing his college hockey at Illinois.

Bessone's unique ability to laugh and to find humor where others didn't often made light of even the most uncomfortable of situations.

"One time we were on the road in Madison, Wisconsin, and it was Amo's birthday," recalled Tom Ross, MSU's all-time leading scorer, a star in the early-to-mid 1970s and one of Bessone's favorite players. "So we ordered a cake for him, we brought it out at the hotel restaurant and we all sang 'Happy Birthday' to him. Then I kind of made some comment to the effect of, 'Hey guys, what do you say I throw this cake in Amo's face?' No one really responded to that. Everyone just kind of stood around and looked down and didn't say anything. The guy I think it really hurt was Amo.

"So then Amo says, 'Hey guys, what do you say I throw this cake in Roscoe's face?' And everyone said, 'Yeah, yeah, yeah ...' So Amo picked up the cake and he smashed it right in my face, right there in the restaurant. The guys loved it.

"I got him back later on. Every year we used to have a spaghetti dinner at (teammate) Denny Olmstead's place; his dad had a farm. So Amo was sitting there in a lounge chair and we were giving him some kind of presentation and I ran up with a whipped cream pie and nailed him."

Bessone no doubt enjoyed an equal chuckle on both occasions, for common sense and practicality were also Amo trademarks.

"We upset Michigan State (7-6 in triple overtime at Munn Arena) and were able to go on to the Final Four and win the national championship in 1976," Brooks said. "That was one of Amo's really fine teams and I know how crushed he was. "But within an hour after that game he was saying, 'Come on over to the house and have a bite to eat,' and 'good luck.' How he could shift gears and, again, always see the big picture, was so unique."

"One time we were stuck in a snowstorm in the Denver airport, and we were there for something like 26 hours," recalled Doug French, a defenseman from 1965-66 through 1967-68. "At first Amo kept walking around saying, 'You guys are all representing Michigan State University, so let's act like gentlemen.' Finally, after about 10 hours, Amo walked by again and Mike Coppo said, 'You know Coach ...,' and Amo cut him off and said, 'Rook, I think you're right,' and away we went. We spent the next eight or 10 hours at every gin mill they had in that airport.

"But that was Amo. I mean, at first we tried ... But after a while, what were you going to do?"

Another time in Minneapolis, Bessone caught French and several other Spartans breaking curfew the night before a series with the Gophers. The next day, the guilty parties were summoned before Bessone.

"There were about six or eight of us," French said, "but we had Gaye Cooley and Jerry Fisher with us. So the next morning Amo calls us all in and says, 'Normally, I'd send every one of you guys home. The thing that saved you is Fisher and Cooley, because we don't have anybody else to play goal.' "

Supporting his players was also a Bessone strong suit. If one of his guys got into trouble, there was literally nothing Bessone wouldn't do to back him up.

"One time at Colorado College, Rick Hargreaves got into it with a guy and they both ended up getting kicked out of the game," said Sandy McAndrew, an MSU winger from 1964-65 through 1966-67. "Well, the dressing rooms there were both at the same end of the rink, one to the left and one to the right.

"So Rick is going out and the other guy is going out, and as they open up the doors behind the net at the one end, the crowd all of a sudden starts swarming down around them. All of a sudden we realize there's really something going on over there, but by now they have the doors closed again.

"Amo didn't care. He jumps off the bench, runs down the ice, goes around behind the net, jumps up over the plexiglass and wades his way through the crowd like a gorilla. When he finally gets through the crowd, there's Rick ... on top of this guy and just pounding the shit out of him. So Amo stands there looking around for a little while, and then finally he says, 'Hey Rick, you better stop that.'"

All the players had to put up with in return was the occasional outburst ("When I yell it means I see them doing something out there," Bessone often noted. "I tell them that when I don't yell at them, they have something to worry about."), his habit of signaling for line changes by putting a pinky in each corner of his mouth and emitting a shrill whistle, and the foul smell of the large, half-smoked cigar that could usually be found resting in Bessone's mouth when his pinkies weren't.

And even on those rare instances when Amo felt the need to get on one of his boys, he did so with equal amounts of tact and temper.

"He never acted like he was superior. He treated you like an equal," said Joe Selinger, the Spartans' goalie from 1956-57 through 1958-59 and the school's first first-team All-America selection in 1959. "He'd never take people and just chew 'em out from one end to the other in front of other people. Sometimes in the games he'd get a little excited and holler at some guys, but basically, in handling people, he'd never make you feel bad."

"A lot of the players that came in there, they were from Canada, unknown parts of Canada," Ross noted. "They'd come in a lot of times with no direction. And the person they looked to for direction was Amo, especially early in his career. Amo was a fatherly figure.

"When it got to our era, he'd give us a lot of direction, too, and not just what to do on the ice, either. A lot of his talks in the locker room would be life stories more than hockey stories. He wanted to win as badly as anyone else. But he wanted us to mature and to grow up to be good people, too.

"Guys would be drinking beer, having a party, something like that, and Amo would say,

Longtime Bessone assistant coach Alex Terpay obviously didn't have Amo's flare for hats.

'Anybody can drink beer, you guys. Don't make this a profession.' He'd say, 'You want to drink beer? I can drink beer. You want me to sit down and drink beer with you? Any drunk can drink beer. I can drink beer with you all night long. But we have a game to play tomorrow night and I don't think it's a smart thing to do.' Instead of him just saying, 'Don't do that,' he'd say, 'Here's why you shouldn't do that.' That was incorporated a lot of times in the locker room when he'd talk to us about things and it was motivating.

"It got to the point where a lot of my determination came from playing for him. I wanted to win for Amo. I wanted to score points for me, but I wanted to win for Amo. I had a vested interest in him, too."

Added Selinger regarding the Spartans' overtime loss to North Dakota in the 1959 National Championship Game: "All the guys liked Amo and we were most disappointed that we lost and he didn't win. Something like that, you mostly do it for somebody; you don't do it for yourself.

"We were trying to win it for him."

Bessone cared as much for opponents as he did his own.

"When I started coaching, one of his best friends, John Mariucci, who had been his counterpart at the University of Minnesota, told me, 'Stay close to Amo,'" Brooks said. "And Amo, in a lot of ways, sort of adopted me and helped me through my formative years. He was like a big brother to me.

"He was a real special guy, and is today."

Bessone's coaching philosophy was as uncomplicated and unpretentious as his personality. His career preceded the "professionalization" of the college game, where tapes are intensely scrutinized, players work out year-round and undergo a battery of physical tests (even one to determine their percentage of body fat), opponents are thoroughly scouted, and complex strategies are concocted around the strengths and weaknesses of the other team. Under Bessone, the Spartans worked mostly on conditioning, fundamentals and special teams. They did what Bessone thought they did best night in and night out, no matter what team was sitting on the other bench. When they were good enough, they won. When they weren't, they didn't.

To Bessone, the on-ice part of it really was that simple.

"Amo was a great guy," said John Sturges, a former teammate of Ross' on the firewagon, thrill-a-minute Bessone

The magnitude of the Spartans' trip to the 1986 Final Four in Providence, RI, demanded that Amo Bessone be brought in to address the Michigan State faithful.

teams that always won at least 22 games a season between 1972-73 and 1975-76. "Was he a great coach? Amo was a great guy."

More often than not that was more than enough. There wasn't much adjusting from week to week in Amo's days, the lines didn't change much and it has been said that you could attend a practice in 1965 and attend a practice in 1975 and it would be the same practice. There wasn't a lot of strategy. It was pretty much throw 'em out and play the game.

"But the thing about Amo, probably his strongest point was he tried to get your maturity level up and he tried to keep you together as a team," Sturges said. "He didn't let people try to be individuals. If he had let the talent get to the point where guys were 'reading their press clippings,' and five or six players were perceived as 'better than the rest,' I don't our team would have performed very well. But he was able to keep that talent together.

"He was never a father figure to me the way he was for Tommy Ross, but I still have a lot of admiration for him. How could I ever say anything bad about Amo? He brought me to Michigan State, I got a great education, I got my degree and I had a great career. And when my family would come to town, or when anyone's family would come to town, he would invite them over and it was expected that you would go to his home because he welcomed you there. Mary Bessone had arthritis and she couldn't really get around, but she was still like a mother to everyone. After the games were over and it was time to interact, that's when it was like a family."

It didn't matter the season or the era.

"Amo's idea of the game was to keep it simple, stupid," Brooks said. "But he was a smart hockey man. He could sit and talk X's and O's all day long, but he didn't believe in book-coaches.

"We have too many book-coaches today, and they get so academic that while the game is going on, they have to take time out and run for the library. Amo's strengths were his ability on the ice and on the bench to adjust. Amo did a lot of things very instinctively.

"I think we need more coaches like Amo Bessone and less of the book-coaches we have today."

"He was an interesting guy," said Don Heaphy, a defenseman in the mid-1960s and a co-captain of Bessone's 1966 national championship team. "I don't know exactly how you would describe him ... He was a little gruff when he spoke, but he always had good stories to tell. He was a good guy to play for, a really good guy ...

"He was almost like a friend ... And his wife made great spaghetti sauce."

"A gem of a guy," McAndrew said. "A wonderful, wonderful person."

"A good man," French added.

Sometimes he won. More often, he lost. But win or lose, Bessone always distinguished himself as a caretaker of the program at Michigan State and the college game.

Initially, he fought merely to have a standard practice time and to get a few scholarships thrown hockey's way. Later, he was a staunch proponent of the Big Ten Conference annually crowning a hockey champion, something it eventually did between 1959-1968 from among Michigan State, Michigan and Minnesota and, from 1969-81 with Wisconsin included as well (Ohio State competed, too, in 1969, '71 and '81; Bessone's Spartans finished first five times). Bessone also championed causes such as requiring schools to play in arenas that were able to manufacture ice and thus be heated, allowing for more comfort for players, coaches and fans (he even threatened to never again bring MSU to North Dakota after a 1967 series in which it was 28 below zero outside and 7 below inside in Grand Forks); and supported regulations that limited older, more experienced Canadian players' opportunities to compete against younger Americans for spots on college rosters.

As the game emerged into the spotlight and the NHL began to finally take regular notice of all that collegiate talent in the mid-1970s, Bessone was outspoken in his beliefs that players should stay in school for four years before turning pro, and that the NHL teams that drafted them should award the college programs $4,000 per player once the player's career was over, as was once the practice with Canadian junior teams.

Bessone, and men like him who thrived despite the climate of the times, helped take college hockey from the days when the players were regarded as "Friday's children" into an era where they have attained near-equal status on some campuses with their revenue-producing brethren in football and basketball.

He even managed to add a personal touch to Munn Arena, which hosted its first game on Oct. 25, 1974, in part as a tribute to all Bessone had accomplished since the early 1950s and in part without Bessone's blessing.

"It was like going from a Model A Ford into a Cadillac," Bessone said of the move from Dem Hall to Munn. "But I would have been happy if we had just moved into Jenison (Field House).

"I can't remember the exact year, but at one point they called me in and asked me if Jenison would make a good hockey rink. They needed a new basketball arena, but we had started to go pretty good. I think we were like the No. 2 revenue-producing sport there for eight or nine years. So I said, 'Christ, this would make a great rink.' We would have been able to seat 8,000 or 9,000 in Jenison. But then Bert Smith, I think he was the AD at the time, he decided to go for a new hockey rink.

"We weren't pushing for it. We would have been happy playing in Jenison. And the only thing I did in regard to the construction of the new rink ... I remember they were just putting the finishing touches on the bench on our side, and I discovered we couldn't get one of the two doors open if they left it the way it was. So there was this carpenter there and I said, 'Wait a minute, this bench is too long. The door won't open. Cut it off right here.' And he said, 'I can't do that. The plans don't call for that.' So I said 'gimme that saw,' and I sawed the damn bench off myself."

Alas, all good things must come to an end, and Bessone's career was no different. Recruiting dropped off, attendance sagged and finally, as his health began to become an inconvenience, Bessone decided to retire at the conclusion of the 1978-79 season at the age of 63. His last game was on March 3, 1979. The Spartans beat Michigan, 5-3, at Munn.

"I couldn't go on the ice anymore (for practice)," Bessone explained. "I had to have a knee replaced, so I said, 'Aw, what the hell ... '

"The retirement party was great."

Bessone spent two years working as the assistant rink manager at Munn after that, and eventually relocated to Florida. He still catches all the hockey he can on his satellite dish, plays a little golf and travels when he can back to his native Massachusetts or to catch Michigan State in the NCAA Tournament. The Spartans still fly him in for the hockey banquet at the conclusion of each season.

"Michigan State has been very good to me," Bessone said.

And Bessone has been very good to Michigan State. Good enough that, decades later, it can be revealed in print that before winding up at Illinois (where he starred in hockey), Amo Bessone actually considered going to college-gasp!-in Ann Arbor.

"I almost went to Michigan," Bessone said. "I was accepted at Michigan. And then Vic Heyliger, who was the one that really recruited me, got the job at Illinois. Vic hadn't been coaching at Michigan but he had been helping them recruit, and he said, 'Hey Amo, how about coming with me to Illinois? Everything I promised you at Michigan will go through at Illinois.' You know, they promised you jobs and everything else ...

"Well, I didn't really know Vic Heyliger, but my brother Pete said, 'Go with Vic, he's a good guy.'"

That's how close one of MSU's most beloved athletic figures ever came to matriculating at Michigan. Yet in retrospect, Bessone probably would have eventually been forgiven even for a transgression of such magnitude, all other things being equal.

Such a man, after all, can not be justly summed up merely by what it says on a diploma, or even in the record book.

March 3, 1979: A tribute to Amo Bessone precedes a 5-3 victory over Michigan in Bessone's final game as coach at Michigan State.

One hell of a place to coach...

CHAPTER
6

Chapter 6

When Ron Mason arrived at Michigan State in the spring of 1979, Spartan fans, students and alumni were riding what had to be an all-time high. Although the football team had been on probation in 1978 and was thus ineligible to participate in the Rose Bowl, the Spartans had still won the Big Ten championship with a 7-1 mark and gone 8-3 overall. After a slow start, Kirk Gibson, Eddie Smith and friends had jelled and become one of the most feared teams in the country. They knocked the snot out of Michigan, 24-15, in Ann Arbor. They hammered Indiana, 49-14, and they wasted Wisconsin (55-2), Illinois (59-19), Northwestern (52-3) and Iowa (42-7). They were awesome.

The basketball team was even better.

The spring of '79 was indeed a time of Magic in East Lansing. Of Kelser, too. And Donnelly (Terry, not Mike), Brkovich, Vincent and Charles. This was the time when Earvin Johnson led State to its first and only national championship by pounding Penn and then grounding Larry Bird and Indiana State at the Final Four in Salt Lake City, Utah. The State News had said it all when it said "We're #1" in big, green type on its front page on March 28, 1979.

Unfortunately, hockey failed to share in the unbridled euphoria that was sweeping through campus and the community.

The 1970s might have been an era to remember on ice, but the decade ended with a crash-and-burn rather than in a blaze of glory. Yes,

there had been Michigan State's first Great Lakes Invitational Tournament championship in 1973. And the opening of state-of-the-art Munn Arena, a palace any program would be proud to call home, in 1974. And there had been 20-win seasons from 1971-72 through 1975-76. Unfortunately, the triple-overtime, 7-6 loss to Minnesota that closed the books on the 1975-76 campaign one step short of the Final Four proved to be MSU's last hurrah for quite some time, and coach Amo Bessone's last ever.

The Spartans went 14-21-1, 7-27-2 and 15-21-0 in Bessone's final three seasons, and finished eighth, 10th and eighth in the WCHA.

"Their hockey team had one of the worst records in the country at that point," Mason said.

Mason, who had moved from Lake Superior to Bowling Green in 1973-74, was at that point responsible for one of the best.

His Falcons had gone to the Final Four in 1977-78, becoming the first non-ECAC or WCHA team to do so, and had finished third. The next season BG missed out on the Final Four but continued putting up numbers (37-6-2) and gaining national attention. The team was even featured in Sports Illustrated's March 12 issue in '79. By recruiting the likes of Mike Liut, Brian MacLellan, John Markell, George McPhee, Ken Morrow and Mark Wells, Mason had built a program capable of consistently "knocking on the door nationally."

Is that the Bee Gees? Not quite, although Ron Mason's first staff at Michigan State (he's flanked by assistants John Mason, left, and Shawn Walsh) looked as if they'd have been right at home experiencing a little Saturday Night Fever with John Travolta.

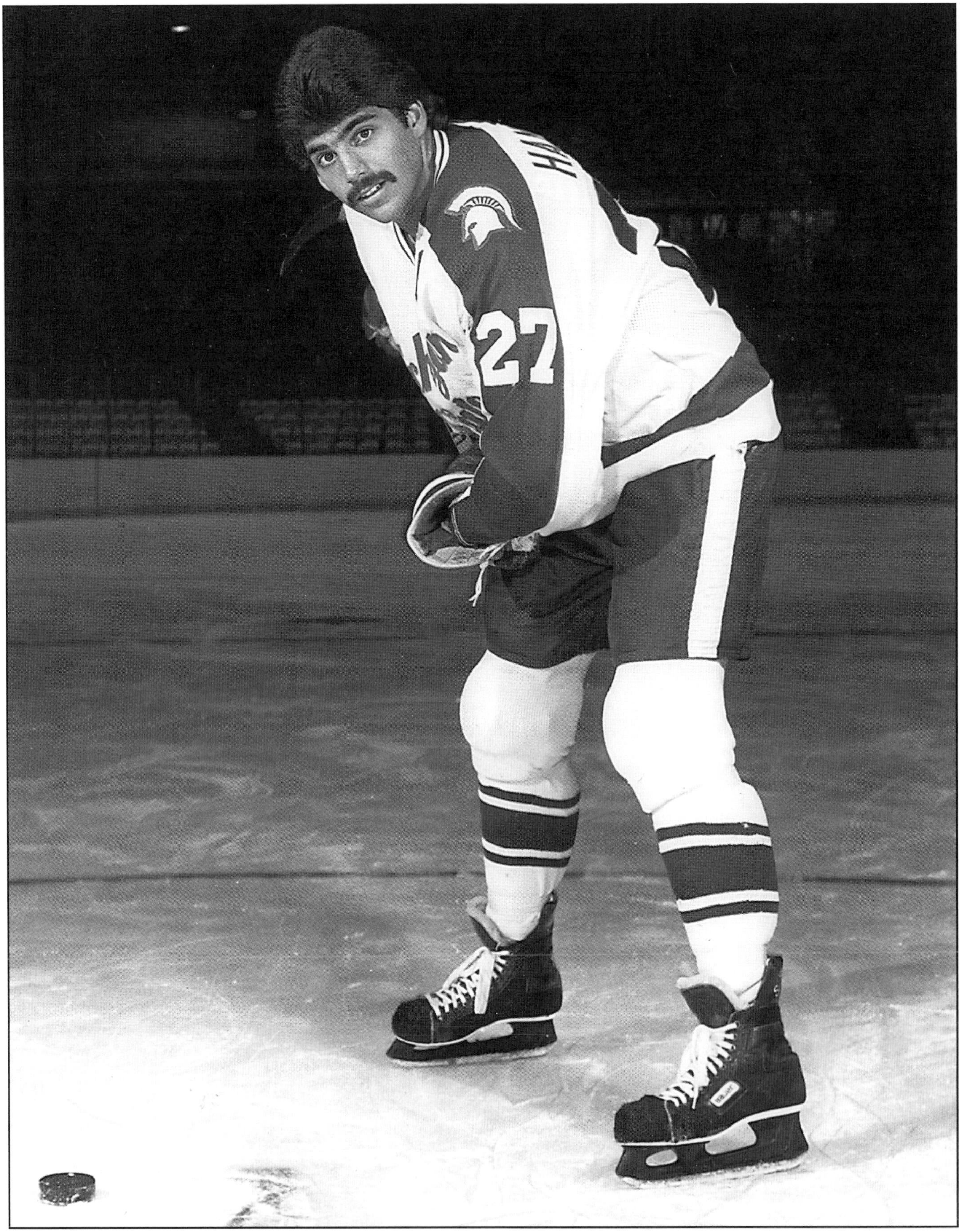
27

That's why, when Athletic Director Joe Kearney finally offered Mason the job Bessone had vacated by retiring, Mason said, "I need a night to think about this." Once Mason said that, Kearney didn't know what to think.

"I think I kind of shocked him a little bit," Mason said.

So Mason thought it over. He thought about the time he had hosted a coaching clinic early in his Lake Superior career, and how Bessone had pulled up in a car that had "Michigan State" stenciled on the sides. "I thought, 'Geez, is that ever something ... they have their own cars.'" And Mason thought about the time BG was busing home from Ferris State a year or so earlier, and how he had thought while passing the I-96 exit for East Lansing, "Michigan State ... now that would be one hell of a place to coach" And he thought about the strong team he'd be leaving, and the weak one he'd inherit ...

"Finally, I thought, 'Heck, I've been to Lake Superior, I've been to Bowling Green, I'll make this program work, too.'" Mason decided.

He was introduced to the local media on March 30, 1979. He was 39 years old, had a 13-year coaching record of 289-110-14 and had never had a losing season. The future couldn't have been more exciting.

"At first, Ron, (assistant coach) John Mason and myself were living in a two-bedroom apartment in married-student housing at Spartan Village," recalled Shawn Walsh, a longtime assistant of Ron Mason's at Bowling Green and Michigan State who went on to become the head coach at the University of Maine. "All we had was furniture. We were never there because we were always in the office or out recruiting.

"But one thing I'll always remember is dri-

Mark Hamway led MSU's 1980's resurgence on and off the ice with a persona and presence that won him universal acclaim and admiration.

ving back to Bowling Green after one of our first weeks (at MSU). We were going back to BG to get some of our belongings or something, and the three of us went back in two different cars. It was the day that Kirk Gibson hit the home run that clinched the Big Ten title for the baseball team (Gibby was also a baseball star at MSU).

"We were listening to the game on the radio. I think we were right around Brighton, and all of a sudden we started honking our horns at each other. At that point, I knew were Spartans."

Mason's unofficial "Welcome to East Lansing' was extended shortly thereafter.

"It was at Ron's first Ralph Young Fund dinner, and (basketball coach) Jud Heathcote and (football coach) Darryl Rogers were there," Walsh explained. "Ron was a little uncomfortable. It was his first speaking engagement in front of boosters old and new. He just got up and said he wanted to improve the program and then sat down to polite applause. Then Darryl got up and then Jud got up.

"Well, before they had introduced Ron, they had given out this Spartan of the Year recognition award. It went to some guy who had lost 150 pounds. So when Jud got up, he had been seated next to Ron, he said, 'Don't think this Mason guy is all that humble. He turned to me when they introduced Joe back there as the Spartan of the Year and said, 'What did that fat slob look like 150 pounds ago?'

"The place went crazy. Jud was just telling a joke, but Ron turned about eight shades of red. That was typical Jud. That was his way of welcoming Ron to Michigan State."

Unfortunately for State, although Mason was indeed welcomed on campus, he wasn't the second coming of Magic. At least not at the outset.

Even for Mason, it takes players, and in his first season at MSU, he simply didn't have enough to be successful. Despite the almost universal approval and enthusiasm Mason's hiring had generated, his first season played out much as Bessone's final one did. The Spartans went 14-24-0 and finished eighth in the WCHA. They gave up 11 goals once against Minnesota, 10 to Wisconsin,

Rugged defenseman Ken Leiter, a longtime friend of Mark Hamway's, was another essential cog in Ron Mason's first recruiting class at Michigan State.

nine to Minnesota, Notre Dame, North Dakota and Wisconsin, eight to Denver, Minnesota-Duluth, North Dakota and Western Michigan ...

Yet even as the losses mounted, so, too, did Mason's optimism. For taking their lumps out on the ice at Munn were two players who would eventually help hoist the program onto their shoulders and hoist trophies on high at Joe Louis Arena.

One, Mark Hamway, was a forward. The other, Ken Leiter, was a defenseman. Together, they became the first two blocks upon which a program was rebuilt.

"They were the key guys," Mason said.

And how. Both were initially supposed to play for Mason at Bowling Green. But when Mason made the move to East Lansing, both initially hedged. In the interim, Mason awarded a scholarship to forward Rico Martin, from Candiac, Quebec, and honored an invitation Bessone had extended to Nigel Thomas, a forward from Victoria, British Columbia. But the new coach still wanted Hamway and Leiter badly.

Leiter eventually accepted a scholarship, too. But when it came time for Hamway to decide between Michigan State and Michigan, there was no scholarship money left.

"I had to go to Joe Hamway (Mark's dad) and see if he could help us," Mason said. "Kenny Leiter needed the scholarship; Hammer really didn't. So Mark, Joe and I sat down and we talked it out. I leveled with him and he agreed to pay his own way the first year.

"He ended up getting a scholarship the next year, anyway. Still, it was a real coup getting Mark Hamway."

A native of Detroit, Hamway would go on to score 98 goals and record 201 points during his four seasons at Michigan State. But much more than scoring, Hamway brought a personality to the program. He not only became a captain during his days at State, but a prime example of all the Spartans hoped their players would become.

"He was gregarious, he helped encourage other players to come, he was well-liked, he was a good player, he was all the right things you were looking for," Mason said of Hamway. "He had skill, he had talent, he was well-dressed and well-spoken, he went to school, he got his degree ... Mark Hamway had it all."

Even the best-looking girlfriend.

"Of all the years I've ever played, he was the best captain of any team I've ever been on," said forward Tom Anastos, who joined the program in the fall of 1981. "He just had a way about him-self, he made people feel good about themselves. He really made an effort to make people feel a part of everything, whether you were a top scorer or a player that just practiced (but rarely got to dress for games). He went out of his way to make people feel comfortable.

"That was an important part of the team, and Hammer probably doesn't get as much credit as he deserves for that. He really tried to create a team environment. Plus, he was a hell of a hockey player."

So was Leiter, another Detroit native and "a tough kid from the tough side of the tracks,"

according to Mason. Both had size and strength. But Leiter wasn't nearly as outgoing as Hamway, nor as popular.

No one was. No Spartan probably has been since.

"Kenny was more of a leader by example because he worked really hard in games, worked really hard in practice and worked really hard off the ice. But he didn't do the things Mark did in a social environment, and that's as big a part of it as

Ron Mason's second recruiting class was also vital in turning State's fortunes around. Brought to MSU in the fall of 1980 were, front row, from left: Andre Lamarche (Drummondville, Que.), and Jeff Eisley (Redford, MI). Back row, from left: Ron Scott (Guelph, Ont.), Newell Brown (Cornwall, Ont.), Gary Haight (Edmunds, WA), and David Taylor (Charlottetown, P.E.I.). That's Mason kneeling between Lamarche and Eisley.

anything," Anastos explained. "When you have guys coming in from Pilot Mound, Manitoba, and Regina, Saskatchewan, and some of these places, you have to really make them feel a part of it. They're not raised in a culture where going to a U.S. college is really a critical thing, so a lot of these guys come in and ... I remember (Pilot Mound native) Lyle Phair once telling me he had seen more cement in riding in from Capital City Airport to campus than he had ever seen in his life. Hammer deserves a lot of credit for being able to create an environment where these guys felt comfortable."

Or, as Dee Rizzo put it shortly after joining the program in the fall of '81, "We're teammates, we're basically the same age ... and to a certain extent Mark Hamway is my hero."

The Spartans needed one at the time, too, because they had yet to become a team under Mason. The recruiting class for 1980-81 produced goalie Ron Scott, center Newell Brown and defensemen Gary Haight, Jeff Eisley and David Taylor, all of whom would go on to either become stars or prominent players at Michigan State. But the group that dressed together in the locker room was still divided between Amo Bessone-players and Ron Mason-players and they weren't all on the same page.

Ron Scott's teammates certainly appreciated the Guelph, Ontario native's dazzling ability.

The atmosphere was such that some players were privately considered by others to be satisfied merely with being an athlete and a campus big shot. Some were accused by others of being more concerned about smoking pot than playing hockey. Some, it was said by others, didn't really care who won or lost as long as they got their letterman's jacket. Others insisted they found MSU a great place upon their arrival, wanted to give as much back to the school as they could and wanted a compelling future as a group.

At this juncture Munn Arena was indeed a house divided.

"The right Amo players cared," Mason insisted. "The ones that wanted to win, they rallied. Kenny Paraskevin was my captain one year, plus we had Teddy Huesing, Russ Welch ... those guys wanted to win.

"But there weren't enough of them. Other guys resisted that I wanted to do this or that. They thought, 'He's favoring his players.' That wasn't the way it was at all."

The 1980-81 season was also painful. Thanks to Scott, an acrobatic and brilliant puck-stopper from Guelph, Ontario, the goals-against dropped significantly (from 227 to 144). But so, too, did the goals-for (116, down from 158). Mason's second year ended up worse than his first

-at 12-22-2 overall and 7-20-1 and last in the WCHA.

At the two-year mark, the rebuilding of the program was still at ground-level (actually, it was below ground-level; it was in the basement). And yet, a series of events and experiences throughout that second year had ensured that the ones that followed would be something special.

One was a second talented class of freshmen getting baptized by fire in the rugged WCHA.

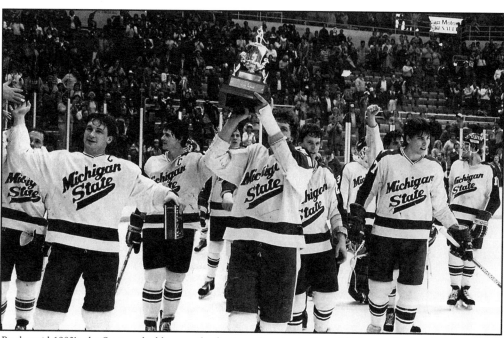

By the mid 1980's, the Spartans had become the dominant force in the Central Collegiate Hockey Association. Joe Louis Arena became a second home for this powerhouse and was dubbed "Munn Arena East".

"A lot of us had no idea what college hockey was all about," said Brown, who had played with Scott on a Memorial Cup-winning Cornwall Royals team in the days when Canadian major junior players were still eligible to move on to the college ranks. "But when you go into Wisconsin and the band is leaning over the glass and the trombones are almost taking your head off, or you're in North Dakota and people have flashing lights and sirens on their heads ... That was a whole new experience for a lot of us.

"In juniors you'd have 70 to 75 games a season and you'd pace yourself. But there was so much more emotion in those type of buildings (where college hockey was a big-time happening) ... We learned a lot that year as a team."

Another was that 1980-81 would be State's final season in the WCHA. In 1981-82, MSU was scheduled to switch to the much-less-publicized and much-less-prestigious Central Collegiate Hockey Association, along with Michigan, Michigan Tech and Notre Dame. Instead of playing Minnesota, Wisconsin and Denver on a regular basis, the CCHA's new teams would be meeting the Lake Superiors, Ferris States, Illinois-Chicagos and Miami of Ohios of the college hockey world.

And although the expanded CCHA soon grew into a loop that was as tough as any nationally, the CCHA in the early 1980s simply wasn't in the WCHA's league—literally.

"I can remember talking with (Athletic Director) Doug Weaver about it, and that I didn't want to move back into the CCHA," Mason said. "I had left the CCHA and moved to Michigan State because I wanted a team in the WCHA. That was the league where everything was happening.

"But all of a sudden, because Notre Dame and Michigan had said they were going to leave the WCHA, Doug said we had to leave, too. He said we couldn't be playing in one league while our two nearest rivals were in another league. He convinced me it was best in the long run. I objected to it initially, but of course I didn't have much of a choice.

"A lot of people didn't like the move, but we had to stay with Michigan. Then Michigan Tech came, too, along with Notre Dame, Michigan and ourselves. Well, you plug those four schools in with Bowling Green, Northern Michigan and Ohio State, which was pretty darn good in hockey at that point, and all of a sudden you have a real

Ron Scott's spectacular goaltending saved Michigan State on a regular basis, and gave the Spartans a much-needed mental edge as they began to contend for championships.

viable league real fast. That credibility was automatically there with the four traditional hockey schools coming in."

So was the opportunity to win a championship, something the Spartans did during their first venture into the CCHA playoffs.

"I don't know that we could have done that in the WCHA," Mason admitted. "But even that second year (1980-81), with Ronnie Scott, we were losing games but we were in every game. He was making 50 saves a night, but I said, 'Geez, all we need is another line and a couple of defensemen and we're going to be as good as these teams.' "One thing I always think about when I look back on it—I spent two years in that league and we couldn't win. I never had a chance to stay in that league and build a winner. That kind of bugs me a little bit. But during those development times, I was more concerned about making the team competitive and good than I was about who we played or where we played. I knew if we brought in the right players, the same type of players the (WCHA) teams were bringing in, that we were going to be fine."

Five more of those—Anastos, Gord Flegel, Dan McFall, Kelly Miller and Phair—signed on prior to the 1981-82 season. Once they did, it was look out, CCHA.

"We put together a heck of a recruiting class again, and that was the one that put us over the top," Mason said. "We plugged that class into the other two and we finally turned the corner."

"Mark Hamway and Ken Leiter were important because they were the two highest-profile guys in Detroit at the time, and Ron felt it was important for Michigan State to step up to the plate and start going head-to-head with Michigan for that kind of player," Walsh remembered. "They were building blocks because they were also role models and because they were two guys intent on playing at the next level (and did—Leiter played in 143 NHL games with the New York Islanders and Minnesota; Hamway skated in 53 games as an Islander).

"And Newell and Ronnie were obviously key because they were just pure, blue-chip winners. They were coming off that Memorial Cup winning team (Cornwall, Ont.) and they were guys that just didn't want to lose, and that was an important ingredient we needed to bring into our locker room.

"The phrase we always used back then was we wanted to gain on the top programs. To do that we thought we'd have to hit on four of five recruits every year because we thought it took 16 players to compete for the national championship. Well, we went through a stretch there where we didn't make any mistakes at all in recruiting."

Knowing that, and understanding that they finally had a team that could seriously compete, the coaching staff turned up the intensity level next. Mason, Walsh and Terry Christensen (who had replaced assistant John Mason after Ron Mason's first year in East Lansing) began to work on the players' attitudes as much as their abilities.

The offices had been remodeled, the program had been streamlined (as far as off-ice organization and the support staff was concerned) and the phrase "Spartan Hockey: We're Moving Up" had been painted on the tunnel wall leading from the home locker room to the ice at Munn. The coaches had even gotten the team to take up singing "The MSU Fight Song" to celebrate victories prior to a bus ride back to campus.

Now, it was time to really get serious.

Walsh and Christensen showed up in the fall of 1981 with an edge that never softened. They reacted during games as if each was the seventh of the Stanley Cup Finals, screaming and swearing at officials from the press box, pounding the table in front of them in frustration and occasionally snapping a pencil or two in anger (and that was when State was winning). They produced such regular and repeated outbursts of emotion that a pane of plexiglass was eventually installed, separating the coaches' station from the media in the press box. They kept their game faces on not just on Fridays and Saturdays, but throughout the week (although this wasn't really difficult for Christensen, of whom defenseman Brad Beck once said, "Coach C could be intense going to the bathroom."). And they studied the game tapes over and over when the Spartans lost, determined to discover something that would prevent such a calamity from ever happening again.

Mason would, too.

"His immediate impact on me was his intensity level," Anastos said. "His intensity level was enormous. In practices he was intense. In games he was intense. Never in my life have I seen anybody who hates to lose as much as he does. He just hated it.

"Initially, when you'd see the coaches acting like they were in third grade, a lot of guys didn't quite understand that. But then you'd see it start to permeate through the players, that attitude that we weren't going to accept losing."

"Everybody on the staff was fiercely competitive," Christensen agreed. "It didn't matter at what. And the thing was, there were always three games being played at Michigan State. The biggest of those were the real games, the games played on Friday and Saturday nights. Then there was the recruiting game. That was a game in itself and nobody on our staff ever wanted to lose that game. And then there were the 'off-ice games' ...

"It could have been golf, a game in the weight room with the assistant coaches ... I can remember times after practice where we'd stay out on the ice and make bets over who could hit the crossbar with the puck, and we'd stay out there sometimes until somebody had to tell us to get off.

"As coaches we were extremely competitive, and in some ways that created an arrogance about us. But did that rub off on the players? No question about it."

In 1981-82, the Spartans didn't lose their first CCHA game until they had already played five. They opened the season by beating Lake Superior and Bowling Green twice and getting a tie at Ferris State. Still, that didn't mean a 4-3 loss at home to Ferris was considered acceptable simply because losing a few along the way was inevitable.

"We didn't know what to expect that first year in the CCHA, and it just kind of snowballed on us," Anastos said. "I remember we had a real emphasis on freshmen, and that I was shocked by that. At our first formal practice we were working on the power play, and we were all thrown right in it, except for Kelly (Miller). Then we started winning right out of the gate.

"Then, after we tied at Ferris, we came home and Gary Haight made a turnover in the last 15 seconds and we lost. I'll never forget coming off the ice. Haight was in front of me, and Ron was waiting for him at the door to the locker room. As Haight walked in, Ron grabbed him and pinned him up against my locker and said, What the (expletive) were you thinking? It's the last minute of a period and you're trying to beat a guy one-on-one?'

"The guy had stripped Gary of the puck, walked in and scored, and then come over to our bench and basically taunted us. Mason was livid. And I'm thinking, 'Ok, what do I do? Do I just stand here? Do I try to get in my locker?' I had never seen people take a loss with as much intensity as I began to see there. I started to learn how important every single game was."

Celebrations were intense as well.

"When we went into Bowling Green and won, the coaches were jumping up and down and hugging each other in the doorway to the dressing room," Anastos said. "At the time I didn't appreciate what was happening. But here was a set of coaches that had worked hard for a couple of years. Now, it was starting to happen.

The players really got caught up in it.

"That year turned out to be a great year."

Intensity had a lot to do with that. So did Scott, now a sophomore sensation who was making a difference rather than merely making the games closer.

"When you have a great goaltender like that, he can win games on his own," Anastos said. "When people played us, they were a little intimidated by who they had to face in goal. It was mental warfare, almost, and we already had an edge because of Ron Scott."

Just 5-foot-8 and 155 pounds (that's what he was listed at, at least), Scott never appeared very athletic. His favorite food, as reported one time in a New York Rangers Media Guide, was pizza, and he was once described in The State News as a guy who looked like a physics major from Battle Creek. But he could play. What Scott could do in the crease was flat-out amazing at times.

And Ronzo didn't lack anything in the intensity department, either. No one wanted to be near him while suiting up for games, because Scott would be chewing his fingernails and spitting them in all directions while strapping on the pads. And God help the player who made the mistake of putting one past him during warmups. Frank Finn did that once at New Hampshire and Scott responded by digging the puck out of the net and firing it back at Finn. Scott hit Finn in the back of the head with it, too.

The way Scott played night in and night

out, Finn could live with it. Scott ended up a two-time All-American and a three-time academic All-American before foregoing his senior season to sign with the New York Rangers. And although he tops none of the Spartans' career charts (playing only three years had something to do with that), Scott is remembered as perhaps as good a goalie as MSU ever had. And MSU, remember, had All-Americans at the position in 1959 (Joe Selinger), 1962 (John Chandik), 1969 (Rick Duffett) and 1972 (Jim Watt) prior to Scott's arrival.

"Let's not kid ourselves," Anastos said. "Our team was pretty good, but we had a great goalie."

Thanks to Scott's sparkling play, the new influx of talent and the new attitude, the Spartans ended up second in the regular season to Bowling Green. They also beat BG three out of four times head-to-head in the regular season, went 3-1 against Notre Dame and 3-1-1 against Michigan. MSU got on such a roll against UM after dropping the first game of the series that fall that the Spartans went 3-0-1 the rest of the 1981-82 season against the Wolverines, starting streaks that would hit 9-0-1 over the two schools' next 10 games and 15-1-1 for the good guys in January of 1985.

The league playoffs (this was another new experience) opened at home against Lake Superior. MSU won the first game of the two-games, total-goals series, 9-1, then dropped the second, 4-3. It didn't matter. Motivation wasn't expected to be a problem the next weekend in Motown at the Joe Louis Arena.

It wasn't. MSU beat Michigan Tech, 3-2, in the semifinals, then dominated Notre Dame, 4-1, to win the CCHA playoff championship.

"We brought a ton of character with us to Detroit," Brown said. "That's the one area

where Ron and Shawn and Terry really did an outstanding job. They brought in talented people with character, people who really wanted to win."

"I don't know if we expected to win, but we certainly weren't nervous," Anastos said. "Going down there, we just continued to ride the wave."

It didn't even matter much that the NCAA Tournament bid the Spartans had earned by beating Notre Dame, MSU's first since 1967, was wasted on 3-2 and 6-2 losses at New Hampshire. The table had been set for the Amazing '80s and beyond.

The players were here.

The championship precedent had been established.

Finally, it was full speed ahead again.

"After that second year, I was wondering if we were ever going to win," Mason said. "I thought, 'My God, I've upgraded the talent and nothing's happening.' Then, the next year you could just see ... you could see it in the Green & White (preseason) game ... Now we've got a hockey team here!"

And Michigan State was indeed one hell of a place to coach once again.

It wasn't long after Ron Mason's arrival that fans were once again packing Munn Arena and enthusiastically expressing their opinions of the Spartans.

We won everything but what
we wanted to win...

CHAPTER
7

Chapter 7

The offense came pretty easily most nights for just about everyone on this team. Here fourth-liners Jeff Parker (No. 11) and Mike Donnelly (No. 14) celebrate yet another goal against Ohio State.

They had come agonizingly close to capturing the national championship in 1983-84 during a run to the Final Four that finally ran out of gas in Lake Placid, N.Y. You can't, after all, come much closer than losing 2-1 in the semifinals to a Bowling Green team that would go on to capture the national championship in a four-overtime thriller over Minnesota-Duluth, as the Spartans had done.

They returned to Munn Arena determined to finish the job the following fall.

"From a competitive standpoint, that might have been a turning point," Spartan winger Tom Anastos said of MSU's first Final Four appearance since 1966-67. "We felt like, 'Hey, just getting here isn't good enough. This is something we need to win.'"

As it turns out, the little chip Bowling Green had left on MSU's shoulder by denying the Spartans' national championship dream at the Olympic Arena turned out to be the final ingredient in what would ultimately come to be known as "The Dream Team." That lingering sting of defeat left at the conclusion of the Ron Mason era's fifth campaign added tenacity to a mix that already included talent comparable with anyone else's and facilities that were second to none. For the first time a season-ending loss wasn't met with sighs of,

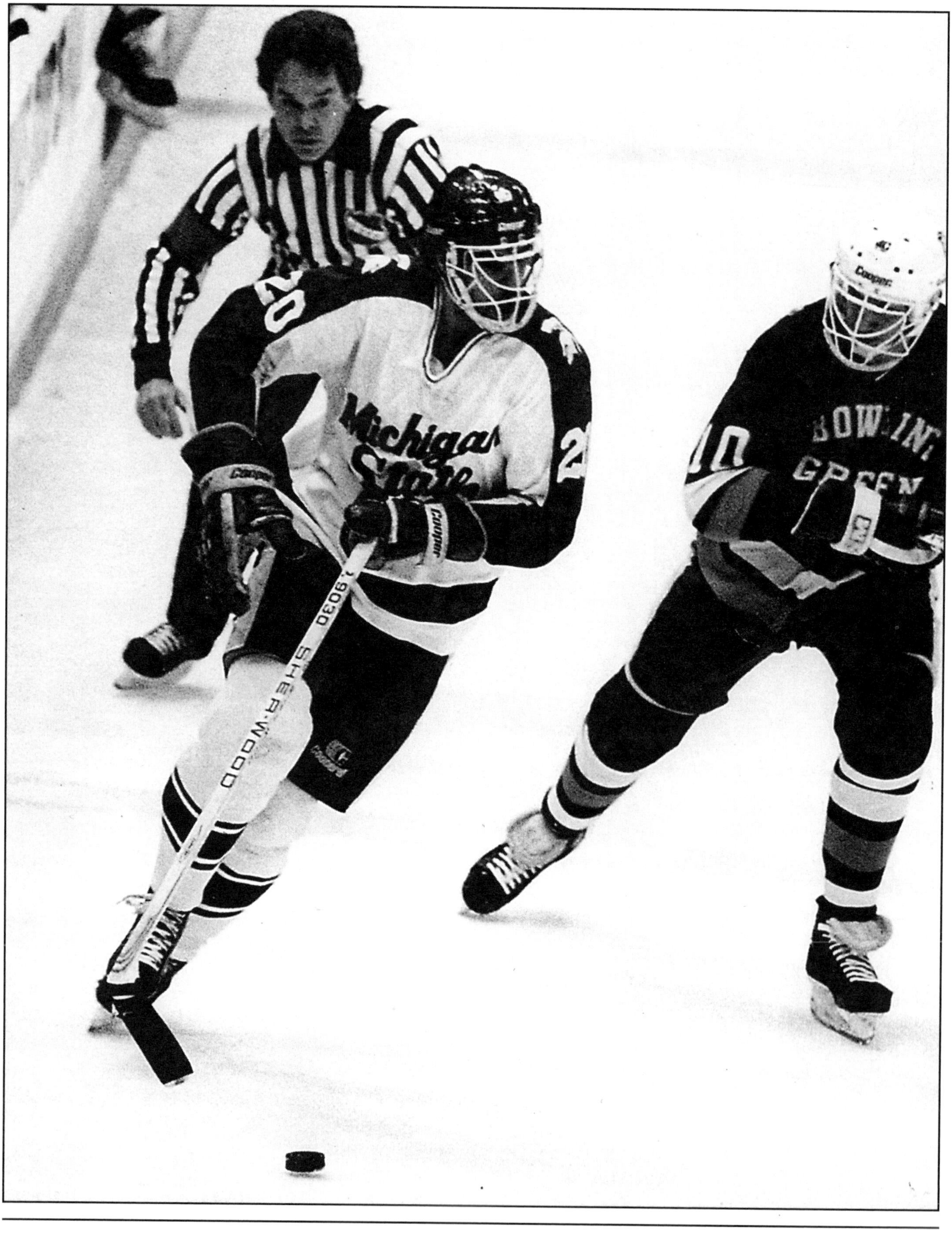
Michigan State
20
BOWLING GREEN
10
SHER-WOOD
Cooper

"Oh, well, we still came a long, long way." Suddenly, expectations had been raised. Finally, the Spartans were more than prepared to meet them.

Gone were longtime stalwarts Newell Brown, Jeff Eisley and David Taylor. But this time, only three blue-chip recruits (forward Kevin Miller and defensemen Sean Clement and Tom Tilley) would be counted upon, as opposed to eight the previous season. This time, inexperience wouldn't be a problem.

Neither, apparently, would anything else.

In 1984-85, the Spartans returned 20 letter-winners from a team that won a school-record 34 games and scored a school-record 241 goals. Among them were 13 of the top 15 scorers from the previous season, including sophomore center Craig Simpson. Just 17 years old and destined to become the No. 2 pick in the 1985 NHL draft, Simpson had led the team in scoring as a freshman (14-43—57) despite being a mere 16 years of age when he first arrived on campus, and was on the verge of becoming what Mason would later call "a Bryan Trottier-type center."

"The thing that was really incredible to me was he had three goals up until Christmas his first season, and he wound up being the leading scorer on a team that went to the Final Four as a 16-year-old turning 17," then-assistant coach Terry Christensen recalled. "Now, that is pretty impressive.

"I don't know if that will ever happen again."

Equally impressive was this: During his two seasons in Green, Simpson would lead the team in goals once, in assists twice and in points twice. He had great hands, great vision, great anticipation, a great knack for passing and a great ability to hold the puck in the attack zone at the blueline (Simpson

Everyone, it seemed, from Bowling Green to referees, had a hard time keeping up with flashy Tom Anastos and Michigan State's 1984-85 "Dream Team."

also played one of the points on the power play).

Now that he was a sophomore, had filled out a bit physically (6-foot-2, 180 pounds) and had improved his skating, Simpson was expected to really shine. He was a special player blessed with special talent, and he was far from alone in that regard. A total of 13 Dream Teamers would go on to play in the NHL someday. As for now, however, they were poised to dominate the college ranks. This was a team that was loaded in every sense of the word.

Thanks to freshman sensations Bob Essensa and Norm Foster in goal and a rock-solid, experienced defense, the Spartans had allowed fewer goals per game than any team in the country in 1983-84 (2.80). And thanks to an abundance of forwards with size, speed, strength and savvy, the Spartans had averaged more goals per game (5.24) than the other three national semifinalists. Because of his age and teen-idol appearance, Simpson had become one of the Spartans' highest-profile players. Still, he was far from the only one who was deadly around the net.

What's more, Gary Haight was back. One of the most talented and explosive defensemen ever to play at Michigan State, Haight had spent the 1983-84 campaign with the U.S. Olympic team. He was so fast he could build up Paul Coffey-like speed in just a couple of strides, and so strong Haight could snap off a wrist shot from the goal line and clear the glass at the other end of the ice. The Spartans hadn't had a defenseman blessed with that kind of natural ability before Haight's arrival in 1980 and haven't had one since. Still, Team USA coach Lou Vario had somehow included Haight among the final cuts, so he missed the Olympics. But with one year of eligibility left, Haight wasn't about to miss this.

Even fate seemed to be on the Spartans' side. For this year, the Final Four was scheduled to be held not in Grand Forks, N.D., or Lake Placid, N.Y., but in Detroit's Joe Louis Arena. The same Joe Louis Arena where MSU had amassed a 10-game winning streak. The same Joe Louis Arena where near-capacity and occasionally overflow crowds dominated by Green-and-White clad Spartans enthusiasts gathered whenever Mason's team was in town. The same Joe Louis Arena The State News had for two or three years now been referring to as "Munn Arena East" because it was nothing if not Michigan State's second home whenever Michigan State played there.

"It's there waiting for us if we want to go get it," Anastos said of the national championship.

The details of the regular season had to be attended to first.
Although a Freon leak at Munn Arena forced them to practice for a while at the Lansing Ice and Gymnastics Center and play their first six games on the road, the Spartans started strong, as expected. They won six of their first seven and were unshaken even by an early-season defection.

That occurred during a 9-1, 5-1 sweep of Miami in Oxford, Ohio. It was at that point—six games into what potentially would become Michigan State's greatest season ever—when sophomore defenseman Neil Davey decided he had seen enough of MSU and college life. Frustrated by a lack of playing time, the once-promising recruit packed his belongings and headed home to Edmonton, Alberta, while his teammates were in Ohio.

"It's somewhat of a surprise, but I have no hard feelings," Mason said. "I'm sorry it didn't work out for him, but it's not going to have a big impact on us."

You bet it didn't. The Spartans won 10 of their first 12 before falling to Bowling Green at home on Nov. 24. That loss, of no great consequence in the grand scheme of things, was still somewhat frustrating. A unanimous pick to win the Central Collegiate Hockey Association regular-season title in a preseason poll of the league's coaches, MSU had only days before been ranked No. 1 in the country by Houghton, Mich., radio station WMPL (one of the authorities of the day on such matters). Now, that No. 1 ranking would surely be given back.

State dealt with the disappointment by refusing to lose or tie for the next 2 1/2 months.

From Nov. 29 (an 8-2 win over Illinois-Chicago) through Feb. 15 (a 6-2 win over Illinois-Chicago), the Spartans were literally unbeatable. They won by shootout (8-4 over UIC, 9-4 over Michigan), by shutout (7-0 over Ohio State, 7-0 over Michigan Tech) and by sweating it out (4-3 in overtime over Western Michigan, 3-2 in overtime over Miami). They won an NCAA record-tying 22 consecutive games, mostly by lighting opponents up almost at will. The Spartans scored at least seven goals in a game 13 times during the run, including 10 or more four times and 15 once (a 15-1 payback to Bowling Green on Feb. 8, a mere seven days before Simpson's 18th birthday).

"That's when I really started to wonder," forward Mitch Messier said. "I said to myself, 'Wait a second, Bowling Green was pretty good the year before (when the Falcons had won the national title). Sure, they lost a few players. But if we're beating teams this good by this much ...'"

Mason was thinking the same thing. He admitted as much sometime after the streak had reached the teens when he told the team after yet another blowout, "I won't kid you boys; we're going to have to find ways to challenge ourselves in practice."

As it turned out, that wasn't hard to do, either.

"Our practices were probably as beneficial (in terms of player development) as the games," Anastos said, "because we were playing against some of the best players in college hockey every day in practice."

In the games it was one mismatch after another. Michigan Tech was beaten by a touchdown, 7-0, in the Great Lakes Invitational Tournament finals on Dec. 29. The Spartans' third straight GLI championship was witnessed by 21,576 at Joe Louis Arena, then the largest crowd ever to watch a hockey game on the continent of North America, and ran State's winning streak at the JLA to 12. Michigan was trashed, 11-2 and 9-4, in late January. The second victory, achieved in the hated Wolverines' Yost Arena on Jan. 26, clinched the CCHA regular-season title, MSU's first regular-season league championship of any kind on ice. That the flag was wrapped up a week before Groundhog Day (that's somewhat akin to a baseball team clinching the pennant by Labor Day), captured on Michigan ice and secured by beating Michigan for the 15th time in 17 tries (including one tie) made it all the sweeter.

"This is a milestone for our program," Mason said.

"They're definitely the best team we've seen this year," said Michigan coach Red Berenson, whose team had also been swept recently by Rensselaer Polytechnic Institute.

The streak finally ended when upstart UIC surprised State, 7-4, at Munn, on Feb. 16. Even more surprisingly, another loss against Lake Superior State followed on the regular season's final weekend, costing the Spartans -- who had long since been reinstated atop the WMPL poll -- the No. 1 ranking again.

It didn't matter. The streak had said all that needed to be said about this team and where it stood in relation to the rest of the nation's best.

"We were just so balanced it was unbelievable," defenseman Brad Beck said.

"It has to be the best team we ever had because we had depth at every position and we had talent at every position," Mason said. "And it had character. It was a team that had every ingredient needed to win a championship.

"I could change systems with that team dur-

The goaltending duo of Bob Essensa and Norm Foster, here flanking No. 3 goaltender Tom Nowland, was just one of the elements that made the Spartans almost unbeatable in 1984-85.

ing a game when things weren't going right, they'd react to it and we'd win. Or, that team could just take over and do it and the game would be over in the first period. It didn't matter where we played, it didn't matter what kind of game we were in ... It was just a team that had all the ingredients."

Including a bit of an attitude.

"That's one ring down, one to go," winger Kelly Miller said after the CCHA regular-season title had been won.

The playoffs were expected to be little more than a by-the-numbers march toward wrapping up that second ring, the one that would read "1984-85 National Champions." They started out that way, too. A squeaker in the opener of a first-round, two-games, total-goals series against Miami, Ohio (4-3) was followed up by three consecutive post-season blowouts (7-1 over Miami, 8-0 over Ohio State in the semifinals and 5-1 over Lake Superior in the CCHA playoff finale). The Joe had been packed again for the Spartans' fourth consecutive league playoff banner-clinching, but this party—it was assumed—would be nothing when compared with the one destined to convene in a few weeks for the Final Four. All that was left before then was a bye week, and then a two-games, total-goals series at home against some poor, unfortunate team from the East, which, after a series of upsets, turned out to be Providence College.

The Friars had made it all the way to the Final Four in 1982-1983, but had been drummed out of the ECAC playoffs in the first round in 1983-84 and had gone only 17-15-5 overall and 15-14-5 in the newly-formed Hockey East in the 1984-85 season. This was not a team completely without players who would go on to make a name for themselves in the NHL. Goalie Chris Terreri and defensemen Peter Taglianetti and Paul Cavallini would become established in the pros; Taglianetti and Terreri would eventually see their names engraved on the Stanley Cup. But it wasn't a team that scared anyone, either.

Terreri, the Hockey East Player of the Year, was the main concern. He stood only 5-foot-9 and weighed just 160 pounds, but most of it was heart.

He was fearless in the crease and, even better, almost never gave up rebounds. And after recording a 3.49 goals against average and a .905 saves percentage in the regular season, the dean's list student in business management had made 33 saves in a 5-2 upset of Boston University in the Hockey East semis, and then 65 more in a 2-1, double-overtime triumph of Boston College that got Providence this far. He was, without a doubt, the dreaded "hot goalie," the type capable of taking over a playoff game or series that all teams feared at this time of year.

Still, the Spartans weren't sweating.

Once again they were setting offensive records and piling up fantastic stats. By season's end 11 of their 12 forwards who played regularly would score at least 10 goals, led by Simpson's 31. Six of those 12—Simpson, Anastos (29), Kelly Miller (27), winger Mike Donnelly (26), winger Dale Krentz (24) and winger Lyle Phair (23)—would net at least 20. So potent was the Spartan attack that MSU was even a threat to dent the net when playing a man down. State would wind up allowing 31 power-play goals and scoring 21 times while short-handed.

Yes, Terreri posed a threat, but not one that most everyone wasn't sure the Spartans could overcome as the Final Four and
The Joe came clearly into focus.

In retrospect, though, there was cause for concern, for by now the Spartans were systematically taking opponents apart at something less than 100 percent.

Just before the start of the playoffs, Essensa had been lost in an off-ice mishap that almost defied explanation. Upon returning to Wonders Hall after a night out at the bar, the sophomore sensation got into an argument with his girlfriend, Jeanine, while on his way up to his room. In a fit of frustration and emotion as rare as Essensa reacting visibly to anything that transpired around him on the ice, he slapped a glass partition in an elevator lobby. When he did, his hand penetrated the divider, which apparently both stunned and scared Essensa. He next attempted to quickly jerk his hand back through the hole that had been created, and as he did the rest of the glass came crashing down. Essensa's wrist and arm were cut severely enough that immediate surgery was required.

Once that happened, a goaltender with a 15-2 record and a 1.64 g.a.a. was removed from the national championship picture.
The circumstances surrounding Essensa's injury were "without a doubt" as bizarre as any Mason had come across in his coaching career.

"I was at the hospital at 2 a.m. looking at this kid with his arm sliced open to the point where you think he's never going to play hockey again," Mason said. "The doctor said it could be career-ending. I thought it was.

"And he was a guy you never, ever expected anything like that to happen to. It was like a bad dream."

Indeed, Essensa was as soft spoken and unemotional as they came, and remained that way in his NHL days with the Winnipeg Jets, Detroit Red Wings and Edmonton Oilers. He was also very, very good. Good enough that he used to entertain himself by giving shooters room on the glove side and then snatching would-be goals away with the flick of his wrist. Good enough that he'd feed his pinball habit (Essensa also excelled at hand-eye coordination exercises such as Nintendo and pinball) by taking money from his teammates during tests of skill in practice.

"We used to do this drill, him against me and Simmer (Simpson) and Mel (Donnelly) and (winger) Kevin (Miller) and (defenseman) Donnie (McSween)—we're talking about some guys who can shoot and score," Messier said. "We'd line up the pucks between the (face-off) circles and Bob would put his toes on the goal line with his ass and everything inside the net. We could take slap shots, do whatever we wanted. If we scored, it was a buck for us. If he stopped it, it was a buck for him. I think we must have paid him $50 a practice.

"I think I might have just signed over one of my scholarship checks to him at one point."

Once he was hurt, Essensa was forced to take an extended break from pinball. Unfortunately

for the Spartans, he couldn't play hockey, either, not that anyone held becoming suddenly unavailable over a fight with a girlfriend against Essensa.

"(Stuff) happens," Messier reasoned.

"He married her, so it was worth it," Mason said.

Maybe for the Essensas. For the Spartans, however, Essensa's mishap eventually proved fatal. At 6-foot, he was bigger than Foster (5-7). And although Foster had been superior the previous season when the two were freshmen, in 1984-85 Essensa had been better. Essensa relied on playing the angles just right and acrobatics when all else failed much less. He was good enough that he could depend mostly on his reactions and reflexes and still make it look easy. Now, suddenly, all the pressure was on Foster.

The first indication that something was indeed wrong came in the opening game against the Friars. Michigan State outshot Providence, 36-20, but won by only a 3-2 count. Worse, the largest crowd in Munn Arena history (6,841) had to wait until 17:12 of the third period for the heavily-favored Spartans to take the lead for good, which they did on a rare unassisted goal by Beck.

In the Spartans' locker room there was mild surprise, and a lingering conviction that a similar effort the next night might easily result in 10 or more goals being scored. Across the ice, however, Terreri did his best to convince any media member within earshot that Michigan State hadn't won anything yet.

Yes, Michigan State was ranked No. 2 in the nation and was seeded No. 1 in the West in the tournament. And yes, Providence was unranked nationally and a No. 4 seed out East. Still ...

"They're not God and the angels," Terreri insisted of the Spartans.

He and the Friars were greeted by, among other things, a "Welcome to Heaven" sign the next night, when another Munn record crowd (6,895) assembled to witness the kill. But a funny thing happened on the way to The Joe ...

The puck was dropped and Providence got a goal from John Deasey at 2:26. Then another from

Gord Cruickshank at 3:49. Then another from David Wilkie at 5:30, this one off a short-handed, two-on-one rush.

Foster, who was no slouch and wound up 22-4 on the year with a 2.63 g.a.a., had cracked. Playing on back-to-back nights for the third straight week after Essensa had been lost, Foster had allowed three non-goal scorers (Wilkie's goal was his first of the season, Deasey's his third and Cruickshank's his eighth) to get the best of him. Worse, they had done so on "soft" goals. Bad goals. Goals Foster normally could be counted upon to stop.

"Both Normie and Bobby had been used to splitting Friday and Saturday nights," then-first-year assistant coach George Gwozdecky explained, "and Bobby was our 'hammer' guy, so to speak. When all of a sudden he couldn't go, it put a lot more weight on Normie's shoulders.

"Then early in the (second) game, they got a couple of real, real softies. After that, it was like 'Holy Jesus' ..."

Less than six minutes into the second game, the Spartans found themselves trailing the series by two goals.

"Had Bobby Essensa been there they probably wouldn't have gotten the goals they got," Mason said.

But Essensa likely wouldn't have scored any, either, which would have left him in the same sinking ship as most of his teammates on this most baffling of nights. The Spartans started swarming, as they had through much of Game 1, soon after falling behind, and Clement got one back at 15:17 of the first. But this was to be Terreri's night.

One by one they challenged him. And one by one Terreri turned aside the best collection of offense in college hockey. Posts were hit. Open nets were missed. But mostly, Terreri played the part of a fanatical acrobat, doing whatever it took to get a piece of himself or his equipment on the puck just before it entered the net. As he did so, the crowd moaned and groaned. And as the time relentlessly ticked away, a sense of desperation enveloped Munn. Although the players never panicked as the

fans did, they never figured Terreri out, either.

It was 4-1 Providence entering the third period. Phair, off assists from Beck and Gord Flegel, got the Spartans back to within one in the series count at 10:07, but that was as close as they would get.

Terreri finished with 50 saves in the Friars' unthinkable, 4-2, series-clinching victory, which ran his weekend total to 83. Foster stopped 16 of 20 Providence shots in what remains one of the most frustrating events in Michigan State athletic history.

It was one of the saddest, too, and not just because Terreri—who began hot-dogging it as the saves piled up and the crowd became more and more annoyed by his antics—and the Friars were pelted with garbage as they celebrated punching their Final Four tickets on Spartan ice. Providence forward Tim Sullivan left the arena almost immediately after the game had ended (he took off his skates but otherwise stayed in uniform) and was rushed to Lansing's Sparrow Hospital to be with his father. John Sullivan, 59, had been sitting a few rows behind the Friars' bench before collapsing during the third period. As paramedics attended to and removed him via a stretcher, the final minutes of the series were played out with the Friars exchanging nervous glances out onto the ice and up into the seats.

The heart attack John Sullivan had suffered claimed his life later that night.

All Michigan State had lost was a hockey game. And yet, "It was like your heart had been pulled out of your body," Gwozdecky said, "or like somebody had punched you and you were out of breath. That next day, that next week, that next month ... was like a funeral.

"There had been such great expectations of us advancing in three or four days down to Joe Louis for the Final Four and all of a sudden it wasn't going to happen. It was just ... it was just awful. Even though I was the young guy on the staff and had only been there for about eight months, it was just horrible to see what it did to Ron and Terry and the rest of the people that had been around the program for a number of years."

The Friars ended up holding a practice in preparation for the Final Four at Munn on Monday.

The Spartans cleaned out their lockers.

"I'll never forget coming to the rink on Monday and listening to the sound of Providence pucks banging against our boards," Christensen said. "I think that was a feeling that stayed with everybody."

few couldn't do so with dry eyes.

"I saw Kelly Miller in tears," recalled Dee Rizzo, a scrappy forward-defenseman who had been red-shirted in 1984-85, mostly because there was simply no place for a player of Rizzo's limited skills on a team this talented. "I know how bad a guy like Kelly wanted it. So did the other guys. It wasn't from a lack of effort."

Craig Simpson accepts the Outstanding Offensive Player Award at the MSU hockey banquet in April 1985. Simpson would next be called to a podium when the Pittsburgh Penguins made him the second overall pick at the NHL Entry Draft in June.

Especially the seniors. As it turned out, the Providence game was the final game in the Spartan careers of Anastos, winger Dan Beaty, Flegel, Haight, defenseman Dan McFall, Kelly Miller, Phair and reserve goalie Tom Nowland. Juniors Krentz and winger Harvey Smyl had also used up their eligibility. All had intended to go out with national championship rings on their fingers, not like this.

In the locker room, they faced the music and met the media, anyway, although more than a

In a way, that's what made the Dream Team's demise so difficult to accept. They hadn't gotten cocky or over-confident. They hadn't looked past the Friars and played poorly as a result. They had, in fact, thoroughly dominated both games, but they couldn't score enough goals. When they needed it most, the Spartans' firepower had somehow failed them.

"That's the most heartbreaking defeat I've ever come across in sports," Beck said. "Why did we lose? Two words ... Chris Terreri. We couldn't beat him. We peppered them. The play was in their end for two games. And one guy beat us. They had a .500 hockey team, or something like that, and one guy carried them."

"It was fate," Mason reasoned. "There was nothing more we could have done."

Well, almost nothing. Rizzo, a player who was effective because he employed fists and elbows and whatever else was necessary while he was on the ice, even thought of something while sitting in the stands and watching Terreri single-handedly destroy what should have been a dream season. "Somebody should have somehow, some way run into Terreri," Rizzo pointed out. "Stand in the crease and let him chop you, then chop him back,

or, if you're forechecking, forecheck a defenseman into him. He was so hot... and we were hitting posts ...It was crazy.

"That's why I would have done what I could have to get right in front of that crease and let Taglianetti or Cavallini just beat me, beat me right into him. And while they were beating me on the back of my head I'd have been beating Terreri on the front of his."

Mason, however, didn't want to play it that way.

"What we could have done, if it was professional hockey, was run Terreri and get into a big fight," Mason explained. "That's what they'd do in the NHL. But you know what? That's not the character of college hockey. And if I'm going to represent college hockey, I'm going to represent the character of college hockey. I've always done that and I always will."

So they never did run Terreri, who didn't run out of gas until taking Providence all the way to the NCAA final, where it was beaten by RPI.

The Dream Team, quite possibly the greatest team never to win an NCAA Championship. Pictured are, front row, from left: Assistant coach Terry Christensen, Tom Anastos, Lyle Phair, Gary Haight, Kelly Miller, head coach Ron Mason, Dan McFall, Dan Beaty, Dee Rizzo, Gord Flegel, and assistant coach George Gwozdecky. Middle row, from left: Team physician Dr. John Downs, trainer Dave Carrier, Norm Foster, Tom Nowland, Harvey Smyl, Dale Krentz, Bill Shibicky, Don McSween, Rick Fernandez, Mike Donnelly, Brad Beck, Bob Essensa, student manager Stuart Allen, equipment manager Tom Magee. Back row, from left: Tom Budnick, Dave Arkeilpane, Joe Hamway, Sean Clement, Jeff Parker, Mitch Messier, Craig Simpson, Tom Tilley, Dave Chiapelli, Kevin Miller, and student manager Steve Brown.

"We'd have kicked RPI's ass," Beck said.

As it was, they had to settle for setting 18 team and 20 individual school records, for winning an NCAA record-tying 22 straight games and an NCAA-record 38 overall, for winning the Great Lakes Invitational Tournament, the CCHA regular-season title and the CCHA playoff crown, for placing five players (Essensa, Haight, McSween, Kelly Miller and Simpson) on the All-CCHA first team, three (McFall, Kelly Miller and Simpson) on the West All-America team and two (Kelly Miller and Simpson) among the 10 finalists for the Hobey Baker Award, college hockey's version of the Heisman Trophy.

"We won everything but what we wanted to win," Anastos said. "To this day, I don't know that there's been a team in college hockey as good as that one. Even (NCAA champion) North Dakota in 1987. Even the Maine team that won 40-plus games (and the national title in 1992-93). I don't know that there's ever been a team as balanced offensively and defensively as our team.

"And it was a fun team to be on. Of all the teams I've been on, that one was the most enjoyable because it was a good group of guys who got along well. There were some guys who were a little different in their ways, but everyone was accepted. Sometimes, if a guy has an awkward personality or something about him that doesn't quite fit, he's kind of an outcast. On this team, everybody accepted you for the way you were. I thought that was kind of unique."

The Dream Team was nothing if not unique, even in defeat.

1966 NCAA National Champions

Front Row, from left: Gaye Cooley, Matthew Mulcahy, Don Heaphy, Gerry Fisher, Mike Coppo, Tom Purdo, and Larry Roche. Second row, from left: Trainer Clyde Stretch, Sandy McAndrew, Tom Mikkola, Mike Jacobson, Dainis Vedejs, Ron Roth, Doug Volmar, Tom Crowley, Wayne Duffett, and coach Amo Bessone. Third row, from left: Team Manager William Smith, Richard Bois, Bill Faunt, Doug French, Nino Cristofolli, Robert Fallat, John Schuster, and manager Ralph Faust.

Overall: 16-13
WCHA: 9-11

Colorado College	L	0-4
Colorado College	L	3-4*
St. Lawrence	L	3-5
Clarkson	L	3-6
St. Lawrence	W	6-4
NORTH DAKOTA	W	11-5
NORTH DAKOTA	L	3-5
DENVER	L	6-8
DENVER	W	4-1
COLORADO COLLEGE	L	4-5*
COLORADO COLLEGE	W	6-2
MINNESOTA	L	5-7
MINNESOTA	L	1-5
MINN.-DULUTH	W	6-5*
MINN.-DULUTH	W	5-2
Minnesota	L	5-6*
Minnesota	W	4-3
MICHIGAN	W	8-7
Michigan	W	4-2
Wisconsin	W	3-1
Wisconsin	W	5-3
Michigan Tech	L	4-8
Michigan Tech	L	2-4
MICHIGAN	W	7-1
Michigan	L	0-1*
Michigan%	W	4-2
MICHIGAN TECH%	W	4-3
Boston University!	W	2-1
Clarkson!	W	6-1

* Overtime
% WCHA Playoffs
! NCAA Final Four

Lansing native Kip Miller, the sixth member of his family to don the Green & White, is the first and only Spartan to have won college hockey's most coveted individual prize, the Hobey Baker Award. Kip earned the award following a 48-goal, 53-assist campaign in 1989-90.

HOBEY BAKER MEMORIAL AWARD
PRESENTED ANNUALLY TO THE OUTSTANDING COLLEGIATE HOCKEY PLAYER
IN THE UNITED STATES BY THE
DECATHLON ATHLETIC CLUB OF BLOOMINGTON, MINNESOTA
KIP MILLER
MICHIGAN STATE

More than a bookstore...

MSU Clothing & Souvenirs • Hallmark Card Shop
ArtCarved Class Rings • School & Office Supplies
Art & Engineering Supplies • Books: Gift and Reference
Computers: Hardware, Software, Supplies & Books

"Go Grand Rivering"

Student Book Store

421 E. Grand River Ave., East Lansing
Phone (517) 351-4210 • (800) 968-1111 • Fax (517) 351-2568
30 Minutes FREE Validated Parking in Large Colorful Ramp Behind Store.
Hours: Mon.-Fri. 9-7, Sat. 10-6, Sun. 12-5 Check us out on the Net at http://www.sbsmsu.com
Serving MSU & East Lansing since 1960

After building winning programs at Lake Superior State and Bowling Green, Ron Mason rebuilt the Spartan program to a championship level. Mason-coached teams have won one national title, four CCHA regular season titles, and seven CCHA playoff championships.

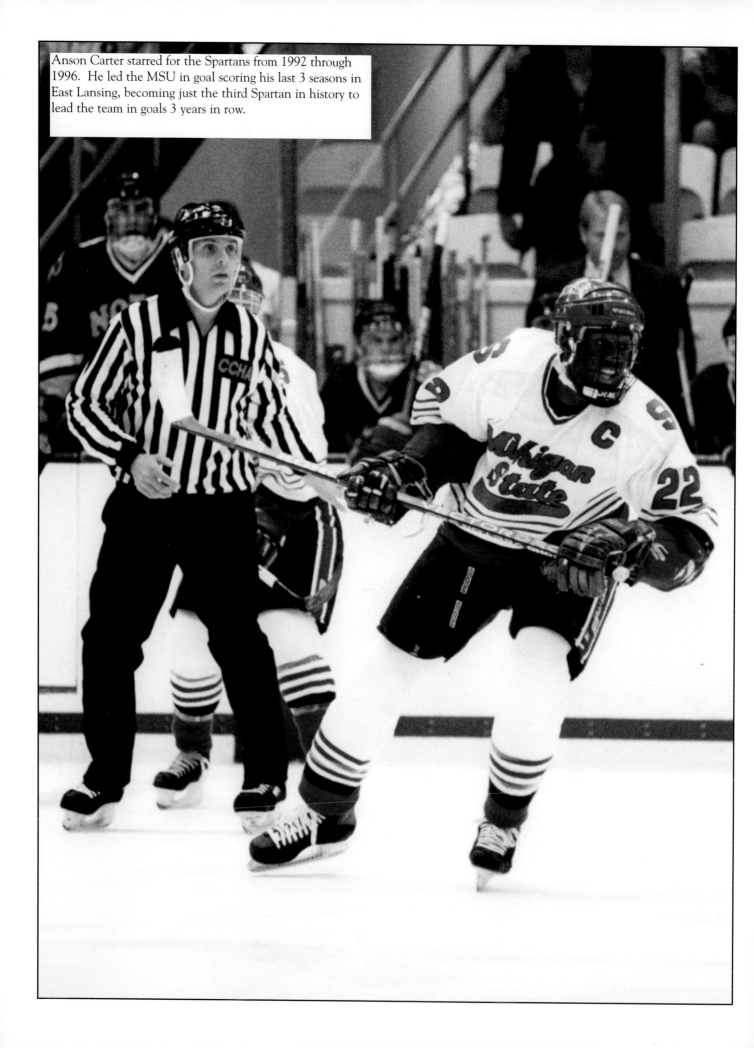

Anson Carter starred for the Spartans from 1992 through 1996. He led the MSU in goal scoring his last 3 seasons in East Lansing, becoming just the third Spartan in history to lead the team in goals 3 years in row.

MSU BOOKSTORE

Your offical
Michigan State University Bookstore!

NCAA
TOURNAMENT
CHAMPIONS
1966

NCAA
TOURNAMENT
CHAMPIONS
1986

Congratulations MSU
for your
Collegiate, Amateur and
Professional Hockey Excellence
in the
Past, Present and Future

STORE HOURS
MONDAY-FRIDAY
8:30 AM - 7:00 PM
SATURDAY
10 AM - 5 PM
SUNDAY
NOON - 5 PM

MSU
BOOKSTORE
YOUR OFFICIAL UNIVERSITY BOOKSTORE
INTERNATIONAL CENTER • ON-CAMPUS
(517) 355-3450

the College Store

More Green & White Apparel Than Munn Arena On Game Day

We've Got The Goods!!

FREE PARKING

the College Store

4790 S. Hagadorn • East Lansing, MI 48823
517-333-0505 • 1-800-336-0586 • Fax: 517-333-9802
E-mail: storecol@pilot.msu.edu
Web Site: www.thecollegestore.com

We invite you to visit

SPARTAN COUNTRY

featuring

A unique collection of clothing & gifts for the entire MSU family

Meridian Mall, Okemos

Spartan Hockey - Pride, Tradition, Excellence

ANOTHER SPARTAN CELEBRATION!

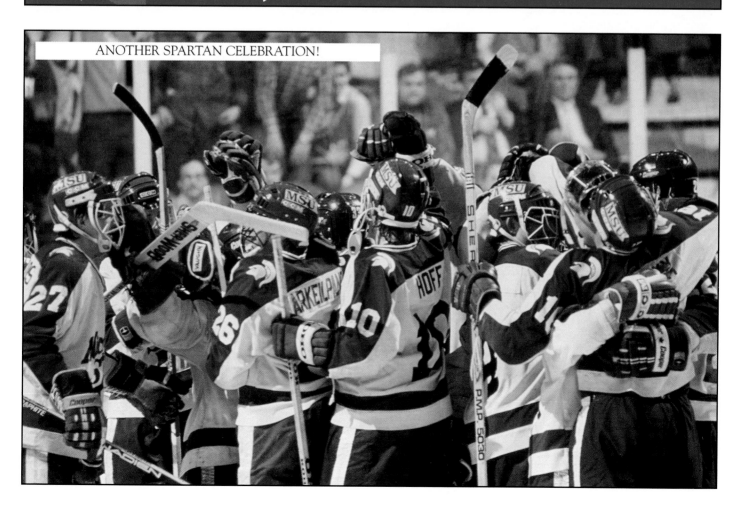

The scoreboard says it all!! The Spartans captured their first CCHA playoff title with a decisive 4-1 victory over Notre Dame at Joe Louis Arena in Detroit. This was the first of four straight CCHA playoff titles for MSU.

Showing off the hardware! Ron Mason and the seniors on the 1986-87 Spartan team smile easily with the 1986 Championship Trophy. The Green & White fell just short of defending their title, losing to North Dakota in the 1987 NCAA Championship game. Front (l-r) Mitch Messier, Ron Mason, Don McSween. Middle (l-r) Bob Essensa, Norm Foster. Back (l-r) Dave Arkeilpane, Bill Shibicky.

1986 NCAA National Champions

Front Row (left to right): Norm Foster, Asst. Coach George Gwozdecky, Bill Shibicky, Mitch Messier, Rick Fernandez, Dee Rizzo, Head Coach Ron Mason, Mike Donnelly, Brad Beck, Don McSween, Jeff Parker, Asst. Coach Terry Christensen, Bob Essensa. Middle Row (left to right): Team Physician Dr. John Downs, Tom Tilley, Danton Cole, Rick Tosto, Chris Luongo, Sean Clement, Dave Chiappelli, Bobby Reynolds, Kevin Miller, Dave Arkeilpaine, Student Manager Troy Tuggle. BACK ROW: Equipment Manager Tom Magee, Trainer Dave Carrier, Geir Hoff, Jim Lycett, Mike Dyer, Bruce Rendall, Brian McReynolds, Joe Murphy, Brad Hamilton, Student Manager Steve Brown

Overall: 34-9-2
CCHA: 23-7-2

Ohio State	W	6-2		Illinois-Chicago	L	2-3		NORTHERN ARIZONA	W	9-3
Ohio State	W	5-2		Lake Superior	L	3-7		Bowling Green	W	7-4
Western Michigan	L	1-5		Lake Superior	L	5-6*		BOWLING GREEN	W	6-4
WESTERN MICHIGAN	W	4-3		OHIO STATE	W	6-5*		ILLINOIS-CHICAGO	W	4-2
MIAMI	W	5-2		OHIO STATE	W	8-0		ILLINOIS-CHICAGO	W	7-2
MIAMI	W	7-2		NORTHERN MICHIGAN	L	2-3		LAKE SUPERIOR	W	8-5
FERRIS STATE	T	5-5*		Michigan Tech (J)+	W	2-1*		LAKE SUPERIOR	W	5-4*
Ferris State	W	5-3		Rensselaer (J)+	W	8-3		MICHIGAN@	W	4-3
Michigan	L	4-5		WESTERN MICHIGAN	W	4-2		MICHIGAN@	W	5-2
Michigan	W	6-2		Western Michigan	W	8-5		Lake Superior (J)@	W	3-2
TEAM CANADA (ex)	L	3-5		Miami	W	8-3		Western Michigan (J)@	L	1-3
TEAM CANADA (ex)	W	5-4*		Miami	W	6-3		BOSTON COLLEGE!	W	6-4
BOWLING GREEN	W	4-3*		Ferris State	W	8-6		BOSTON COLLEGE!	W	4-2
Bowling Green	L	5-6*		FERRIS STATE	T	9-9*		Minnesota#	W	6-4
Illinois-Chicago	W	6-4		MICHIGAN	W	7-5		Harvard#	W	6-5
				Michigan	L	3-5				
				NORTHERN ARIZONA	W	12-2				

* Overtime, @ CCHA Playoffs, ! NCAA Tournament, # NCAA Final Four, + GLI, (J) Joe Louis Arena

As good ONCE as they ever were...

CHAPTER
8

Chapter 8

As painful as the collapse against Providence had been the previous spring, as impossible as it was to enter Munn Arena all summer and not wonder how a playoff series and ultimately a national championship that was widely perceived to be in the bag could have slipped away, the coaching staff began initial preparations for the 1985-86 season with an even more distressing problem on its hands.

"I remember about two or three months after the Dream Team debacle, we were analyzing our needs for the upcoming year," said then-assistant coach George Gwozdecky, the current head coach at the University of Denver. "We were all sitting there and the first thing Ron said was, 'OK, we have no offense returning. Who is going to score?'

"We were feeling sorry for ourselves, I guess, is the best way to put it. We were sitting there thinking, 'Who the hell is going to score?'"

It was a legitimate concern.

Among the 12 players who had departed from head coach Ron Mason's 1984-85 Dream Team were the likes of Tom Anastos, Gord Flegel, Dale Krentz, Kelly Miller, Lyle Phair and Craig Simpson, who left after his sophomore year and was selected No. 2 overall by the Pittsburgh Penguins in the NHL draft. Those players had scored 175 of the Spartans' MSU-record 262 goals the previous season. And they had been dominant personalities in the locker room, leaders on and off the ice. They had comprised much of the heart and

Michigan State won its fourth consecutive Great Lakes Invitational Tournament championship before yet another record crowd at Detroit's Joe Louis Arena, which by now had become a second home for the Spartans.

soul of a squad that had registered an NCAA-record 38 wins despite failing to reach the Final Four.

In their place would be 10 freshmen and a myriad of questions.

The goal, as it always is for Mason-coached MSU teams, was a top-four league finish and home-ice advantage in the first round of the CCHA playoffs. But this year, Mason and the Spartans weren't being modest. This year, expectations were almost non-existent because even though the league coaches had voted MSU No. 1 again in their annual preseason poll, no one really knew what to expect.

"We're going to have to be real patient," Mason told the press. "It's going to be frustrating at times. It's going to be a real interesting year. I think it's going to be a fun year, but at the same time it's going to be frustrating."

On the plus side, the Spartans' top four defensemen—Brad Beck, Sean Clement, Tom Tilley and Don McSween—were back. So were standout goalies Bob Essensa and Norm Foster. And that gargantuan freshman class included winger Joe Murphy, who had already become a household name in Canada and was destined to become the NHL's No. 1 overall pick in 1986. Thanks in no small part to the recruiting efforts of assistant coach Terry Christensen, Mason's unusually large group of recruits contained in Murphy perhaps the most heralded freshman ever to migrate to East Lansing.

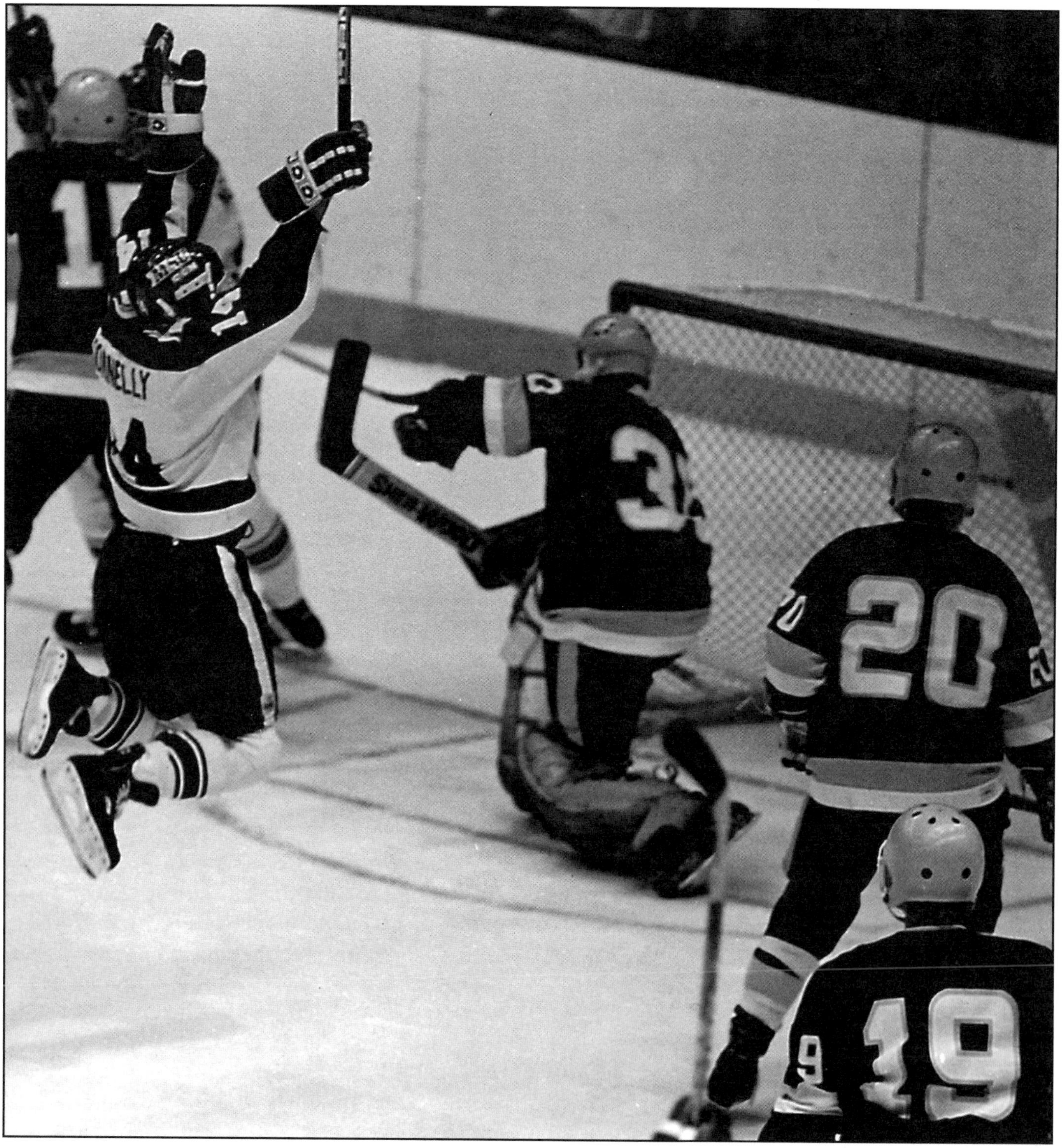
20
19

"There were things Joe did that you just didn't teach," Christensen remembered. "He had excellent skating skills at the college level, he had outstanding hands skills and he could see the ice very well with the puck on his stick.

"He could have gone to any major college that had hockey that he wanted. And the toughest thing we had to do wasn't beat out the other colleges, it was to beat out major junior hockey. Joe was offered money, at that time a significant amount of money ... the rumors were that he was offered $50,000 Canadian to play for Verdun (in the Quebec Hockey League). Now, that was just a rumor, so I don't know if it was true or not. But I know one thing, when he decided to go to college they all thought we were cheating, and we weren't."

"We were all very excited about seeing Joe Murphy play," Gwozdecky said, "and we thought we had a pretty good class coming in."

So the season didn't open without hope.

"I sort of look at this year like I did two years ago," McSween, one of the Spartans' captains, acknowledged. "It was a replacement year then and it's a replacement year now, more so than a rebuilding one."

Forward Danton Cole, one of the 10 incoming freshmen, was also optimistic.

"The tradition factor makes it a little bit easier," Cole, a Lansing, Mich. native, explained. "And the ability to win is here. If (the freshmen) can spread the scoring around a little bit and help the team, we should have a good season."

The start certainly didn't lack much of the usual Spartan fanfare. Mason achieved career victory No. 450 with a 6-2 drubbing of Michigan at home on Nov. 9. A few weeks later the Spartans stood 8-2-1 following a 4-3 overtime win over

Mike Donnelly stayed in shape by jumping for joy after scoring goals in bunches all season long.

Bowling Green at home, had split an exhibition series with Team Canada and were ranked No. 2 in the nation. That same weekend on ESPN, the New York Rangers, with former Spartan stars Kelly Miller and Ron Scott, battled the New York Islanders, and former Spartan stars Ken Leiter and Mark Hamway. All seemed as it should be.

Then reality kicked in. BG won the November rematch in Ohio, 6-5. Next came a split against Illinois-Chicago and a sweep at the hands of Lake Superior. Suddenly, MSU had dropped four of five and had fallen out of the Top 10 nationally for the first time in four years.

"We were still excited about the freshmen," Gwozdecky said. "But we were also still deeply involved with getting them in tune with how we wanted them to play and fitting them together."

Two events in December galvanized not only the freshmen, but the entire team. The first was junior winger Mike Donnelly scoring eight goals in a 6-5, 8-0 sweep of Ohio State on Dec. 14 and 15. The second was an 8-3 thumping of Rensselaer Polytechnic Institute in the championship game of the Great Lakes Invitational Tournament on Dec. 29—the same RPI that had stolen the 1985 national championship the Spartans had considered themselves destined to win the previous spring.

"You just got that feeling," is how Beck described it. "You got that special feeling, almost that you were invincible, and that if you played to your capability every night nobody was going to beat you."

Only arch-rival Michigan—which saved its best hockey for State throughout the year—did the rest of the regular season. MSU went 14-1-1 in the second half and captured the CCHA regular-season championship. And thanks to Donnelly, the staff finally relaxed and stopped wondering who the hell was going to score.

A senior winger from Livonia, Mich., Donnelly had first tried to make the squad as a walk-on in 1981. And the only reason he even tried that was because the University of Michigan had tried to pull a fast one with Donnelly's scholarship the previous spring.

"I had gotten an offer, but they were waiting for my grades from my final term (in high school) to make sure that I was accepted," Donnelly remembered. "What happened was, I ended up getting accepted, but when I went to sign my letter-of-intent—I was going to get like a half-scholarship or a three-quarters scholarship—their coach, John Giordano, said that because they had had to wait for my grades, they had given my scholarship away. He still wanted me to go there.

"My dad had gone with me to Ann Arbor. We just looked at each other ..."

Then Donnelly went up to Michigan State, as a student who thought he might take a shot at joining the hockey team. His speed got him noticed, and Donnelly was able to survive the open tryouts players over the years have come to refer to as "The Gong Show" and make the team. But after practicing in anonymity for a couple of weeks, Donnelly decided he wasn't quite ready for college hockey or college life just yet.

He left campus as quietly as he had arrived. "I ended up making the team, but I don't know that I was ready," he said. "I think my skill level was OK, but I don't know that I was mature enough at that time. I was 17, I didn't like school ... so I quit.

"I went back home and played junior hockey (with the Waterford Lakers) with plans to go back again the next year, and I ended up playing really well, well enough that I got a few offers from colleges. One of them was from Michigan Tech (Michigan wasn't in the picture this time), but (MSU assistant coach) Shawn Walsh came to one of my games and I had a meeting with him afterward and he said they really wanted me back at State.

"He said they couldn't give me any money, but that they thought I could develop in their program and that they'd consider me a 'recruited walk-on' this time. And you know how Shawn is ... He's quite the salesman. So I ended up back at State, and this time I was a lot more comfortable."

Three comfortable and productive seasons later, Donnelly became downright combustible.

After scoring 51 goals in his first three seasons (including 26 as a junior) and working mostly as a role-player and third-line winger, Donnelly had been expected to contribute as a senior. Instead he exploded, recording an NCAA-record 59 goals.

Playing regular shifts with winger Mitch Messier and center Kevin Miller, playing on the power play, killing penalties...the former walk-on became an All-American.

He also became almost unstoppable.

"Teams tried to shadow him and double-team him, but his speed and acceleration were just tremendous," Gwozdecky said. "That's why he was able to play so long in the National Hockey League (from 1986-87 through 1996-97 Donnelly appeared in 465 NHL regular-season games and scored 114 goals with the New York Rangers, Buffalo Sabres, Los Angeles Kings, Dallas Stars and New York Islanders), because of his speed and quickness."

By the time he was a senior, Donnelly, 5-foot-11 and 180 pounds. had finally learned to create space with his legs. Once that was accomplished, he simply waited for someone to get him the puck, then took advantage of what Mason had long described as a "scorer's shot."

"It was a combination of a kid working awfully hard to develop his shot and awfully hard to develop his confidence and it all came together in one year," Mason said. "It got to a point where it was almost laughable how many goals the guy was scoring. And he was scoring them against everybody ... Lake Superior, Bowling Green, whatever, he got his goals. And when he got on fire, Holy Jesus, look out.

"He probably could have had more. But a lot of times, if we were ahead by four or five goals, I didn't play him. Then, when he started getting close to 50, I tried to get him into positions to let him go because this was a chance to do something phenomenal."

"After a while, every game we knew Mel was going to pop one or two goals," Beck said. "It was just automatic. And that kind of rubbed off on everybody else. (Freshman winger) Bobby Reynolds started playing really well. So did (fresh-

Senior night at Munn Arena was an emotional night for , from left, Brad Beck, Dee Rizzo, Rick Fernandez, and Mike Donnelly.

man center) Brian McReynolds...everybody contributed.''

Especially Donnelly, a soft-spoken, easy-going star known to his friends then and now as "Mel." That's a nickname Donnelly first picked up as a sophomore at State, after a TV announcer mispronounced his first name. When roommates Harvey Smyl and Jeff Eisley heard that while watching a Friday night game replay one Saturday morning, "Mike" Donnelly might as well have never existed.

"Mel" has stuck ever since.

"Everyone calls me that now," Donnelly said. "I don't even know if they know my first name is Mike in East Lansing. It's even followed me to the NHL."

Donnelly, who never took himself too seri-

ously and always appreciated a good joke, even when the joke was on him, never minded—then or now.

"He had speed, he had quickness, he had a shot...There were just so many things he had," Mason said. "Plus, he had a good heart; he was a team guy. He was the kind of guy that didn't get all caught up in himself and I think that helped him, because all of the guys on the team wanted to help him.

"A lot of times, if a guy gets all caught up in himself, the other guys start thinking, 'Screw you, I'm not passing you the puck.' Our guys loved to help Mel out. They wanted him to have success."

"He had always had great speed, but he never knew how to use it," Gwozdecky said. "Then, all of a sudden, as a senior he's one of our go-to guys, he started playing on the No. 1 power play with (center Bill) Shibicky and Messier and he started getting some confidence.

"Those three guys were deadly, I mean they were just deadly. Shibicky was a magician with the puck on the half-wall. He'd get it to Mitch or Mike...And when Mike got in the scoring area that year, he'd just snap his wrist and the puck would go where it's supposed to go, in the net, or the goaltender would make a great save. As many goals as he scored that year, goaltenders made a lot of great saves on Mike.

"Boy, I'll tell ya, he was a dynamic player for us that year, just dynamic."

Dramatic, too. Donnelly scored goal No. 52—snapping Tom Ross' MSU record of 51 in 1975-76—on the last day of the regular season. Despite the absence of Murphy, Messier, Tilley, Clement and freshman defenseman Chris Luongo, the Spartans beat Lake Superior that night, 3-2, and clinched the CCHA title. A Munn Arena record crowd of 6,897 was on hand as seldom-used or under-publicized players such as Dave Arkeilpane, Dave Chiappelli, Rick Fernandez and Dee Rizzo filled in for the missing, and freshman forward Geir Hoff played defense for the first time in his career.

"This win just goes to show you how great this team is," Donnelly said in a jubilant winners' locker room. "We're missing four or five guys, and other guys just go out there and do a great job. That's the whole key to this thing right here."

On a personal note, of all the goals Donnelly scored in 1985-86, No. 52 might have meant the most.

"It happened on like the first shift of the game," Donnelly said. "After I scored it Ron Mason came over from behind the middle of the bench to where we would go on and off the ice. I was getting a standing ovation and I came over—I don't know why I did that because our line was staying on the ice—and when I got over to the door Ron Mason leaned over and hugged me.

"That really sticks out in my mind because Ron was never really one to show his emotions. I mean, he showed 'em as far as getting mad, but you never really saw that side of him. That's why that's something I'll always remember."

Also memorable in retrospect was the team's overall level of talent. Contrary to those early-season fears, the cupboard wasn't exactly bare after all. Miller and Messier, for example, became so good they were even capable of improvising lethal moves on their own after a while.

"Kevin used to do this little thing on the power play where he'd fake a shot, take a step around a guy, then take a slap shot and miss the short side of the net on purpose," Messier explained. "It would rebound off the boards and come right to my stick on the other side of the net. I'd just stand there and everybody would rush to the other side or the slot once Kevin made his move. Or, if a defenseman stayed with me I'd just cross-check him in the back and push him into the slot, and I'd be wide open on the other side. I'd be all alone every time with a wide-open net. That all started from Kevin saying, 'Hey, try this...' one day in practice."

Other tricks were just as effective.

"On two-one-ones with Mel, I'd actually pass him the puck off the goalie," Messier said. "The goalies always thought I'd go between their legs so they'd keep their sticks down real low, and the defensemen usually stuck with Mel. So I'd just snap a low wrist along the ice. It would hit the goalie's stick and rebound right to Mel and he'd rip it home. On draws, I'd shoot right off the drop while Mel was going straight to the net and he'd score on the rebound. I'll bet he scored 15 out of the 59 goals on plays like that."

Still, that in itself doesn't account for Donnelly's unheard of jump in production.

Years later, even Donnelly still has a hard time grasping it.

"That's scary, isn't it?" Donnelly said. "Guys I played with in the NHL have asked me, 'God, how'd you score all those goals in 40-something (44) games?' I tell 'em I don't know.

"I do know that of the six or seven guys that were really highly skilled, we played a lot. Maybe the year before, when we were constantly rolling over four lines, the higher skilled players didn't get to play as much as we did. But my senior year, we played a lot.

"We had five forwards on the power play—myself, Mitch, Kevin, Joe and Billy Shibicky—and I know I scored a lot of the power play (a team-leading 27 times). Also, there was no red line (no two-line pass rule, unlike the one the NHL employs), and I was getting breakaways all the time. We had some set plays off faceoffs in our own end, we did a number of things with my speed and without the red line that really benefited my game.

"I know I had worked extremely hard in the offseason because almost all of the guys on the team had been drafted (by NHL teams) and I hadn't been and that pushed me. And I know my roommate for a few years, Harvey Smyl, had a better grasp of the game than I did and that I really learned a lot from him. And I know playing in the Spartan program for four years really helped.
"But I really can't explain how I went from 26 goals (as a junior) to 59."

While Donnelly clearly led the way, Messier and Murphy both ended up with 24 goals in 1985-86 (Murphy added 37 assists for 61 points, which wasn't bad for a freshman). Miller had 19 goals and 52 assists. Three other freshmen, McReynolds (14 goals), Cole (11) and Reynolds (nine) were also heard from regularly in the offensive end. And for this team, on a lot of nights, things just went right.

"When Mel had the eight goals against Ohio State, I set him up on every one," Messier said. "I had two that weekend and on both of mine, he set me up. I remember talking to him after that and he said, "Man, this is just sick...""

On game nights, they played together. Other nights, they partied together. Football on TV, foosball at the house Donnelly, McSween, Messier and Miller were living in, team "meetings" at popular East Lansing nightspots; you name it, these Spartans stuck together doing it.

"After a Saturday night home game, we'd have a party, and out of 25 guys on the roster, 19 would be there," said Rizzo, a senior swingman who provided grit rather than goal scoring. "Every Tuesday, eight or 10 of us would go out for all-you-can-eat spaghetti. During Christmas break, we'd practice at 10 a.m., and then 12 of us would go see the new Stallone movie at the Meridian Mall. Instead of making the freshmen walk from the dorms to the team meal on Saturday morning when it was 20 below, we'd make sure somebody would swing by and pick them up.

"The freshmen were never initiated. We never treated them like shit just because they were freshmen. And when we went into the corner, we knew they'd be there to back us up."

The playoffs opened with a sweet sweep of Michigan—a sub-.500, second-division team that had managed a regular-season split (2-2) against State in the regular season mostly by rising to the occasion of the rivalry—at Munn. MSU won on the first night of the series, 4-3, and escorted Red Berenson and Co. into the off-season, 5-2, the next. Neither win was what you'd call pretty.

"If they'd just play the game instead of clutching and grabbing us all the time, we'd blow them out," Tilley complained.

That they didn't was no big deal. Unlike the previous season, when after a while nothing the Dream Team-juggernaut did seemed to be good enough (and ultimately wasn't), wins were all that mattered this time around.

"Last year if we won 5-1, people would ask us why we didn't win 10-1," Messier said. "This year, while we aren't like last year's team, we're mature enough to realize we've reached the standards we set for ourselves."

"I think our fans have a better feeling about this team," Mason added. "They understand they can't compare it to last year's team. As a result, I don't think the fans' expectations are as big as they were last year."

MSU next headed to Detroit for the CCHA Final Four, hoping to extend its 16-game Joe Louis Arena winning streak. The Spartans did, too, but only by one game. A 3-2 victory over Lake Superior in the semifinals was followed up by a sobering, 3-1 loss to Western Michigan in the play-off-championship clash.

"We were nervous tonight and I don't know

why,'" Mason said.

"This is a milestone for our program," Western Michigan coach Bill Wilkinson said. "We're trying to build a program like Michigan State's."

What the Broncos had done in the interim was lock up the CCHA's automatic bid in the NCAA Tournament with the victory. The loss left the Spartans, No. 2 in the nation prior to the conclusion of the league playoffs, at 30-9-2 overall. It also made everyone more than a little bit nervous. Although MSU still hoped and expected to get an at-large bid to the tournament, it couldn't be certain its season hadn't suddenly ended (the CCHA in the mid-1980s always seemed to get the short end of the NCAA stick regarding at-large bids) until the call officially came in.

Once it did, the loss to Western—State's first in 12 games—was much easier to keep in perspective.

"I think it actually helped us," Beck said. "I think we were starting to get to the point where our confidence was becoming over-confidence. That just brought us down to earth a little bit."

Once the NCAA invitation arrived, the Spartans prepared to host Boston College. MSU had finished fifth in the final coaches' poll (behind Minnesota, BC, Denver and Harvard), but had been awarded home ice based on its ability to fill the seats at Munn.

"Last year at this time we thought we were the best team in the country and that we would win the national title, and we should have," Mason said. "This year we're more of an underdog. We're just trying to stay alive."

"The advantage was the Final Four was in Providence, R.I.—a long way away," Gwozdecky said. "People were excited, they wanted to follow us, but they were concentrating on the next game that we had to play. The media wasn't talking about the Final Four, our fans weren't talking about the Final Four and our players weren't talking about the Final Four.

"Our focus was on playing them one game at a time, if you'll pardon the old cliché. That was

the real difference in how everybody approached the games down the stretch from one year (1984-85) to the next (1985-86). Everybody was excited when BC came to town because everybody was excited to still be playing."

BC was excited, too—and with good reason. The Eagles, who had fallen at Munn in a two-games, total-goals NCAA quarterfinal series in 1984, came to town this time with the likes of Doug Brown, Ken Hodge Jr., Craig Janney, Kevin Stevens, Bob Sweeney and Tim Sweeney. Coached by NCAA-legend Len Ceglarski (who had been behind the Clarkson bench in the title game when State won the NCAA championship in 1966), Boston College posed a serious threat.

MSU responded with surprisingly easy 6-4 and 4-2 victories to take the two-games, total-goals series, 10-6. The first win featured Donnelly's sixth hat trick of the season—goals No. 55, 56 and 57, which bested the 56 Denver's Jerry Walker had netted in 1960-61 and tied Dave Merhar of Army's NCAA-record 57 in 1968-69. The goaltending, meanwhile, was superb (Foster made 33 saves the first night; Essensa 36 in the second, including 18 in the third period) in both games. One year after what seemed like a sure thing had exploded in their faces, the Spartans were back in the Final Four.

Up first was Minnesota, which featured a pair of future NHL goalies (Frank Pietrangelo, once heavily recruited by MSU, and John Blue) and star forwards Corey Millen and Paul Broten (two more NHLers in-the-making). It was a typical Golden Gophers team—fast, relentless, tenacious and a little undersized.

"I remember thinking they were small, quick and fast, and that if we'd just hit them, hit them, hit them and wear them down, by the third period we'd be able to take over. And that's what happened," Beck said. "Ron had a great gameplan. He said, 'Let's stick with them for two periods and just pound them, pound them, pound them.' We were hitting them all over the place for two periods. And by the third period, they weren't going into the corners anymore."

Minnesota wouldn't have had to if Foster

hadn't repeatedly risen to the occasion in the nets in the early going. But after allowing an early goal, he stood on his head for stretches in holding the Gophers at bay until the Spartans found their equilibrium. State escaped the opening 20 minutes ahead, 2-1.

After the disappointment of the previous spring, Foster had bounced back and then some with a brilliant effort.

"Normie played phenomenal in that first period," Gwozdecky said. "He made some tremendous saves. We were playing nervous, we weren't playing with a lot of composure, and Normie really kept us in there while Minnesota was dominating.

"After that first period we kind of settled down, and got a little pissed off, if you will, that we were playing as stupidly as we were, and started to execute the way we were capable of executing. It was a hell of a game."

It had a hell of a finish, too. The Gophers fell behind by counts of 4-1 and 5-2, but rallied to pull to within 5-4 at 18:17 of the third. Their comeback hopes weren't officially dashed until Jeff Parker's empty-net goal at 19:24 started Michigan State's countdown to the NCAA Final. Foster finished with a career-high 42 saves.

Suddenly, the coveted national championship was only a game away. And suddenly, this team that opened the season with little or no expectations of greatness was on the verge of doing something only one other MSU team had been able to do. And by now, the questions had been all but erased. By Donnelly. By Parker, who had emerged as a physical force. By Murphy, the CCHA's Freshman of the Year. By Messier, Shibicky, McSween, the goaltenders and so many others...

And now only Harvard stood in the way. And the Crimson would be forced to play State without Hobey Baker Award-winning defenseman Scott Fusco, who had been injured in Harvard's semifinal win over Denver.

"It's strange how fate plays a hand," Gwozdecky said. "Who knows what would have happened if Fusco had been in the lineup for

For some ridiculous reason, 59 goals and an NCAA title weren't enough to get Mike Donnelly the Hobey Baker Award. At least The Hockey News understood Donnelly's standing in the college hockey game in 1985-86.

them?"

What happened without him was impossible to top as far as the Spartans were concerned.

Harvard took a 2-1 lead into the first-period intermission, which turned into an extended break when the Providence Civic Center's Zamboni machine broke down and a replacement had to be driven in from Providence College across town. The Spartans coped with jokes and with card games in the locker room. Then, after 40 minutes had been

former walk-on who was mostly what hockey types refer to as a "shit disturber" during his days at State, Rizzo—a player who was never shy about delivering an elbow, a slash or a verbal barrage on an opponent despite standing only 5-foot-7 and weighing in the neighborhood of 150 pounds—took it upon himself to speak to his teammates from the heart.

"I can't remember exactly what I said. It was something like, 'This is the last (expletive)

Nerves were evident on the bench in the third period of the NCAA Championship game against Harvard. All eyes were riveted on the ice except those of Bobby Reynolds (no. 15), who anxiously glances up to sneak a peek at the Providence Civic Center clock.

played and Harvard had established a 4-3 advantage, the Spartans coped with emotion.

Rizzo, who was playing on defense in the Final Four because the staff had lost faith in Luongo, decided a little pep talk was in order. A

time I'm ever going to wear this (expletive) uniform, and I don't intend to go out a (expletive) loser. If any of you guys are thinking about quitting now, don't even (expletive) come out for the third period,'" Rizzo recalled.

He had recorded just five assists that season, and totaled only two goals and 17 helpers for his career. Still, on many nights when he wore the

Green and White, Rizzo's personality made him an asset. This was one of them, for everyone got the message.

"He was always the kind of guy who was a big talker, so the guys didn't always take him seriously," Gwozdecky said. "But with this speech he really hit home."

MSU took the ice flying in the third period and quickly took a 5-4 lead on goals by freshman defenseman Brad Hamilton (at 1:06) and

and so nerve-wracking and there was about 10 minutes left in the game. I remember saying, 'Doc, isn't this great? You work all year to get here and this is just the kind of situation you love to be a part of and no one else can experience this except you and me and the rest of the guys.'

"And I remember looking down at the bench, and Doc was smiling. Then he was laughing. That feeling was so unique ... It was tense and it was nerve-wracking, but at the same time it was a

The boys didn't mind getting a little wet while celebrating their national championship. Pictured are, from left: Mitch Messier, Bobby Reynolds, Mike Donnelly (clutching the NCAA Championship trophy), Norm Foster, and Bill Shibicky.

McReynolds (at 2:15). Harvard came back and tied it at 6:46. And back and forth they went from there, with an entire season's worth of agony and the national championship hanging in the balance.

"I can remember talking with Doc (Dr. John Downs) on the headphones when it was tied in the third period," Gwozdecky, who was stationed upstairs in the press box, offered. "It was so tight

highly-enjoyable situation."

Finally, with just under three minutes left, Donnelly (who else?) decided it.

Murphy, who had replaced Messier on the line with Donnelly and Kevin Miller before the

Final Four, lost a draw in the Harvard end. But Donnelly, positioned as the trigger man at the top of the circle, intercepted a weak Harvard clearing attempt and one-timed the puck toward the net. Harvard goalie Grant Blair, who had a habit of coming out a long way to cut the angles down on draws, couldn't get back to the crease in time. When the red light went on, a mere 2:51 remained.

"Kevin Miller had gotten kicked out of the faceoff and Murph got beat so bad, it went right to

At last, the championship!! A giddy group of Spartans gathers for an impromptu team photo moments after holding off Harvard.

lose it now,'" Beck remembered.

They didn't. Even an empty-net goal that was waved off because of a too-many-men-on-the-ice penalty in the final minute (Jeff Parker's emotions had gotten the best of him and he had left the bench early) failed to derail what had become destiny's darlings' march to the top of the mountain. In the end, Essensa's toughest task wasn't preserving MSU's 6-5 victory, it was surviving the avalanche of happy Spartans that landed on top of him once the game had finally ended.

"Riz (Rizzo) and I were on the bench

their winger," Donnelly said. "But the guy didn't hang onto it, he just kind of pushed it up to me. The guy put it right on my stick and I one-timed it.

"It went in and we went crazy."

"I thought, 'Man, there's no way we can

together as time expired," Beck said. "We looked at each other and hugged. He had tears in his eyes, I had tears in my eyes...It's something I'll never forget, never.

"The year before kind of flashed in front of me and

I remember thinking, 'Wow...who would have ever thought this was possible?"

Who indeed?

Donnelly had been a third-line player the year before. Parker—whose hitting throughout the second half of the season reminded Gwozdecky of the "de-cleaters" and "off the film" blocks regularly delivered by the Spartan football team's All-America offensive tackle, Tony Mandarich—had been a fourth-line winger the year before, and disappointing enough that the coaches were wondering if they'd made a mistake in bringing Parker to State in the first place. His MVP-caliber play in the stretch run ultimately took him to the NHL. Messier, a force at forward who somehow still never quite emerged from Donnelly's shadow in '86, had also been a third-liner the previous season. And the 10 freshmen were just freshmen (even Murphy) back when all of this madness began...

Somehow, it all came together.

"It still seems like a dream to me," Donnelly said some 10 years later. "Winning, scoring all those goals, everything that happened...That's a great memory I'll keep with me the rest of my life.

"That's one of my career highlights, and I played on a line with Wayne Gretzky and Jari Kurri for a year and a half (with the Los Angeles Kings)."

"Last year was like doomsday around Michigan State when we lost in the quarterfinals," Mason said. "This year it's like heaven."

And so another surprise ending had been written, one as satisfying as the Dream Team's demise had been stunning the year before.

"Somebody asked me what it felt like to win it," Gwozdecky said. "I said what I felt mostly was relief...relief that we wouldn't have to go through what we went through the year before again.

"Winning it all that next year...that was really the only medicine that could finally take that disappointment away."

Years later, the 1985-86 team is remembered with reverence around East Lansing, and for much more than merely easing the sting of a bitterly disappointing and totally-unforeseen defeat the previous season. But the 1984-85 team, the Dream Team, the one that didn't win it all, is still remembered as the better hockey club, as the best hockey team in MSU history, in fact.

So be it. That doesn't make the national championship won by the 1985-86 team any less spectacular.

Their triumph was best summed up by former MSU Sports Information Department assistant John Hahn, who told Greg Lapinski of The State News, "This team may not be as good as they once were, but they're as good once as they ever were."

Throughout the unlikely ride 1985-86 provided, that was more than good enough.

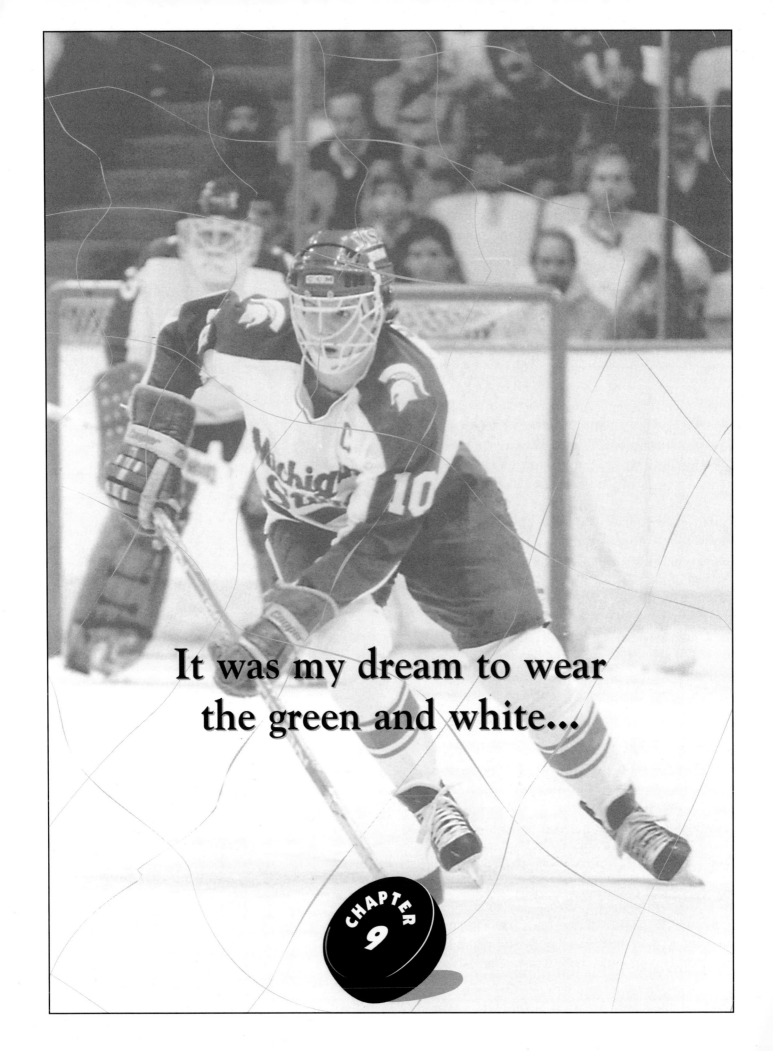

It was my dream to wear
the green and white...

CHAPTER
9

Chapter 9

What's most responsible for the Miller phenomenon at Michigan State?

Pop.

Not pop as in Lyle Miller, father of Kelly, Kevin and Kip, but pop as in Pepsi or Vernors or Orange Crush or whatever it was the boys liked to polish off while visiting the Spartan locker room following another exciting night of college hockey.

"They used to have this pop machine in their locker room and it was always a lot of fun to have a pop after the game," remembered Kelly, who along with his brothers was treated regularly to the Demonstration Hall-Jenison Field House MSU hockey experience by father Lyle, an MSU alum and former Spartan icer who often worked the games as either a public address announcer or a linesman.

"We'd also look around for broken sticks and end up trying to tape 'em back together.

"I had so many fond memories of being around Michigan State hockey and looking through that screen at Dem Hall and wanting to be out there some day."

Enough that when the time came in 1981, Kelly Miller, the oldest of Lyle Miller's three sons, couldn't pass up the scholarship Michigan State was offering. He considered playing junior hockey in Peterborough, Ontario. And he considered play-

Butch Miller's love for MSU convinced brother Lyle (pictured here) to attend, and Lyle wound up setting the Spartan record for sons produced that went on to become stars at Michigan State.

ing on the collegiate level elsewhere, most notably at Harvard, Notre Dame and Wisconsin. As his class valedictorian and the owner of a 4.0 grade-point average in high school, Kelly definitely was no cement head. Although he was a Lansing, Mich., native, this was not a decision he was going to make hastily.

Still, when push came to shove, Kelly followed his heart.

"They were all excellent schools, so it really made for a tough decision," he explained. "But in the end, the thought of playing in my hometown was too powerful.

"I grew up watching Michigan State. Their players were my heroes when I was growing up. And it was my dream to wear the Green and White. That's why I ended up picking Michigan State."

Once Kelly had done so, the Miller Movement was off and running again.

It had started in 1955, when Lyle's brother Butch decided to leave Regina, Saskatchewan, for East Lansing. A hard-hitting defenseman who scored only three goals in his MSU career ("I heard he was famous for his hip-check," Kelly offered), Butch Miller was a member of State's 1959 NCAA finalist, the team that was denied a national championship by North Dakota, 4-3, in overtime.

His experiences were enough to convince Lyle to follow in his brother's footsteps. Lyle

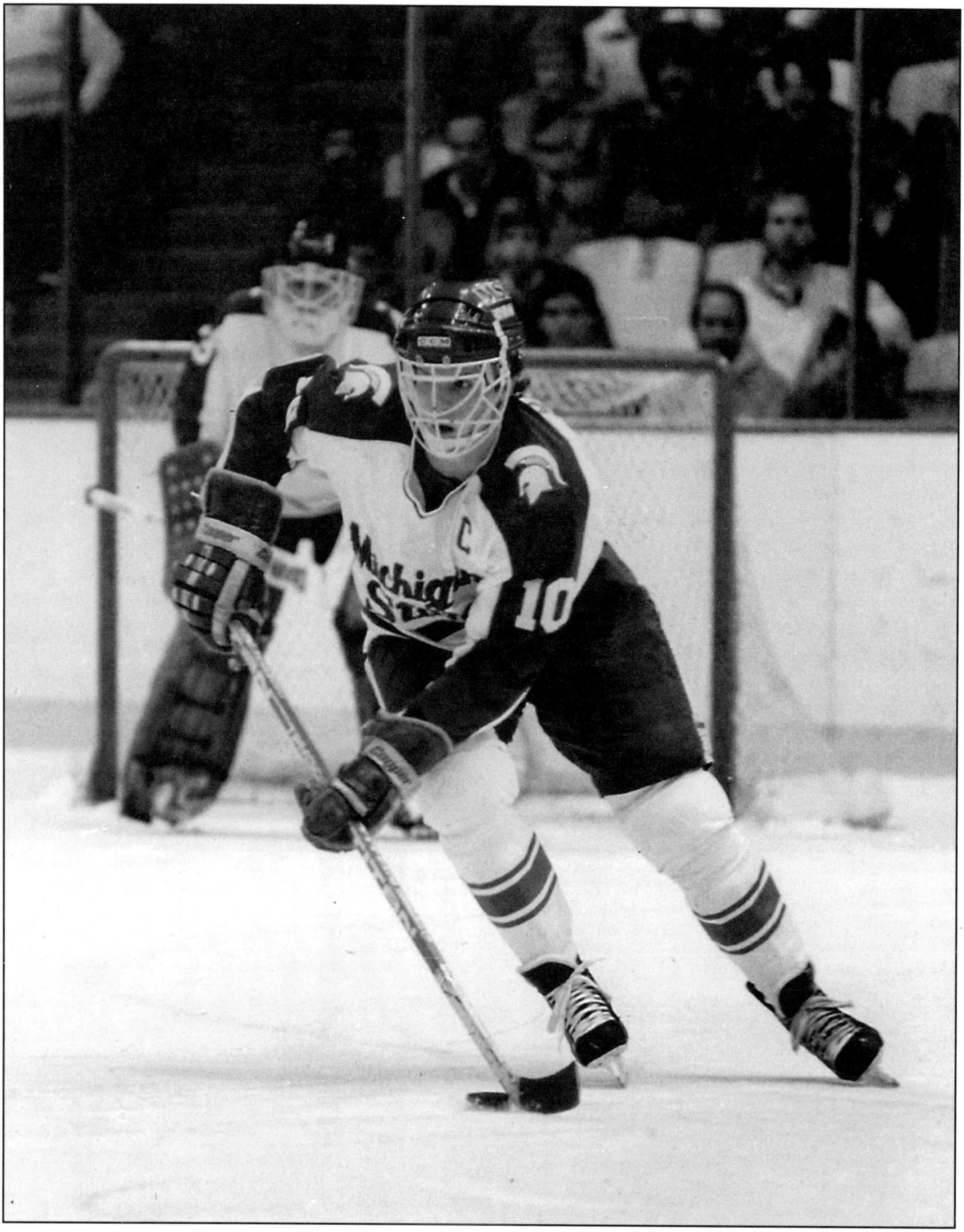
C
10

played some as a sophomore (freshmen weren't eligible), got married when he was a junior and earned his only letter as a senior in the 1963-64 campaign. The MSU community, meanwhile, grew on him the entire time.

"I really came because Butch loved the place," Lyle is fond of explaining. "I just haven't left.

"Probably the campus was the thing Butch liked best, and of course the hockey and of course (former coach) Amo (Bessone). Me, I never thought about going anyplace else.

"And as soon as I got here, as soon as I saw the campus. I knew that this was someplace special. Everything just seemed to fit. It was kind of scary at first. At that time I think there were about 20,000 students, but it was still like a city of its own. It was scary, but it was an exciting scary."

Butch's son Dean skated for the Spartans in 1977-78 and 1978-79 (Bessone's final two seasons), scoring four goals and recording 14 points and rounding out a nice, little story, or so it seemed. But when Kelly came onto the scene in the fall of 1981, the Millers were well on their way to becoming the First Family of Spartan Hockey.

Brothers Kevin and Kip soon followed, and the three combined to help inspire an unprecedented, nine-year run that lifted the program from also-ran status to that of a national power.

Their collective resume reads like a diary of State's "Amazing '80s" decade. It includes nine straight winning seasons, four Central Collegiate Hockey Association regular-season championships, seven CCHA playoff titles, nine straight appearances in the NCAA Tournament, four trips to the Final Four, two berths in the NCAA title game and one national championship (1985-86, Kevin's the only one of the three with a ring). Michigan

State's combined record during the nine seasons when at least one of Lyle Miller's sons wore the Green and White was 294-94-14.

No wonder Kelly became a first-team All-American in 1984-85, and Kip followed in 1988-89 and 1989-90 (joining Tom Ross and Ron Scott as the only Spartans to be so honored twice).

No wonder Kelly (in 1983-84 and, along with Dale Krentz in 1984-85) and Kip (1989-90) were selected as MSU MVPs.

No wonder Kelly (in 1984-85) and Kip (in 1988-89 and 1989-90) were finalists for college hockey's version of the Heisman Trophy, the Hobey Baker Award (which Kip won his senior year).

No wonder Kevin was chosen for the 1988 United States Olympic Team, where he played along with future NHL stars and future NHL counterparts Mike Richter, Brian Leetch, Craig Janney and Kevin Stevens.

"The team had been struggling for a number of years, and it just seemed that when Kelly hit the school it just started something," Lyle said. "Of course, I'm not saying it was just those guys. They brought in a lot of good players."

That they did. Still, the Spartans haven't hung a banner from the Munn Arena rafters since Kip Miller departed in 1990.

"Kelly gave 'em great leadership, and Kevin gave 'em great leadership, and they could play," Lyle said. "And Kip just absolutely... well, I don't think there has been anybody over this last little while that has dominated college hockey like he did for two years straight."

Kelly set about trying to make the most of what MSU had to offer from the first moment he set foot on campus.

He had an edge growing up, as did his brothers, because Lyle's pursuits also included running the Lansing Ice and Gymnastics Center. The boys could skate to their hearts' content there or on the backyard rink their father fashioned for them in the winter. But an abundance of ice time alone didn't turn Kelly Miller into an All-American or an NHL stalwart (initially with the New York Rangers

---

Captain Kelly Miller, who literally worked and willed himself into becoming an All-American, resurrected the family tradition of attending MSU and blazed a trail for his brothers.

and then with the Washington Capitals).

His work ethic did.

"Probably the hardest worker I've ever seen," current coach Ron Mason said. "There are only a few players that have Kelly Miller's work ethic. Everything he did in life, he had that work ethic. Rod Brind' Amour was like that, in that category of individual.

another 109 in the playoffs (but not so much as one shift in the minor leagues) later, Kelly Miller remembers it worked out that way by design.

"I owe most of my success to just simply outworking some of the people that were in a position similar to me," he said. "I really tried to put to good use all the time I had, whether it was off-ice training, working on my shot or puckhandling, or

Butch Miller (far right, pictured with Glenn MacDonald, Joe Selinger, and Amo Bessone) had no idea he'd be starting a trend when he migrated from Regina, Saskatchewan to Michigan State.

"Kelly, because of his determination and his competitiveness and his desire to be the best that he could be, that's what got him where he's at."

Over 900 NHL regular-season games (939, to be exact, through the 1996-97 season) and

just thinking about the game.

"I tried to be a smart player and to understand the game and really know the game. I'd ask the coaches questions and analyze the game and try to attack hockey from every angle and work hard at every practice."

Even at Monday optionals, when some of the team would be screwing around in a pickup game at one end of the ice, Miller would be at the other, lining up pucks and blasting them at an unguarded net. Even after he had grown from an eager freshman into a team leader.

Kelly's relentless attack on the game even included positive-thinking tapes.

"'The Psychology of Winning,'" Kelly remembered. "I think it was my sophomore year, I was over at my girlfriend's, well, now my wife's house, and her dad had these tapes. They looked interesting. I said, 'Do you mind if I listen to these?' I was always looking for an edge.

"After that I started getting into visualization pretty big. I'd visualize myself doing certain moves on he ice, making certain plays. It's amazing, but even today in the pros, if I see a guy that's struggling or someone that maybe needs a little bit of help, I talk to them about some of the things that helped me. One of them is how you talk to yourself mentally in terms of visualization and things like that."

He first showed up, in Mason's estimation, as a "good, prized recruit," but wasn't considered a lock for stardom. Eventually, Kelly Miller turned himself into a more-than-capable goal scorer (55 over his last two seasons, including a team-leading 28 as a junior, and 82 for his career), a tireless skater, a tenacious penalty killer, a coach on the ice, a leader in the locker room, a captain and an All-American. His career totals of 82 goals, 82 assists and 164 points don't begin to reveal all that he meant to Michigan State.

"He didn't have the gifted hands to be a scorer, but he had everything else," Mason said.

"He's as good as anyone we've seen in either the CCHA or the Western Collegiate Hockey Association," Northern Michigan coach Rick Comley observed during Kelly's senior season.

Kelly Miller the collegian was perhaps best summed up by former New York Rangers scout Chuck Grillo, who was absolutely lavish in his praise of the Rangers' 1982 ninth-round draft pick.

"He's a positively infectious player," Grillo once said. "He has a chemistry about him that's catalystic and it causes other people to look at themselves and say, 'Hey, it's degrading if I don't work a little harder...look at that guy.'

"His assets fit his coach. It doesn't make any difference who the coach is. If you don't want

Dean Miller, the third but hardly the last of his clan to wear the Green and White.

Kelly Miller on your team, you probably don't want to coach. Kelly Millers have made more coaches than coaches have made Kelly Millers."

And finally, "If I had a kid and I wanted him to grow up and be like somebody that plays the game the way it's supposed to be played, I would want my boy to know Kelly Miller," Grillo said.

Alas, even Kelly Miller's stuff-that-dreams-are-made-of days at State didn't end without a little angst. As great a player and as respected an individual as Miller became, he still couldn't stop the "Dream Team" from toppling at the hands of Providence in a shocking NCAA quarterfinal upset that ended his MSU career in the spring of 1985.

"No question the most disappointing loss I've ever been involved with," he said. "I still think about it. We had just a fantastic team. I wish I could have that game over again."

Brother Kevin was with him on that record-setting, ultimately frustrated 1984-85 bunch. He too, had considered playing his college hockey elsewhere. But like Kelly, Kevin had grown up around MSU's rinks, rubbing elbows with MSU's players.

"My cousin Dean went through when we were at a good age, so we could remember all of his buddies and got to hang out with them a little bit," Kevin pointed out. "We were always around Michigan State hockey.

"And it's hard, growing up, not believing in it, that's for sure."

Still, MSU had offered only a partial scholarship at first, which allowed Providence College to initially sneak into the Kevin Miller sweepstakes.

"I was looking for a full ride," he recalled. "I wanted to take the burden off my parents and make my way through college on my own.

"State ended up coming to me later in the year and offering me a full ride. As soon as that happened, it was a sure thing."

Kevin played mostly a third- or fourth-line role as a freshman on the "Dream Team," but quickly established himself as a sophomore. His

rapid development, along with that of several others, paved the way for 1985-86's unexpected national championship run. And while Mike Donnelly was scoring an NCAA-record 59 goals, Miller was piling up an MSU-leading 52 assists, many by setting up Donnelly. Miller's 71 points, meanwhile, trailed only Donnelly's 97 on the '86 champs.

Miller was also going into the corners and getting in opponents' faces with regularity, aspects of his game that he appeared to enjoy as much if not more than scoring.

"He had great skills and he was feisty," Mason said of Kevin. "He didn't have the same work ethic that Kelly had, but he was he kind of player who could do anything in a given situation. He was a better scorer than Kelly, and could have been every bit as good a checker but didn't want to be.

"But if the chips were down, you could count on Kevin Miller. In the big games, in the big situations, at the times when you really needed a player, I never hesitated in putting Kevin Miller on the ice because that's when he came to the forefront."

Kevin continued to shine as a junior in 1986-87, during MSU's defense of its national championship. He scored big goals (including the OT winner against Bowling Green in the CCHA playoff championship game), he made plays (again leading the team in assists, with 56), he banged people and he excelled on special teams, and the Spartans made it all the way to the NCAA Championship Game against North Dakota. At that point, all Michigan State needed to do to capture back-to-back national titles was win another game in its second home, Detroit's Joe Louis Arena, where it had already won 21 of its last 23.

It was then that Kevin Miller's career took a frustrating turn, as Kelly's had in 1984-85 against Providence.

"We made a critical mistake," then-assistant coach George Gwozdecky admitted.

The mistake was putting a defensive yoke around Kevin Miller by asking him to shadow

North Dakota's Tony Hrkac, rather than to go out and win the game for Michigan State.

"All year long all you had heard about was Bobby Joyce and Tony Hrkac, about the 'Hrkac Circus' and how good they were and how nobody could stop that line," Gwozdecky explained. "They had Eddie Belfour in goal and some other players who went on to play professional hockey, but all you heard about was Hrkac.

"And all we heard from our coaching peers and people who had had success was, 'You gotta shadow Hrkac, you gotta match lines.' Hrkac (who had 46 goals, 125 points and won the Hobey Baker Award that year) and Joyce were like (former Edmonton Oilers greats Wayne) Gretzky and (Jari) Kurri; it didn't matter who was on their left side. And I can remember Rick Comley and Shawn Walsh telling us, I think both Northern Michigan and Maine had beaten North Dakota during the season, and they said the way they had done it was to put a checking line against the Hrkac line and shadow him.

"We had never done that, but we made the decision late on the Saturday of the game that we were going to use Kevin Miller (then a right winger) to shadow Hrkac (a center). I remember at the team meeting Ron made that announcement as we were going through our 15-minute battle plan and I'm looking around the room and there are looks of disgust, looks of 'Why are we doing this?' No one said anything, but you could just see it in their faces."

After 20 minutes of play in the title game, it was the Spartan coaches who were visibly upset. North Dakota was ahead, 3-0.

"Ron, (then-assistant) Terry (Christensen) and myself, we were just disgusted with ourselves, absolutely furious," Gwozdecky said. "We had put so much emphasis on the Hrkac line that all we were doing was thinking defense and we got no offense established and after the first period, the game was basically over at that point."

One of the reasons Mason decided to play it that way was that Bobby Reynolds, an excellent two-way forward, had been lost in the semifinal victory over Minnesota after suffering a concussion. The lines and special teams were going to have to be re-shuffled somewhat, anyway, Mason reasoned, so why not listen to the advice of men he knew, respected and trusted?

"I've been kicking myself in the ass ever since," Mason said.

"That's what you call over-coaching," Gwozdecky said. "We over-coached that game. We should have just done what got us there.

"After it was 3-0 we said, '(The heck with) it, let's just play our game.' And we did and we played well and we created offense...Who knows what would have happened if we had just played their game against our game (from the outset) and let the chips fall where they may? We may have lost by seven, but we may have won by seven."

Kevin Miller, the player most affected by the staff's decision, wasn't critical of it following the Fighting Sioux's 5-3 victory. Nor was he critical of it a decade later.

"You can always look back and say we would have won (had the Spartans played it normally), but who knows?" Miller said. "Who is to say it would have been any different the other way? They had a great season, a strong team...It's always easy to second-guess.

"But it would have been interesting to see, if we would have played it straight up, what would have happened."

The North Dakota game more or less finished Kevin Miller's career at Michigan State.

He joined the U.S. Olympic Team the following season—he had long held playing in the Olympics one notch above playing in the NHL on his list of career goals—and returned to MSU in March of 1988 to try and help out in the playoffs. Alas, there was nothing left in the tank.

"Kevin was so tired, so burnt out, he looked like he really didn't want to play," Gwozdecky said. "It had been a long year prepping for the Olympics with all the traveling that team did. He came back, but he just wasn't the Kevin Miller we needed."

He left for good following MSU's 8-5, two-games, total-goals loss in an NCAA quarterfinal series at Minnesota with 61 goals, 140 assists, 201 points, 277 penalty minutes and one national championship to his credit.

Next it was on to the New York Rangers (who had drafted him on the 10th round in 1984), Detroit Red Wings, Washington Capitals (where he was reunited with Kelly for all of 10 games), St. Louis Blues, San Jose Sharks, Pittsburgh Penguins and Chicago Blackhawks. Pens General Manager Craig Patrick (who had drafted Kelly and Kevin while working as the GM of the Rangers) added Kevin to solidify his team for what he hoped would be a Stanley Cup run at the NHL's trading deadline in March of 1996, and in the process summed up why Kevin Miller is often in such demand.

"He's a guy who can play well both offensively and defensively, can play on one of our top lines, he can play all three forward positions and he gives you experience," Patrick said.

It didn't take long for Kevin to become a fan favorite in Pittsburgh, just as Kelly has long been in Washington.

Just as Kelly and Kevin had been at Michigan State.

"I suppose if he had waited (after the Olympics) and come back for a full year (in 1988-89), he probably would have been an All-American," Mason said of Kevin. "He might have even been the Hobey Baker winner, he was that good."

So was Kip.

Like Kelly and Kevin, the rink, either the Miller's backyard version or the sheet at the Ice and Gymnastics Center, had been Kip's second home ("My friends and I would be out at 11 o'clock at night for a pickup game, but my parents knew we were out, so there weren't any problems") growing up. And like Kelly and Kevin, Kip had skating in his blood (sister Kristen was a competitive figure skater, mother Marie was a figure skating instructor). But unlike the first and second of Lyle's sons, Kip had two brothers to admire and pattern himself after and contemplate following on to Munn Arena.

"Being the youngest, I used to always watch Kelly and Kevin play," Kip offered. "I admired them tremendously. I still do.

"I remember watching Kelly his senior year (at MSU) and being the MVP of his team and thinking, 'Wow, what a great honor.'"

By then Kip Miller-to-Michigan State was a virtual recruiting lock. So much so that Mason was confident enough to offer the following in an interview in 1985: "Let's face it, with the history of his brothers and family all going to Michigan State, I would sure think that's where he'd be going."

"I don't think any other schools even asked me. It was basically understood that I was going to play for Michigan State," Kip remembered. "That's where I wanted to go, anyway, so it didn't really matter.

"I pretty much knew where I was going. It seemed like a natural."

Kip even took extra credits to accelerate his high school graduation by a year, a suggestion first made to Lyle Miller by Mason and a plan that would get Kip away from junior competition he was dominating and allow him to continue to develop. He was on the MSU squad that lost the national championship to North Dakota (in part perhaps because of the Kevin Miller-shadow fiasco), and provided 20 goals that season as a freshman. But his offense slipped a bit, to 16 goals, and his overall play in terms of discipline and defense lagged dramatically as a sophomore.

"I think I struggled trying to live on my own with some of the guys," Kip offered. "The first year in the dorm, everything is exciting. Then the second year you get an apartment and you have to learn how to handle all the outside stuff."

It wasn't until late in that 1987-88 season, with Kevin back from the Olympics but fighting illness and exhaustion, that Kip served notice that his time was almost at hand. In the NCAA quarterfinal series at Minnesota, the Spartans lost the first game, 4-2, but bolted to a 3-0 lead in the first period of the second encounter. They did so on the strength of a Kip Miller natural hat trick that was completed in the game's first 15:35.

All of a sudden, Michigan State was leading the series, and was a mere two periods away from the Final Four.

"You just didn't do that at Minnesota back then," Gwozdecky said. "The crowd was so quiet..."

It got considerably louder when the Gophers stormed back to score the next four goals and take the game and the series (the final one, ironically, by center Jason Miller; no relation), but a metamorphosis had apparently occurred within Kip Miller as well.

"He had a good freshman year and a terrible sophomore year," Lyle said. "Then he picked it up the next two years. He really went after it."

"That last series against Minnesota, I think that set the tone for the next two years not just for myself, but for everybody," Kip insisted.

"Our team hadn't really had a good year.

"After that we were really good."

Especially Kip. For the next two seasons, he was, "one of the top, top players that we've had the privilege of playing against," according to Bowling Green coach Jerry York; "one of those players that has the skill and smarts to be the difference in a game," according to Michigan's Red Berenson; and "the heart and soul of Michigan State," according to Western Michigan's Bill Wilkinson.

Kip Miller and teammate Bobby Reynolds tied for the national scoring title with 77 points (Miller had 32 goals and a team-leading 45 assists) in 1988-89. The Spartans won the CCHA regular-season and playoff championships (just the second time that had happened; the "Dream Team" also turned the trick in 1984-85) and made it back to the Final Four, where they lost in the national semifinals to Harvard, 6-3, and defeated Maine in the third-place game, 7-4. Kip was named a Hobey Baker finalist and a first-team All-American.

The following season was even more spectacular, as Kip exploded for 48 goals (including 21 on the power play), 53 assists, 101 points (just the second 100-point campaign in MSU history behind Tom Ross' 105 in 1975-76), repeated as an All-

Senior Captain Kelly Miller poses with incoming freshman Kevin Miller, who would follow his brother's footsteps again by forging a lasting career for himself in the National Hockey League following his MSU days.

America selection and took home the Hobey as the nation's best player.

"At the start of the year, it seemed pretty well locked up that the kid from Boston College (defenseman Greg Brown, the Hockey East Player of the Year in 1988-89 and himself a future NHLer) was going to get it," Lyle Miller said of the Hobey. "All the articles and early publicity suggested there was no competition. Kip was considered maybe third, fourth or fifth (in line).

"Well, that was all Kip needed to hear. He just turned it up a notch. And we went out there to play early in the season (Nov. 17) and it was really a head-to-head battle. They shadowed Kip the whole game. If we got a power play, he would just go stand in the corner. And he still ended up with a goal and two assists, even thought they had a guy with a stick in his (groin) the whole game.

"The other kid (Brown) really didn't do anything and State beat 'em (5-3). After that I thought, 'Now, he has a chance of winning it.'"

Kip did (he always did know how to finish). The downside (after the way Kelly and Kevin went out, you just knew there had to be a downside in here somewhere) was that his Spartans slipped up short of an anticipated trip to Joe Louis for the Final Four—again.

State took the first game of a best-of-three NCAA quarterfinal series against Boston University at Munn, 6-3, but dropped the second, 5-3. Worse yet, key forwards Dwayne Norris (who had missed Game 2 with a knee injury) and Bryan Smolinski (who was suspended for one game after incurring a spearing penalty in game two) would miss the decisive third game.

For a while, it appeared as if MSU would-

Kelly Miller earned respect throughout the CCHA with his skill and determination. He not only impressed those in the college hockey world, but everyone in the National Hockey League as well.

brother Kip was feeling after the unthinkable had happened. Still, Kip departed No. 3 on Michigan State's all-time goals list (116), No. 3 in assists (145; he's since been passed by Peter White's 155 and Rem Murray's 147) and No. 3 in Spartan history in points (261).

Adding another element of frustration to his otherwise storybook career is that, although he's repeatedly produced in college and in the minor leagues, Kip Miller hasn't as yet been able to estab-

After playing for the 1988 United States Olympic Team, Kevin Miller returned to MSU to finish the 1987-88 season.

n't need them, as the Spartans assumed a 3-1 lead midway through the second period (Kip Miller assisted on all three Spartan goals). But the Terriers, led by the likes of future NHLers Tony Amonte and Shawn McEachern, scored the next four, including three straight in the third period to sew up the series.

"Coming in here where Michigan State has had such incredible success and beating them two straight is just unbelievable," BU coach Jackie Parker said.

Kelly Miller no doubt understood what

Kip Miller's extraordinary offensive skills allowed him to accumulate 116 goals and 145 assists for 261 points in his career. His 101 points in his senior season (1989-90) made him only the second Spartan in school history to surpass the century mark in points for a single season. This accomplishment secured him college hockey's most coveted individual honor, the Hobey Baker Award.

Kip Miller's Hobey Baker Award placed him in select company, indeed (in this instance he's pictured with Big Ten basketball MVP Steve Smith and Lombardi Trophy- and Butkus Award-winning linebacker Percy Snow), during a heady era for Spartan athletics.

lish himself in the NHL as his brothers have. Since leaving MSU following the 1989-90 season, Kip has enjoyed only brief stints with the Quebec Nordiques, Minnesota North Stars, New York

Islanders and Chicago Blackhawks.

"It doesn't seem as if I've really been given a chance," he said. "It's getting frustrating. You play well and do things for your (minor-league) team and they promise you things...When you do what you're supposed to do you think you're going to get rewarded, but a lot of times that doesn't happen."

Still, Kip's place among the all-time greats in MSU history is secure.

"I don't know whether he had the same grit and tenacity that Kelly had, or that Kevin had when he wanted to," Mason said. "But in terms of pure talent, Kip had the most of all of them."

At least all of the Millers that have attended Michigan State so far.

"My cousin Dean's kids are starting to come through," Kevin noted in the spring of 1996. "There's a goalie (Ryan) and there's a center (Drew).

"They're quite young yet, but they're pretty good players, that's for sure."

Word has it they also like pop.

The First Family of Spartan Hockey, from left: Kip, Kevin, Kelly, Dean, Lyle, and Butch.

There are no in-betweens...

CHAPTER
10

Chapter 10

As a player who wound up at the University of Wisconsin, as the head coach at Division III Wisconsin-River Falls, as an assistant at Michigan State, and as the head coach at Miami of Ohio and, finally, the University of Denver, George Gwozdecky has seen recruiting from all sides and all angles. Yet all of his experiences, all the trips he's taken and all the tricks he's picked up along the way haven't helped Gwozdecky deal with the stark, bottom-line reality at which the recruiting process—no matter how well it's thought out, how adeptly the calculated moves are executed and how thick a resume a program can offer in selling itself—must ultimately be resolved.

"For any assistant coach, recruiting is his life," Gwozdecky said, exaggerating only slightly. "When you land a good recruit it's like a wedding, and when you lose a top kid it's like a funeral.

"There are no in-betweens."

Not when you spend repeated 10-day stretches in places such as Wilcox, Saskatchewan, courting the next Joe Murphy. Not when the search for the talent to keep the program ahead extends to the far reaches of Canada if it has to, up even "past the tree line" (which, as Gwozdecky once explained to a curious reporter from The State News, is north of where trees are able to grow). Not when the competition includes not just the rest of the NCAA, but junior hockey, the more traditional

The nature of recruiting is such that the Spartans' staff was initially uncertain about whether or not defenseman Don McSween could make it at Michigan State. McSween went on to become an MSU captain as an underclassman, an All-American, an integral part of State's 1985-86 NCAA Championship team and played in the NHL with the Anaheim Mighty Ducks.

path to the NHL and thus, in many cases, the more attractive path in the eyes of the aspiring talent (Pat LaFontaine and Sean Burke are among those who turned down an MSU scholarship offer to play major junior hockey instead). Not when so much is riding on something that's so difficult to gauge.

Not when careers hinge on the decision of nearly every kid pitched.

"You're always asking, 'What's the percentage?' You're always wondering about that," said Shawn Walsh, a national-championship winning head coach at the University of Maine and an assistant to Ron Mason at Bowling Green and Michigan State.

"Ron and I have discussed this a number of times over the years. I'd say recruiting is probably 60 or 70 percent of your program."

In other words, no one wins without talent—no one. And according to Walsh, who has long enjoyed a well-deserved reputation as one of the smoothest recruiters in the business, even the smoothest of recruiters can only do so much.

"You have to remember, it's not the recruiters that get the players; it's the players that get the players," Walsh insisted. "Whenever a player visits your campus, the players already on the team are going to be your key recruiters.

"The Mark Hamways, the Ron Scotts, the Ken Paraskevins, the Newell Browns, the Ken

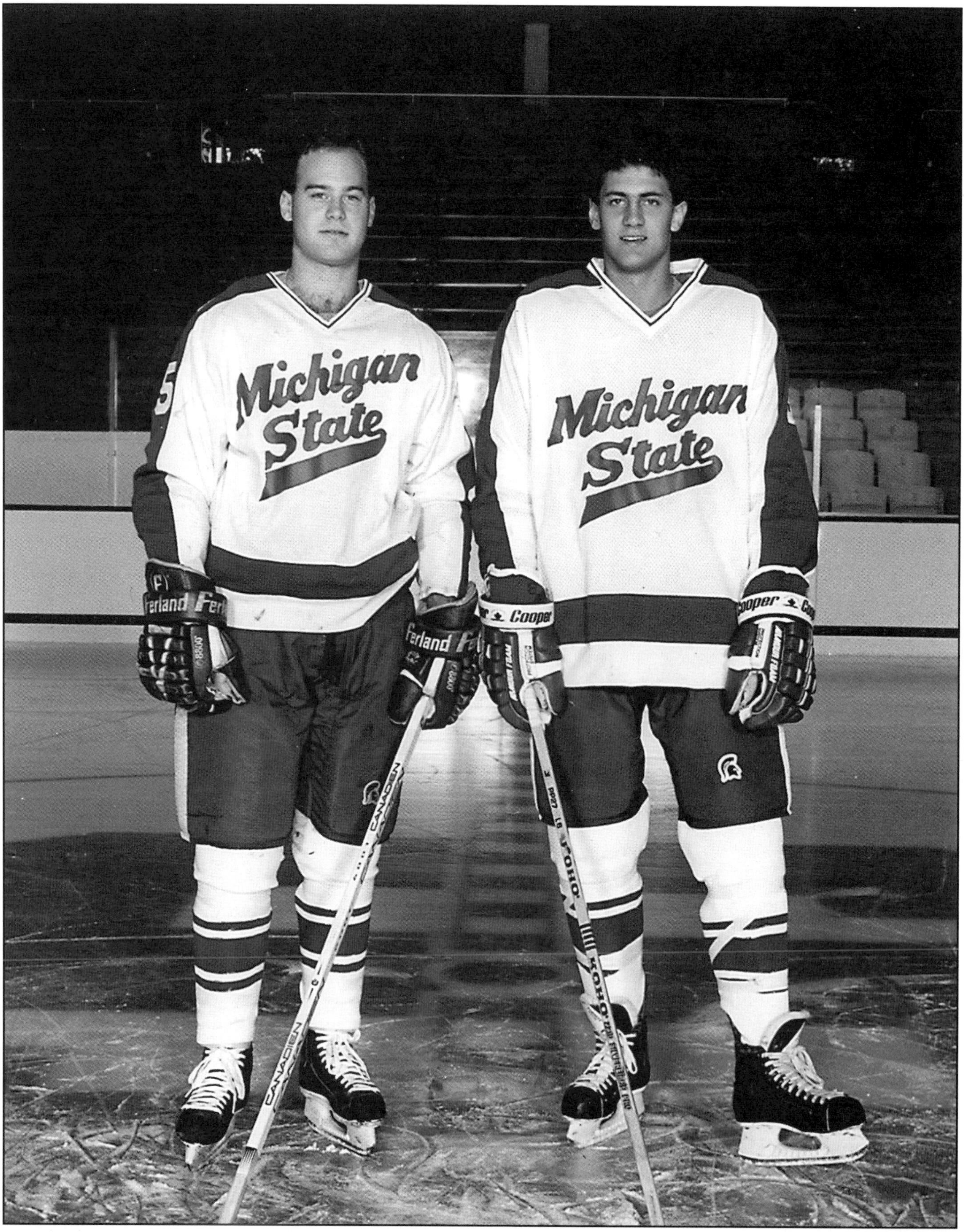
Michigan State
Michigan State
Ferland
Cooper

Leiters...Those are the guys I give the credit to for us continuing with good recruiting years (in Mason's early years at Michigan State), because they were the kind of players a top recruit would see when he came into our locker room and say, 'These are the kind of guys I want to play with.'"

Yet even when they have a locker room full of such players, assistant coaches will go to great lengths—in many cases unimaginable lengths—to keep bringing in more.

"I can remember going to Flin Flon, Manitoba, to watch Dwayne Norris, Rod Brind' Amour and Joby Messier," recalled Brown, a former Spartan center, MSU assistant coach and head coach of the AHL's Adirondack Red Wings who in the summer of 1996 became an assistant with the Chicago Blackhawks. "On the outskirts there are two signs—one points to the mill and the other points to town. There are no trees, there's no grass..."It was like being on the moon."

Mason would no doubt dispatch current assistant Tom Newton to the moon, or even go there himself to lure a potential recruit, if there was one up there that might make the difference between .500 and the Final Four.

Such a trip might not even be the worst Mason has ever experienced.

"The year we were recruiting Brind' Amour and Norris (1987-88), we knew Ron had to get into the (players') homes to meet with the Brind' Amour family and the Norris family," Gwozdecky explained. "But the only time he could do it would be just before Christmas. And just before Christmas we were going to be up at the Nissan Jeep Classic in Anchorage, Alaska, so I set up the recruiting trip from hell."

It went, as Gwozdecky no doubt will never forget, like this:

Bryan Smolinski (left) and Rem Murray, two recruits who made good...all the way to the NHL.

"Right after the Nissan Jeep Classic, which was like Dec. 21st—we lost to Maine in the championship game, by the way—we were going to leave the next morning and fly with the team back to Seattle. Then the team was going to fly back to Detroit and we were going to hit the road.

"Now, Brind' Amour lived in Campbell River, British Columbia, which is on Vancouver Island, which is about the farthest west you can go in Canada. Norris lived on 'The Rock,' St. Johns, Newfoundland, the farthest east you can go in Canada. And this is Christmas time, remember. There's ice and snow and congestion...and our schedule was really tight. The first time Ron looked at the itinerary he said, 'George, there's no (expletive) way I'm doing this.' But I felt it was really important that he get into both homes, so he finally agreed.

"So we left at like 5 or 6 in the morning from Anchorage, got to Seattle, picked up a flight in Seattle and flew to Vancouver, then caught a little puddle-jumper to Campbell River. We had dinner with Mr. and Mrs. Brind' Amour—Roddy was with the Canadian Junior National Team at the world championships, or something; he wasn't there. But the Brind' Amours were very impressed with Ron. I knew at that time there was a pretty good chance we were going to get Rod.

"We had to get out of there by 9 p.m. that night, though, because we had to catch the red-eye to Toronto. So we fly out of there at 9 p.m., get to the Vancouver airport just in time to catch the red-eye to Toronto and we get to Toronto at 7 a.m.—just in time to catch the next flight to St. Johns, Newfoundland.

"So we get to St. Johns at like 4 in the afternoon and we have dinner with the Norris family, but we have to leave by 7 that night because we have to catch a flight back to Toronto because the next day is Christmas Eve. So we have dinner with the Norrises and they get us to the airport and we get to Toronto at 10 or 11 that night and we are just shot. We've had two great visits and we're feeling buoyant about that, but we're just absolutely beat because we've covered so many miles...And Ron, kiddingly, is just cursing and cursing...

"So we checked into a hotel in Toronto. The next morning he had a real early flight back to Lansing and I had a real early flight back to Thunder Bay (Ontario, Gwozdecky's home town), but we decided to go down to the pub in the hotel to celebrate Christmas and the possibility of getting Brind' Amour and Norris. Well, halfway through our first beer we're almost asleep at the bar. Believe me, that never happens to Ron Mason in a bar. But we were so tired...We were just going on adrenaline.

"The next morning we take off again. I finally got into Thunder Bay at about 10 a.m. and its Christmas Eve and I'm running around the mall trying to buy presents for my family. I'm in a women's apparel store, trying to find a sweater for my mother, and I remember I'm sitting down and this sales girl is taking care of me...and then she's shaking me, saying, "Sir, sir...you were sleeping.' It's noon on Christmas Eve and I'm sleeping in a women's apparel store."

The adventure had a happy ending. Gwozdecky got his sweater and Michigan State got Brind' Amour and Norris—but not before Gwozdecky endured a few more sleepless nights.

Brind' Amour was the main reason why. Norris would go on to star at Michigan State, playing four years and scoring 105 goals before moving on to the Quebec Nordiques and the Canadian Olympic Team. But Brind' Amour, who would play just one season in East Lansing before jumping to the NHL with the St. Louis Blues, was perceived as the key. MSU knew it needed a center, but just one. Once the coaches determined Brind' Amour was the one, they turned down Scott Pellerin (who wanted badly to play at Michigan State and would go on to win a Hobey Baker Award at Maine) and wrote off Denny Felsner (who eventually wound up at Michigan).

Of course, they did so before Brind' Amour committed, going on little more than a gut feeling in the process.

"I was on pins and needles from November on," Gwozdecky remembered. "Rod was a real quiet kid. He was looking at a smaller school such as North Dakota, he was looking at Colorado College, he was looking at Denver. Wisconsin was trying to get in on him, too; Michigan really wasn't much of a factor in those days. But I was never sure.

"Finally, one night he calls me out of the blue. It was like 11:30 or something, and I answered the phone and he said, 'George...,' and just by the way he said 'George' I knew he had made his decision and I knew it wasn't going to be Michigan State. So I said, 'What's up?' And he said, 'Well coach, I think I want to be a Spartan.'

"I almost dropped the phone. Hell, I almost shit my pants. I remember calling Ron right away, I was so excited. When I did I could hardly speak. He was such a big 'get' for us. He was such a huge 'get' for us...

"The next year (1988-89) we ended up back in the Final Four."

"I never told them, but I was going there all along," Brind' Amour revealed years later. "I was playing with Joby Messier, and Joby was already going there, and his brother Mitch had already gone there...

"Certainly, you're going to at least look at other schools, and I had looked at quite a few programs, but theirs was top notch."

Former longtime MSU assistant Terry Christensen knew what Gwozdecky was going through, having endured a similar ordeal while recruiting Murphy during the 1984-85 season.

"I remember being at an all-star game in Penticton, British Columbia," Christensen recounted, "and for whatever reason, I just didn't feel comfortable. I sensed there was something Joe just wasn't comfortable with.

"I was supposed to come back home to East Lansing, but I got to Kelowna and I knew Joe's next game was out on Vancouver Island...so I got out my credit card and bought a ticket to Vancouver Island. I didn't tell anybody, I just went. Later on, I told Ron why I was doing it, but at the time I was thinking 'I just can't go home.'

"So finally I talk to Joe again, and believe it

or not, he was unsure of his position on our hockey team, he didn't know if he would fit in."

Murphy went on to star for a national championship team at Michigan State as a freshman, before being drafted No. 1 overall in June of 1986 by the Detroit Red Wings.

"The last thing he should have been worried about was where he was going to play," Christensen said.

Long ago, such an emotional roller-coaster in regard to recruiting was unheard of. When Harold Paulsen tried to drum up talent in 1950 and in 1950-51, he did so over the phone. And when Amo Bessone took over in 1952, his recruiting budget wasn't exactly overflowing.

"My recruiting budget was stamps," Bessone explained. "I did it all by mail."

"Official recruiting visits" were unheard of. When a young Ron Mason wanted to check out Michigan State in the late 1950s, for example, he was able to do so only because he had a sister, Marion, living in North Branch, Mich., who was able to drive him to campus while Mason was in North Branch visiting. Upon arriving in East Lansing Mason—who had been used to playing in palaces such as Maple Leaf Gardens and the Montreal Forum during his junior hockey days—couldn't understand why MSU players had to dress in Jenison Field House and then walk across the street to play in Demonstration Hall. He couldn't understand why there was no scholarship money available, either.

Mason, a native of Seaforth, Ontario, ended up going to St. Lawrence.

"At Michigan Tech I had no scholarships," Bessone said. "Then I went down to Michigan State and I had no scholarships. Then you'd have a few good years and they'd give you a couple of scholarships. We used to split 'em up. Out of probably four scholarships we'd give a few guys room and board, a few their books, a few tuition, whatever. We tried to help everybody out, but it was tough going there for a while. We were the low man on the totem-pole (in the athletic department hierarchy)."

"Up until about, I would say the early 1960s, I probably had four scholarships."

The number at most places these days is 18—it's down from 20, which used to give a top-notch program one for every player that dresses for a game. But that wasn't the case at most places even in the 1970s, so coaches did what they could. As they did, word-of-mouth and tips from friends in places where players could be found became invaluable.

One such place was Copper Cliff, Ontario, a suburb of Sudbury that contained approximately 3,300 residents and one which started sending players Bessone's way in the 1950s and didn't stop even after a national championship had been secured in 1966.

"What the coaches would do, they would just take recommendations from people they knew up here," said Don Heaphy, a defenseman who lettered in 1964, '65 and '66. "Dickie Johnstone (a Copper Cliff native who played at State in 1961, '62 and '63) was probably my biggest supporter. And then when it came to Sandy McAndrew and Mike Jacobson (who were both a year behind Heaphy), it was a take-my-word-for-it type of thing."

Copper Cliff had also been well-represented on the roster of Michigan State's 1959 NCAA finalist in the persons of brothers Bruno and Ed Pollesel.

"I had always wanted to come to Michigan State because I remembered reading about those guys in the paper when I was in elementary school," Jacobson said. "It just kind of stuck in my mind."

When it came time to decide on a college, Jacobson chose Michigan State over St. Lawrence for that reason, and because "the name fascinated me."

Toronto and its surrounding communities were also good to MSU in the years before recruiting became an exercise of great emotion, expense and exasperation.

"There was a gentleman up there by the name of Joe Finegan, whose son had played for Michigan State (Daniel, a defenseman from

Before you can line 'em up, you have to sign 'em up. Recruiting had gone well enough in Ron Mason's early years at MSU that by 1982-83 the Spartans were lining up a team that could compete with anyone.

the mid-1960s until 1974, or something like that."

Eventually, Joe Finegan passed away.

"The recruiting seemed to fall off after Joe Finegan died," Sturges said.

In the days before official visits and early-signing periods, players often arrived on campus sight-unseen. They met Bessone face-to-face for the first time about the same time they were getting their first looks at the campus, which made a first-class arena such as Munn to lure recruits into committing an unnecessary luxury.

More often than not, not having one wasn't a problem.

"I was kind of disappointed in the rink, actually," Jacobson said of his reaction after getting his first glance at Dem Hall. "But I was just amazed by the football stadium. I had never seen anything like that. Being a kid from around Sudbury, Ontario...The furthest we had ever been was North Bay and Parry Sound and Chatham."

"It wasn't as difficult a place to play in as it was to watch a game in," Heaphy reasoned regarding Dem Hall. And besides, "I just loved it there," Heaphy said of MSU. "Just getting out of Copper Cliff, and getting down into a big, new country, at a big school, with a different way of life...It was awe inspiring.

"It was just great."

Even in the relatively rare instances when Bessone managed to get out and establish face-to-face contact during the recruiting process, it wasn't what you might have expected, or what a high-profile recruit would demand from one of his suitor-schools today.

"I can remember the coach from Clarkson, Len Ceglarski, coming up to Espanola (Ontario, which isn't far from Sudbury or Copper Cliff) and talking to me and Richard Bois and Bobby Fallat at

Islington, Ontario, who lettered in 1969, '70 and '71). He was a vital force, I think, in getting a lot of the Toronto recruits," said John Sturges, a forward from Scarborough, Ontario, who played from 1972-73 through 1975-76. "Guys like Mark Calder, Steve Colp, Norm Barnes, Bob Boyd, Daryl Rice, myself...Joe Finegan basically helped Amo recruit the Toronto area.

"He was a good friend to Michigan State and Amo was able to get a lot of good guys from my house," defenseman Doug French said of an experience shared by himself and two players who went on to became his teammates on MSU's 1966 national championship team. "Lenny Ceglarski was...he was a real good guy and he was a real smooth guy. He really gave you the detailed scoop about what kind of program they had, what kind of education you'd get, everything.

"Then we ended up meeting Amo in a restaurant. He was going on a fishing trip, and he walks in unshaven, smoking a cigar and he's saying, 'Yeah, we'll take care of you guys when we get you down there...' I'm thinking, 'Jesus Christ, what kind of outfit is this?' I was really a little leery. But Dickie Johnstone kept promoting Michigan State and we all decided to go there together. I've never regretted that at all."

Such informal visits and descriptions long ago became a thing of the past in big-time college hockey. Great attention to detail dominates the recruiting process today, even when all goes according to plan, which almost never happens. Even when it does, mistakes aren't realized until years later.

Pellerin, who has appeared in uniform with the New Jersey Devils and St. Louis Blues since posing with his Hobey at Maine, wasn't the only big-time talent the Spartans had a chance to land but took a pass on. Goaltender Curtis Joseph, who played his junior hockey at the prestigious Athol Murray College of Notre Dame in Wilcox, Saskatchewan along with Pellerin and Spartans-to-be Joby Messier, Brind' Amour and Norris, also wanted to attend Michigan State.

"I remember it was either in late October or early November, and Joby Messier came up to me and said, 'Coach, Curtis Joseph wants to talk to you,' " Gwozdecky explained. "So I sat down with Curtis. I knew he was a good goaltender, but I also knew we had two freshman goaltenders—Jason Muzzatti and Jamie Stewart, who came in after Norm Foster and Bob Essensa had left.

"Then Curtis says, 'Coach, I'd like to go to Michigan State. I know a lot about it and I've always wanted to go to Michigan State. I know you already have two goaltenders, but if there's anything we can do to work it out...I'll pay my own way the first year, I'll walk on.'

"So I start thinking, 'This kid is really good. This kid could be the difference between being a good team and a great one.' So I call Ron and I'm really excited and he says, I don't think we can do it. It would ruin the chemistry of our goaltending situation and I don't want to put three goaltenders on scholarship.'"

Joseph ended up starring at Wisconsin (Gwozdecky's alma mater), before moving on to

Joe Murphy's awesome shot helped to make him a prized recruit, indeed, even though he only stuck around for one season before being picked first overall by the NHL's Detroit Red Wings.

the St. Louis Blues and Edmonton Oilers.

"I think he and I ended up talking more that year than he did with the Wisconsin coaches," Gwozdecky said.

Which brings to light another key and altogether unpredictable element of recruiting. Sometimes, it's not what you do that matters most, but what the other school does at the same time.

Take what happened when the Spartans went after defenseman Dan McFall in the early 1980s...

"First time I met him was in Buffalo (McFall's hometown), and after that I ended up staying in Ontario all week," Walsh said, setting up one of his favorite recruiting stories. "At that time, there was no junior hockey played on Saturday nights because no one would go head-to-head with (television broadcasts of) Hockey Night In Canada, that tradition. So I saw that Clarkson was playing somebody on Saturday night; I don't even remember who. So I drive down from Cornwall, Ontario, to Potsdam, N.Y. with Brian Gilmore—a good friend of Ron's from Huron Hockey School—and we go to the Clarkson game. Clarkson had given us complimentary tickets.

"So we get there and we end up sitting next to Dan McFall and his parents, who were there for Dan's official visit to Clarkson. I couldn't believe it. I actually had Brian sit between

me and Dan because I didn't want to get accused of going after him, and I didn't want to go after him too hard, on his official visit to Clarkson. But I got my points across.

"We ended up getting McFall and McFall ended up making All-American. It was a good example to us all of how little things can win recruiting battles."

Little things such as, timing, for example.

"In recruiting, you always want to find out who the champion is— the person who will most help the recruit make his decision," Walsh revealed. "In most cases it's the mother or father, or the coach. Well, in the case of Chris Chelios (a Chicago native playing junior hockey in Moose

In Ron Mason's 18 years behind the Michigan State bench 67 of his recruits have been drafted by the National Hockey League. Six first rounders and seven second round selections prove his ability to spot championship calibre talent.

Jaw, Saskatchewan, in 1980), I thought it was the billet (the person housing Chelios while he played his junior hockey in Saskatchewan). And I was close to the billet, close enough that I thought I could sign Chris, even thought he had already verbally committed to North Dakota.

"So on signing day that spring, I thought I could sign Chris. I was already in the Windsor (Ontario) airport getting ready to go out there and then I got paged. It was the billet. He said, 'Don't come to Saskatchewan. Chris has gone on a visit to the University of Wisconsin.' What had happened was, Grant Standbrook, who was an assistant at Wisconsin, scheduled Chris's visit for just before signing day—which you can't do anymore—got him down there and signed him."

So Chelios, who committed verbally to North Dakota and to Michigan State, ended up at Wisconsin before moving on to the Montreal Canadiens and Chicago Blackhawks. And Standbrook would up becoming an assistant at Maine under Walsh. All three laugh about that story today, for if there is one cardinal rule in recruiting, it's that you don't look back.

"If you do, all you'll see is a bunch of mistakes, and nobody admits those," Walsh said. "The biggest thing you have to do in recruiting is figure, 'What happens if Player A doesn't come to you and you're surprised? The second biggest thing you have to do is don't look back."

Having a backup plan helped the Spartans land Dale Krentz, who never made All-America and played only briefly in the NHL but was an excellent college player nonetheless. Krentz stepped in when Tony Granato (who had been wearing a Spartan sticker on his helmet and had become close to Kelly Miller) surprised the staff by going to Wisconsin in 1983. Having enough faith in his primary plans, his backup plans and his own gut feel for the entire often-intolerable process has always allowed Mason to recruit well, especially at Michigan State.

His belief in local players when all else is relatively equal helped MSU land not just the Miller boys, but Lansing products Danton Cole and

Steve Beadle as well. In Kevin Miller's case, that meant MSU took itself out of the running for the likes of Brett Hull (who went to Minnesota-Duluth before going on to the Calgary Flames and St. Louis Blues).

"Hull would have been a battle," Walsh said. "I can't say we would have had him, but we would have been in it."

Bob Joyce (who would help beat Michigan State in the 1987 NCAA Final before moving on to the Boston Bruins, Washington Capitals and Winnipeg Jets) was another pretty good player the staff passed on to concentrate on Kevin Miller. In the short and the long run, however, it was worth it.

So are Mason's instincts in those rare instances when he just throws up his hands, says 'what the heck' and guesses.

"When Don McSween was playing junior with the Redford Royals, we must have seen him play 25 times," Walsh recalled. "He was already out of high school and was working that extra year just to get a scholarship. So we'd go and one week Ron would say, 'I don't think he's good enough.' And the next week it would be, 'Nope, not good enough.' What made it awkward was Donnie skated like an ugly duck, so he was a substance guy, not a flash guy. Fortunately, Ron always looked for substance guys as well as flash guys.

"Finally, it's getting down to the end and Ron says, 'You know what? That guy can play. He just has too many instincts.'"

Ugly duck-like wheels or not, McSween made it at Michigan State. He became a captain. He played on a national champion. He established himself as one of the most competitive and courageous players ever at MSU. And after playing in just nine NHL games during his first six professional seasons, McSween finally became an NHL regular in 1993-94 with the Mighty Ducks of Anaheim.

No one could have predicted that, which is kind of the way it is in recruiting every year no matter what ultimately happens.

A sport of high recognition
and interest...

CHAPTER
11

Chapter 11

The number one line of Fred DeVuono (No. 7), Dick Hamilton (No. 10), and Ross Parke (No. 12) accounted for two goals and five points in the Spartans' celebrated 4-2 win over Michigan in 1958.

They didn't decide national championships. Still, at Michigan State, they are games that have become legendary over the years. Games that, decade by decade, represent all that Spartan hockey was about and all that Spartan hockey has become better than any press release, published

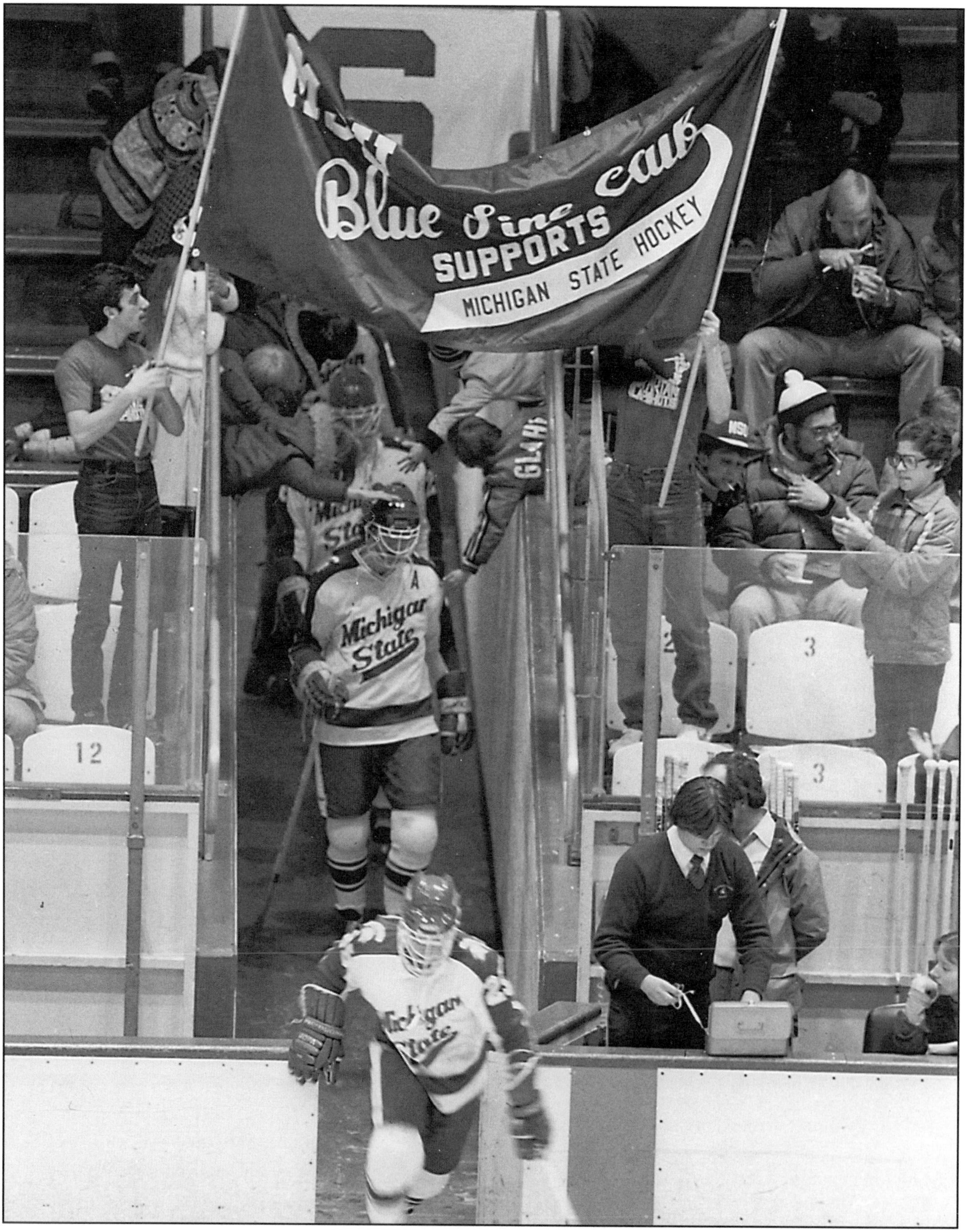
SUPPORTS
MICHIGAN STATE HOCKEY
Michigan State

account, photo, highlights tape or voice-over ever could. Because of the stakes, the setting, the circumstances or all of the above, the following were indeed games for the ages at Michigan State:

JAN. 8, 1958:
MICHIGAN STATE 4,
MICHIGAN 2

This wasn't the first time the Spartans had gotten the best of their arch-rivals from Ann Arbor, but it was the first time it had happened after State had resumed hockey hostilities with Michigan by resurrecting the program in 1950. This was the Spartans' first "modern era" victory over the Wolverines, and the first definitive signal that late in a decade that had been devoted to building from scratch, the program was indeed on the right track.

"Hockey, long a varsity sport at Michigan State, has finally jelled into a sport of high recognition and interest with one big explosion ignited by the thrill-packed, hard-fought, 4-2 victory over the Wolverines of Michigan," The State News gushed on Thursday, Jan. 9. That same story also told of "roughness and frequent fighting," although just three fighting majors and one match misconduct were whistled, and considered the gathering on hand at Demonstration Hall "a near-sellout crowd," even thought only 2,378 showed up in an arena with a seating capacity of 4,000 for hockey.

The Lansing State Journal was even more unabashed in its enthusiasm. "State was supreme throughout!" the next day's editions insisted, while also pointing out that "the last time our pucksters beat Michigan was in 1928."

No wonder everyone was so excited. In the 1920s, it had taken eight tries for the Spartans—known as the Aggies back then—to beat Michigan.

It's always a special night whenever the Spartans take the ice. But by virtue of what's at stake or what transpires, some nights are more special than others.

That happened for the first time on Feb. 5, 1927 (5-2 good guys). It happened again on Feb. 1, 1928 (2-1, good guys). Then the long drought began.

For a while, it looked like it might never end. The Green and White lost the final five meetings before dropping the sport after the 1930 campaign, then went 0-27-1 against Michigan from Feb. 22, 1950 through Feb. 23, 1957. The closest State came to winning a game in that stretch was a 0-0 tie in 1954, and a 3-2 loss in overtime in 1956. Most of the rest of the time it wasn't pretty, as scores such as 10-4, 17-1, 10-1, 11-1, 6-0 and 7-0 would attest.

Late in the decade, however, the worm began to turn. The Spartans dropped all four of their decisions against Michigan in 1956-57, but all four were decided by just one goal. The Spartans were close and they knew it. In their first meeting with Michigan in 1957-58, they finally got over the hump.

"Well deserved and a good job of playing good, hustling hockey," coach Amo Bessone proclaimed once they had done so. "There is no substitute for hustle."

The Spartans hustled their way to the first two goals of the game late in the first period. Bill MacKenzie scored first off a feed from Mel Christofferson at the 16-minute mark. The Spartans got another with just three seconds remaining in the period, when Terry Moroney scored unassisted. Michigan protested this goal, claiming Michigan State should have been whistled for icing seconds earlier, but to no avail. It would not be the last time a Michigan-Michigan State game was highlighted by a little controversy.

State scored again when Ross Parke, off assists from Fred DeVuono and Dick Hamilton, beat Michigan netminder Ross Childs at 8:56 of the second. Then things really heated up. According to The State News "a mass fracas' erupted, one in which "almost all players on the ice were involved in the melee, which lasted for 10 minutes."

Once order was restored, Hamilton and Bruno Pollesel of State were issued five-minute majors for fighting at 10:33. Michigan's Barrie

Hayton, who had drawn a two-minute penalty for spearing in the first period, also received a five-minute fighting penalty, Childs got two minutes for high sticking and the Wolverines' Ross Hudson was issued a 10-minute match-misconduct. With the sides skating three-on-three shortly thereafter, the Wolverines finally got on the board when Bobby Watts beat Spartan netminder Joe Selinger at 12:36.

Michigan got its second goal, cutting the Michigan State lead to 3-2, at 9:39 of the third. But on this night, the Spartans were not to be denied. DeVuono, from Parke and Ed Pollesel, re-established a two-goal lead at 15:45 and Selinger, who finished with 25 saves to Childs' 34, made it stick.

The win turned out to be a springboard for the still-growing Michigan State program. Although Michigan won the next meeting, 4-2 in Ann Arbor, the Spartans came back with a weekend sweep late in the season (3-1 at home and 2-1 at Michigan in overtime) to take their first season series from the Wolverines, 3-1.

It's safe to assume that first victory was easily the sweetest, even if most of the details had escaped Bessone close to 40 years later.

"About all I remember is it was a long time in coming," he said.

It was also well worth the wait.

MARCH 16, 1967:
MICHIGAN STATE 2,
MICHIGAN TECH 1 (OT)

One year after winning their first national championship, the Spartans were making another late-season run. Following a 13-14-1 regular season that included a fifth-place finish in the Western Collegiate Hockey Association, Michigan State dusted off its post-season magic and whipped fourth-place Michigan in the first round of the playoffs. The 4-2 victory over the Wolverines earned the Spartans a date with Michigan Tech in a game that would determine one of the WCHA's two representatives at the NCAA Final Four in Syracuse, N.Y.

As far as the folks at Tech could figure, there wasn't much doubt beforehand as to who that representative would be.

Michigan Tech had won the national championship in 1965, but was upset by Michigan State in the playoffs in 1966. Now, after winning the WCHA regular-season title in 1966-67, Tech made no secret of its fully expecting to extract its revenge this time around. The Spartans found that out shortly after arriving in Houghton.

"We were staying at the Douglass House," winger Mike Jacobson explained. "It was an old hotel and you could listen to just about everything that went on through the heating ducts. So we flew up there and practiced and stayed overnight and just slept most of the time because there was nothing else to do up there.

"But on the afternoon of the game they had a blue line club luncheon. And the president of their blue line club got up and said that they had chartered a plane and sold all the tickets and that everybody was going to Syracuse—I remember that because we were all up in our rooms listening through the heating ducts.

"When it was his turn, Amo got up and said, 'Well, we might as well not even play the game.' It was a big joke to them. Everybody laughed."

Then Bessone got serious.

"I said, 'We didn't come up here for nothing,'" he recounted.

That was all the boys in their rooms upstairs needed to hear. MSU took the ice determined to get the best of Tech again.

Once the puck was dropped, the game quickly developed into a goaltending duel between Gaye Cooley, MSU's NCAA hero from the previous spring, and Michigan Tech All-American (and eventual NHL Hall-of-Famer) Tony Esposito. Unfortunately for the Spartans, Cooley was doing most of the dueling. Tech outshot State 9-1 in the first period, and led 1-0 following the opening 20 minutes.

"After that they really got on Amo's ass," Jacobson said of the Tech fans. "People were always getting on Amo because he was an actor on the bench, but this was really bad. They were yelling "A-mo, A-mo...,' and 'We're No.1,' and really getting kind of rude."

They stayed that way through the second period and most of the third, as Tech protected its 1-0 lead into the final minute of regulation.

"Finally, a whistle blew with 48 seconds left, but the time-keeper didn't shut down the clock," Jacobson said. "It went down to about 30 seconds before he finally shut it off. Well, Amo went bonkers. And the referees went over to the time keeper's box, kicked the time-keeper out and brought the clock back up to 48 seconds.

"The place was really going crazy now. They were all over Amo's ass, just giving it to him because they were winning."

Once order was eventually restored, play was set to resume with a face-off a few feet inside the blue line in the Tech end. Bessone pulled Cooley, allowing the Spartans to attack with six skaters. Five of them—Tom Mikkola, Jacobson, Sandy McAndrew, Bob Brawley and Doug Volmar—were veterans from the 1966 national championship team. As far as solving Esposito was concerned, it was now or never. Their best chance was to get the puck to Volmar off the draw.

An All-American and MSU's leading scorer the previous year, Volmar had been somewhat of a disappointment as a senior in 1966-67. Although he wound up tying for the team lead in goals with Mikkola (21) and finished third overall in points (33), Volmar was also Michigan State's most-penalized player (he was whistled for 38 infractions totaling 100 minutes) by a substantial margin.

That hadn't happened by accident. Although only a precious few college players had gone on to the NHL by the mid-to-late 1960s, Volmar—who possessed what Bessone often described as the hardest wrist shot in hockey—fancied himself becoming one of them. But to do so, Volmar had become convinced he had to inflict damage with his body as well as with his awesome shot. Bessone's contention was that Volmar's wicked shot was useless to himself, the Spartans

and anyone else from the penalty box.

"He was looking at the pros," Bessone said. "The pros had approached him and said, 'You have to be a tough guy to be a pro.' And he was a big kid for that time, but I kept telling him, "With your shot, you don't have to hit anybody—just shoot!" Now, with MSU a mere 48 seconds away from elimination, everyone in the building knew that was what Volmar—who positioned himself in the center of the ice just inside the blue line—intended to do if McAndrew could only set him up.

McAndrew did so. Volmar did the rest.

"He let that son of a (gun) go...man, he had a cannon," Jacobson said. "I still remember, I saw the twine pop before Esposito ever made a move. By the time his hand started to go up the puck was already in the goal. I hadn't even moved from the boards. I was just standing there..."

Volmar's goal at 19:16 tied the game at 1-1.

"Now the place was like a morgue," Jacobson said.

But Volmar wasn't finished just yet. Tech went on the offensive again in overtime, but Cooley somehow held them at bay. He made five saves in the extra session, several of the spectacular variety.

"Cooley was unbelievable," McAndrew said.

On two other occasions, the Huskies blasted shots off a goalpost.
Shortly thereafter, the Spartans went to work.

Catching the Huskies on a line change, Jacobson got the puck in deep. What transpired after that was part pluck, part luck and part poetic justice, at least as far as the Spartans were concerned.

"Jake went through something like four guys to get to the corner," McAndrew remembered. "Then he tried to get the puck to Mikkola in the slot, but it deflected off of him and went right to Volmar, who was about 10 or 15 feet out.

"Now, Esposito was a flop goalie. So to score on him, what you did was you'd drop your shoulder (faking a shoot), wait for him to go down and then shoot high. So Volmar gets the puck right on his stick and he goes in on Esposito and makes his move and goes to shoot the puck over Esposito as Esposito is going down...and he fans on the puck.

"He went to shoot high but it rolled right along the ice and right between Esposito's legs. Game over!"

"It trickled over," Jacobson said. "It was a garbage goal."

"It was not a garbage goal," McAndrew countered. "It was one of the prettiest goals I ever did see."

Whatever, it secured MSU's first win at Tech in nine attempts, dating back to January of 1961 (and first non-forfeit win at Tech in 13 games), and forced a great many plane reservations for round trips from Houghton to Syracuse to be cancelled.

"Now, it's a morgue again, it's complete dead," Jacobson said. "Amo stepped off the bench, walked onto the ice and gave everybody the finger. And we went over and stole this NCAA banner they had hanging up and took it off the ice with us.

"When we got into the locker room, Tom Mikkola said, "I think (the fans) are going to come in here and beat us up.'"

But they never did. On and off the ice, the Spartans somehow survived and marched on to the Final Four.

Their magic ran out in Syracuse, N.Y. Michigan State fell behind Boston University 2-0 in the first period, cut the deficit in half in the second stanza and then fell behind by two goals again when the Terriers' Fred Bassi beat Cooley for the second time just eight seconds before the second-period intermission.

Trailing 3-1 entering the final 20 minutes, the Spartans rallied again when Lee Hathaway set up Mikkola for a goal at 10:08 that trimmed the BU margin to 3-2. Alas, MSU could get no closer. A holding penalty against Nino Cristolfoli less than two minutes after Mikkola's score and Darrell Abbott's breakaway goal at 14:34 effectively squelched Michigan State's momentum, and BU prevailed, 4-2.

BU's victory set up the first all-Eastern final in 18 years (Cornell would ultimately win the national championship) and drew an interesting response from Bessone.

"It proves the Eastern Canadians are catching up to the Western Canadians," he said.

Just as the Spartans' triumph the previous weekend in Houghton, Mich., had proven that Michigan Tech still hadn't figured out a way to solve Michigan State when the games mattered most.

MARCH 14, 1976:
MINNESOTA 7,
MICHIGAN STATE 6 (3 OT)

To many at MSU, this was and remains perhaps the greatest game ever played at Michigan State, and most certainly the greatest game ever staged at Munn Arena. Current Spartans coach Ron Mason is not one of them.

"To me, the greatest game ever played in Munn Arena is not a game you lose," he scoffed.

Good point. Still, the sixth meeting of the 1975-76 season between Herb Brooks' Golden Gophers and Bessone's Spartans is hard to top. Clearly, this epic takes a backseat to no Michigan State game but those in which NCAA Championship trophies were handed out in terms of pure drama.

The Spartans entered hoping to prolong their school-record fifth consecutive 20-win season by advancing to the NCAA Final Four in Denver. To do so, they had to beat the Gophers.

Michigan State had finished second behind Michigan Tech in the WCHA—a feat MSU hadn't accomplished before and would never duplicate again—and was led by the high-flying, record-setting, often-combustible fivesome of seniors Tom Ross, Steve Colp, Daryl Rice, Brendon Moroney and John Sturges. About the only thing that had eluded them to this point was a chance to compete for the national championship. Now, as their careers were winding down, they were a legitimate threat not only to extend the current campaign, but to end it with champagne.

Minnesota was, too. The Gophers had finished third in the WCHA regular season. Although they had managed just one win in four tries in the regular-season series with the high-scoring Spartans, the Gophers were more than capable. Russ Anderson was on this Minnesota team. So was Reed Larson. And Joe Micheletti. And Tom Younghans. And Bill Baker. All of those players would go on to play in the NHL. Baker, along with Golden Gophers teammate Phil Verchota and Brooks, would strike gold with Team USA in the 1980 Winter Olympics first.

No wonder it was such an even series.

The first game of the two-games, total-goals showdown, on a Saturday night at Munn, ended in a 2-2 tie. That forced the teams to reconvene the following afternoon and play at least another 60 minutes, and as many more after that as needed until the issue was decided. Four hours and 15 minutes after they had started, Minnesota finally came up a winner. Left winger Pat Phippen's goal at 6:33 of the third extra session (86:33 overall, for those of you scoring at home) ended what Bessone declared to be "the best hockey game that's ever been played on this campus."

At first it appeared the 6,605 in attendance and the dozens of others peering in from outside through the glass at the Munn Arena entrance gates would witness one of Michigan State's biggest disappointments. The Gophers led 3-1 after one period and 6-2 midway through the second before the Spartans kicked their at-times-unstoppable offense into high gear.

A five-minute, high-sticking major issued to Verchota at 13:22 opened the door. The Spartans made the Gophers pay for the mistake by getting power-play goals from Rice (at 15:46) and Ross (at 17:54). At 6-4 following the conclusion of 40 minutes, it was a game again.

In the third period the Spartans kept coming. Pat Betterly cashed in another power play at 6:55. Finally, as the crowd went wild, Rice completed the hat trick and brought the Spartans all the way back by scoring at 16:26, four seconds after a

high sticking penalty issued to Younghans had expired.

Chants of "We're No.1" and "Denver, Denver..." greeted the Spartans as they took the ice for OT No.1. Why more OTs were needed after that is still a mystery to many, as MSU fired an incredible 17 shots at Gopher goalie Jeff Tscherne (Minnesota managed four), only to be denied every time.

"We should have put it away in the first overtime," Bessone concluded.

Minnesota finally did so in the third while each team was skating one man down.

"Our defenseman, Jeff Barr, had the puck," Ross recalled. "He was in the corner, a left-handed shooter coming out of the left corner. I think he took a couple of strides and got to about the face-off dot in our zone. I turned up ice expecting a pass."

But the puck never got to Ross.

"Apparently the puck hopped over (Barr's) stick and he didn't know it. He kept skating," Ross explained. "One of their guys that was backchecking and trying to catch him just picked it up."

That guy was Don Madson, who quickly turned the turnover into a scoring opportunity for Baker. MSU netminder David Versical was equal to the task on the initial attempt, but Phippen's 20-foot wrist shot off a deep rebound eluded him and, suddenly, it was over.

"The really bad part was we had the puck," Ross said. "I don't know how it hopped over (Barr's) stick. And as I remember, we had a break. We had a three-on-two going up ice because all their forwards were caught in (the MSU zone), and everything changed just that quickly."

Did it ever. The Gophers went on to capture the national championship in Denver. The Spartans were left to wonder what might have been.

"Absolutely, no question about it," Sturges said, when asked if the Spartans might have returned from Denver with another championship in hand had they only gotten by the Gophers. "We had the best team.

"Coming back from 6-2, that tells you what

kind of team we had. We didn't give up. The only problem was, we had to play two lines, probably from about the halfway point of the second period...and we ran out of gas."

Tscherne finished with 72 saves, still a record for an opponent against MSU. Versical wound up with 64, and longed for the opportunity to make a few more.

"I felt good. I was ready to go all night if I had to," he said.

"We beat a great hockey club out there, and one of the greatest coaches in the business," Brooks said then. "I'm just happy the game wasn't decided by a fluke goal, because if I coach another year or 25, we'll never play a team or a coach that

I respect more."

Years later, Brooks' opinion hadn't changed.

"It was an upset," he insisted. "They were a better team than we were. They were a great team."

Losing in triple-overtime may have cost these Spartans a national championship, but it wasn't about to alter how history would remember them.

MARCH 12, 1983:
MICHIGAN STATE 4,
BOWLING GREEN 3 (OT)

If the decision to ditch the WCHA and break relations with the likes of Minnesota and Wisconsin had been met with some criticism—and it most definitely had been in East Lansing—play-

Although Ron Scott often made dramatic saves appear routine (especially when posing for publicity shots), there was nothing routine about Scott's stoning of Bowling Green's Brian Hills on a penalty shot in overtime in the 1983 CCHA Playoff Championship game.

ing Bowling Green on a regular basis at least had helped to make the transition to the Central Collegiate Hockey Association much easier.

The CCHA would come to be ridiculed by some as a "bus league" (schools could bus back and forth to get to games; in the WCHA they flew to outposts such as Grand Forks, N.D., and Duluth, Minn.). And with members such as Lake Superior, Ferris State and Western Michigan, it had little tradition to speak of and even less romantic appeal. But in the early 1980s, the CCHA was on the verge of exploding into prominence. The programs at MSU and BG were big reasons why.

Bowling Green, in fact, had become the first non-ECAC or WCHA team to reach the NCAA Final Four in 1978. The Falcons had done so thanks in no small part to a goaltender named Mike Liut, a defenseman named Ken Morrow and a coach named Ron Mason. Once Mason had moved on to Greener pastures in East Lansing, the Falcons went about the business of maintaining excellence under Jerry York, one of the college game's great coaches and one of its great people. Mason, meanwhile, quickly got the Spartans' house in order to the point where it wasn't long before MSU and Bowling Green were battling for championships on a regular basis.

This quickly became a rivalry that was fun as well as fiercely contested. They even held a "Ron Mason Lookalike Contest" one night at the BGSU Ice Arena, when the prodigal coach returned to his old home with his new team. Fans adorned themselves with fake moustaches and hairdos modeled after the blow-dried, part-it-in-the-middle, disco style Mason sported at the time, and repeatedly threw their arms up in the air all game long, the way Mason liked to whenever referees missed something really obvious. Although some in northwest Ohio were upset Mason had abandoned BG for MSU, they understood. And for the most part they still liked the guy.

MSU fans, too, held a begrudging admiration for BG, even though BG quickly became a team MSU needed to beat. And although some in Spartan country considered themselves inherently superior to this new Mid-American Conference counterpart, losing to BG was nowhere near as devastating as, say, losing to Michigan. The Spartans, after all, didn't hate Bowling Green simply as a matter of principle. They could even live with BG beating them once in a while.

The night of March 12, 1983, however, wasn't one of those times.

The CCHA playoff championship was at stake and, although no one knew it at the time, so was the conference's sole invitation to the NCAA Tournament. It was winner take all between BG, which had just won the second of what would become three consecutive regular-season championships and stood 28-7-4, and MSU, which was in the second year of a tear that would produce a league playoff or regular-season championship banner every year from 1982 through 1987, and had a record of 29-10-0.

There was considerable intrigue as well.

Ron Scott, the Spartans' All-American netminder, had aggravated the right-ankle sprain he had suffered two weeks previously early in the second period of MSU's 8-3 semifinal victory over Ohio State the night before. With backup Jon Brekken out with mononucleosis, the Spartans were forced to turn to seldom-used and previously all-but-unheard-of No.3 tender Tom Nowland. In the little less than two periods that he played, Nowland responded with 16 saves and a 3-1 lead grew into a blowout, so initially, at least, disaster had been averted. But Nowland—who wound up playing a mere 82 minutes in 1982-83—wasn't expected to be able to handle Bowling Green's onslaught the following night. And no one was really counting on Scott making it back, either.
"Even I didn't think he'd be able to play," Mason said.

But Scott was determined not to miss this one. After leaving the Joe Louis Arena on crutches Friday night, he returned to the ice Saturday morning to test a cast team physician Dr. John Downs had fashioned. Scott did so without Mason's knowledge. Once that experiment ended, trainer Doug Locy tried another. He gave Scott a rubdown with aloe vera (a plant extract commonly used to treat burns or as a skin-softening agent today).

"That was a new product at the time," said center Newell Brown, one of Scott's closest friends on the team. "We had Ronnie convinced it was a magic potion."

To the amazement of his teammates and everyone else, Scott suited up Saturday night and took the ice.

"I can still see the Bowling Green fans dropping their mouths when they saw him come out for warmups," Mason said.

As it turned out Scott was just getting warmed up in more ways than one, although initially it appeared the Michigan State goalie wouldn't be much of a factor. Center Gord Flegel connected just nine seconds after the puck had been dropped, and again at 2:41 for a 2-0 Michigan State advantage. The lead grew to 3-0 when defenseman Dan McFall found the net at 6:13.

Those wearing Green in the arena seats were delirious. Those on the bench, however, still expected a severe test.

"We thought Bowling Green was perhaps the best team in the country at that point," Mason said.

BG, which had won the only two regular-season meetings between the teams, battled back to get a couple before the first period intermission. And after the Falcons got the equalizer from defenseman Garry Galley at 6:37 of the second, it became a real battle. Scott hobbled and flopped and did what he had to thereafter. His Falcon counterpart, Mike David, settled in at the other end and refused to be beaten again. The two teams played on through a scoreless third period and into overtime.

It looked as if it would end early once the extra session got started. Scott made a couple of saves, but then Bowling Green's All-American center, Brian Hills, broke in 4 1/2 minutes in. It was all but over...until defenseman Gary Haight, beaten by Hills on the play, did what any self-respecting defenseman who didn't like the idea of being remembered as the goat would have done.

Haight threw his stick.

Referee Dennis Parish in turn made the obvious call.

Penalty shot.

There were some 15,192 people in the stands at the time, and yet, "I can remember the silence in the building just before the shot was taken," Brown recalled. "It was so exciting...It was the two best players in college hockey at that time, going head-to-head...It was unbelievable."

Scott came out on top, sliding across the crease as Hills made his move and then preserving the tie with the save of the season.

"I really wanted Hills bad," Scott later told the press.

It might as well have ended right there. Hills, the Falcons' all-everything, had failed to finish off Scott and the Spartans one-on-one and Bowling Green was stunned. Bowling Green was done, too, as it turned out. Captain Mark Hamway's 29th goal of the season at 6:18 of overtime—just 1:43 after Scott had stoned Hills—was merely the final detail of a classic the Spartans must have been destined to win. An ironic twist was added when Kelly Miller and Haight (who was able to hang onto his stick this time) were credited with assists on the game-winner.

"When Ronnie made that save, that was the hockey game," Mason said, expressing a sentiment many in the winner's locker room echoed. "That was the most exciting game I've ever been involved in my life."

It was also the one that "put us on the map," Mason said. "That game gave us the impetus to move on and become a nationally-recognized team."

That it did, for beating BG not only proved MSU's post-season run the year before hadn't been a fluke, it signaled a new era was off and running. One where success under the bright lights of Joe Louis and regular trips to the NCAA Tournament would come to be expected when the skates were first strapped on in the fall. One in which the national championship would be viewed as a realistic achievement, not a dream.

They had the little goalie from Guelph, Ontario, to thank for it.

"A player like Scott, who played despite his injury, exemplifies Michigan State hockey," Mason said.

No one has ever done so any better.

MARCH 28, 1992:
MICHIGAN STATE 3,
MAINE 2

The two teams had met on Dec. 19, 1991, at The Forum in Inglewood, Calif., and Maine had defeated Michigan State, 4-2, in the Great Western Freeze-Out. Maine had been on top of its game that night, and the effort Michigan State had come up with hadn't been especially impressive. Taking all of that into account, Mason had this to say to his players: "Boys, we're going to play that team

Mike Gilmore liked to chew on pucks before games and then spit them back out at opponents during the heat of a battle. One of Gilmore's most dramatic performances denied powerful Maine a trip to the Final Four in 1992.

again. And next time, we're going to beat them."

The rematch materialized in the second round of the NCAA East Regional, in Providence, R.I. Initially, it looked like a mismatch.

Maine was the No.1-ranked team in the country and the No.1 seed in the East Regional. The Black Bears, in their eighth season under the leadership of Shawn Walsh, had been pointing toward the Final Four all season. They were 31-3-2 overall and 13-0-2 in their last 15 games. They were loaded. Maine boasted the likes of Jean-Yves Roy, Jim Montgomery, Chris Imes, Cal Ingraham, Scott Pellerin, Garth Snow and Mike Dunham. The roster was littered with future All-Americans, future Olympians and future NHLers. Pellerin, in fact, was only days away from winning the Hobey Baker Award, given annually to college hockey's top talent. This was the team that, once freshman Paul Kariya arrived the following fall, would dominate college hockey on its way to the 1992-93 national championship.

The Spartans, by contrast, were a modest 24-10-8 and had been seeded fifth in the NCAA's West bracket. They had finished third in the CCHA in the regular season and had been knocked off in the semifinals of the league's playoff tournament. And they hadn't even been expected to beat Boston University in the first round of NCAA play, but had somehow pulled off a 4-2 upset.

That win set up a more-than-intriguing meeting between Mason and Walsh, who had worked as a Mason assistant from 1976-77 through 1978-79 at Bowling Green and from 1979-80 through 1983-84 at Michigan State. Walsh had also been a member of the Mason family since marrying Ron's daughter Tracey in August of 1989.

"I hate it," Shawn's mother-in-law and Ron's wife, Marion, said of the family feud.

Ron loved it. He had believed what he had told his team in the bowels of The Forum months before. And after dealing with the constant weight of great expectations in seasons such as 1984-85, 1986-87, 1988-89 and 1989-90, Mason was truly enjoying the rare underdog's role his Spartans were playing these days.

It was nice to have all the pressure on the other guy for a change, Mason figured, even if the other guy had married one of your daughters.

"I thought we had had a very average to below-average performance (in the December game)," Mason said. "I thought this time we'd play better, and maybe they wouldn't play quite as well.

"And I knew we had had more of a struggle throughout the year in just getting to that point than they did."

Thus, if MSU could get Maine to play from behind for a change, or do something else that might otherwise frustrate the Black Bears, the opportunity to pull off an upset might just present itself, since frustration was an emotion Maine hadn't really experienced to this point.

It didn't quite work out that way at first. Montgomery opened the scoring, one-timing a pass from Patrice Tardiff into the right corner over goalie Mike Gilmore's shoulder at 5:39. But the Spartans didn't get rattled. They were loose because they really had nothing to lose. They simply kept plugging away until Dwayne Norris tied it with his 42nd goal of the season at 9:33.

Norris, a first-team All-American in 1991-92 (along with Spartan defenseman Joby Messier) who would go on to become an Olympian and play in the NHL himself, untied it at 1:54 of the second. And Bryan Smolinski, who would become a first-team All-America selection in 1992-1993 and who would go on to establish himself as a scorer and an in-your-face type of player with the Boston Bruins, Pittsburgh Penguins and New York Islanders in the mid-1990s got another off a scramble in the slot at 11:22. Although Imes pulled Maine back to within one some six minutes later, the Spartans headed to the locker room after two periods smelling another upset.

It was there that Mason made a key change in the gameplan.

"They were forechecking the hell out of us," Mason said of Maine, which had a slight edge in shots (16-14) through two periods. "I decided we were going to play in our own end, but they were not going to outnumber us in our own end of the rink. We were going to have five guys in there just like they'd have five."

The theory was MSU wouldn't give up anything cheap, and would eventually catch a three-on-two or two-on-one break and use it to put the game away.

"It's just like in practice," Mason explained. "You can take the sticks away from five players and just have them play defense, and it's still damn hard for someone to score on them. And I knew eventually we'd break out..."

They did, too. But by now Garth Snow had decided he wasn't going to give up any more goals. He turned aside all seven attempts MSU registered in the final 20 minutes.

It was up to Gilmore thus, to make the one-goal lead stand up. The 24-year-old graduate student in engineering was more than ready to do so, too. For as big a game as this was, Gilmore had prepared himself for it as he would for any other—by chewing on a puck.

"I used to chew my fingernails so bad that they'd bleed, so now I use a puck," he explained. "I get that taste in my mouth and it's like giving a dog a scent and sending him out on the trail."

Maine came at him in waves in that final period. Swarming the net. Firing from all sides, all angles. Relentlessly attacking in a desperate attempt to salvage its national-championship hopes.

Twenty saves later the Black Bears still hadn't scored. And finally, it was over.

Gilmore and the Spartans had earned the right to chew rubber in Albany, N.Y., at the Final Four.

"It was just one of those nights," Gilmore said. "I just felt like a magnet. Everywhere I went, the puck just hit me. The puck just seemed to bounce my way."

"He made four or five saves (among the 20 in the third period) that were unbelievable. That's something you have to have in big games, great goaltending," Mason said. "And we played a hell of a game and upset a hell of a team."

They had done so in relative anonymity, too. So underwhelming was the momentum MSU had generated in qualifying for the NCAA Tournament, only 50 or so fans had made the trip from East Lansing to Providence for the weekend regional. And the NCAA, using logic that only the NCAA can understand, had ruled that TV feeds back to the hometowns of the participants weren't allowed.

"It was a great, great win for Michigan State, one of the greatest games Michigan State ever played...and nobody saw it because the NCAA was goofy," Mason said. "And the write-up in the paper...I still tell (Lansing State Journal veteran scribe) Neil Koepke about it...It sounded like we were lucky to win the game.

"From start to finish we were the better team. They had a better finish than we had, but we had the better start, so don't obliterate our start with their finish. We didn't just luck out. That wasn't as big an upset as people think."

It was a monumental one nonetheless.

We took it to the limit...

CHAPTER
12

Chapter 12

The 1995-96 campaign wound to a close earlier than many once believed it would, and in a fashion as distressing as the ultimate result was disappointing.

A less-than-capacity crowd was on hand for the NCAA West Regional at Munn Arena. Try as they might, the Spartans, for the second time in three years in a first-round regional at home, simply couldn't solve the University of Massachusetts-Lowell (a lowly branch campus, for crying out loud). And as the final minutes of MSU's 6-2 defeat expired, University of Michigan fans in attendance who would watch their team skate the following afternoon began chanting "Season's O-ver" at the expense of those in Green and White.

Ugh.

At least when the Spartans had lost to Lowell at home in the West Regional in 1993-94, there had been a consolation prize.

The sting of defeat for Spartan fans on that weekend was quickly replaced by a determined effort to temporarily adopt Lake Superior, which met Michigan the next day, into their hearts. And it was well worth the effort. MSU loyalists cheered

the Lakers with seemingly as much intensity as had ever been generated at Munn. The Lake Superior Pep Band continually belted out the "MSU Fight Song" to keep everyone emotionally stoked, and Laker Clayton Beddoes sent everyone home deliriously happy—the previous day's loss to Lowell and all—by scoring in overtime to finish Michigan. The Lakers even saluted the outpouring of MSU support by raising their sticks at center ice, following their usual tradition at home.

It was a beautiful thing.

It was not to be repeated this time around, however. Michigan, compounding Spartan fans' consternation, beat Minnesota, 4-3, the day after Lowell had knocked out Michigan State. The Wolverines celebrated locking up a trip to the Final Four on Munn ice.

Ugh. Again.

It wasn't supposed to end like this. For this was a Michigan State team that had won 22 of 25 games from Oct. 28 through Feb. 3. One that had rebounded from a potentially disastrous 7-1 loss at Western Michigan on Feb. 9 to beat the Broncos at home, 3-2, in a stern character test the following night. One that had been ranked as high as fourth in

Highly touted winger Mike Watt made his presence felt as a sophomore. A second-round draft pick of the Edmonton Oilers in 1994, Watt helped his native Canada win the gold medal at the 1995 World Junior Championships.

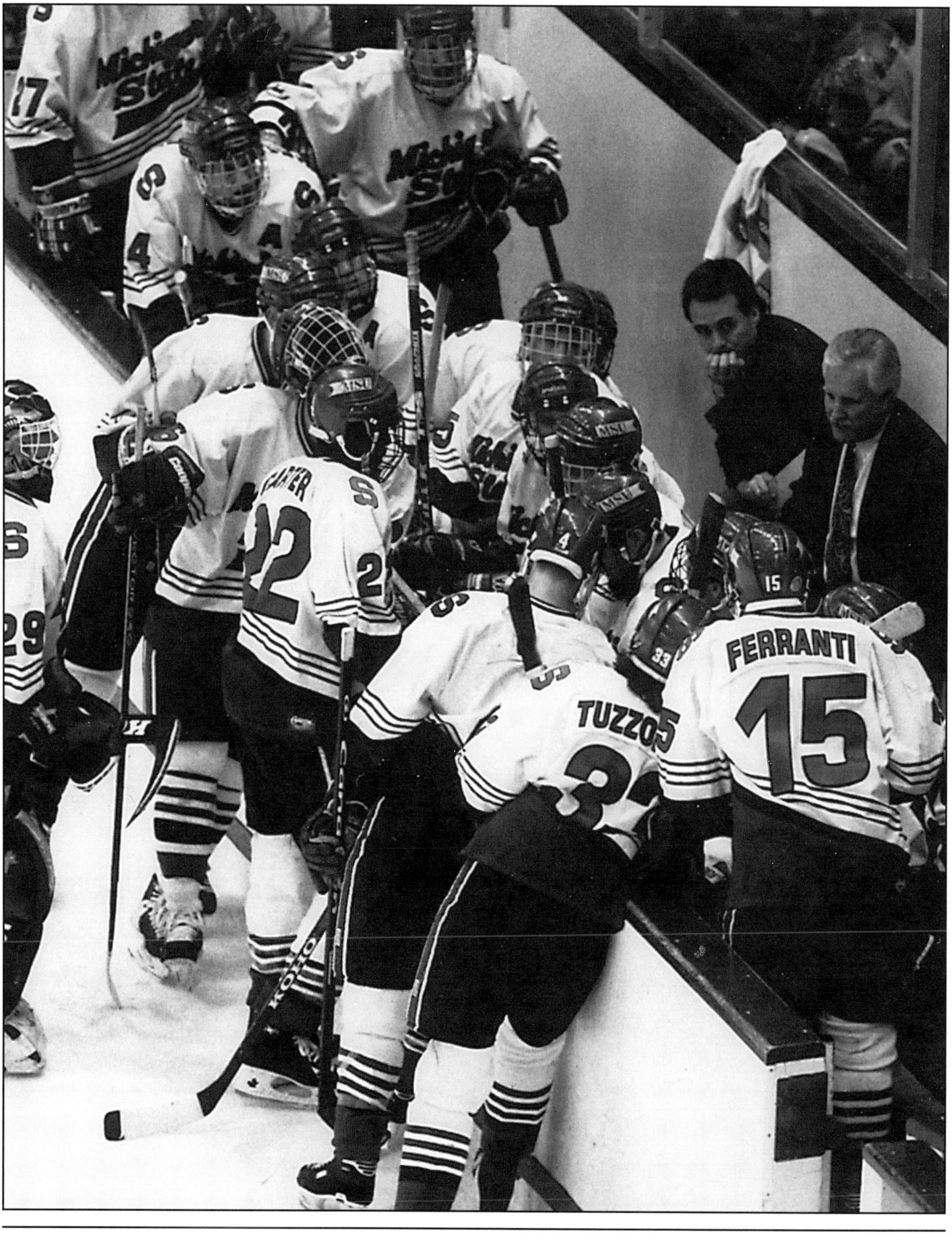
CARTER
22
TUZZO
FERRANTI
15

the nation at midseason. One that rallied from a 2-0 deficit to win, 4-2, on Feb. 16 in Detroit over a Lake Superior team that would go on to sweep Michigan the following weekend. This was a Michigan State team that had led the Central Collegiate Hockey Association since Jan. 6, and had needed just one win in its final two games to wrap up the CCHA regular-season championship.

It never happened.

Instead, MSU finished 2-6-1, including three losses in five tries in the postseason.

"It was kind of an unusual year," coach Ron Mason conceded.

Indeed.

Back when the 1995-96 season began, Mason knew he and his staff had some work to do. The Spartans had opened 7-0-1 and been ranked No. 1 the previous season, but went just 18-12-2 over their final 30 games and finished at 25-12-3. Although returning to the NCAA Tournament had been a plus (MSU had missed it in 1992-93 after an unconscionable loss to Ferris State in the CCHA semifinals at Joe Louis Arena), the season-ending loss to Wisconsin at Wisconsin in the first round of the West Regional had also signaled the end for seven seniors. Among them were leading scorer Rem Murray (whose 218 career points tied him for seventh on the all-time MSU list), playmakers Steve Guolla and Steve Suk, Kent transfer Dean Sylvester (who scored 15 goals and added 15 assists during his only season in Green) and reliable and at times spectacular goaltender Mike Buzak.

Their departures promised to affect MSU in net, on the power play and in killing penalties.

"Those areas are the ones that take a little longer to rebuild," Mason pointed out.

That was obvious early. State lost to Maine

The Spartans came together and got it together in January and took a run at the CCHA title before injuries took their toll.

in the championship game of the season-opening Great Western Freezeout at The Pond, in Anaheim, Calif., 4-3, in part because defenseman Chris Smith inadvertently fired a clearing attempt past startled sophomore Chad Alban and into the MSU goal. The Spartans also lost 6-2 at Bowling Green on Oct. 21, and 4-1 to Lake Superior at home on Oct. 26. Their 2-3 record at that point didn't exactly inspire a lot of confidence.

Winning 12 of the next 13 did.

An efficient seven-game winning streak sent the Spartans to Milwaukee, Wisc., for the Thanksgiving-weekend College Hockey Showcase riding a crest of momentum. They had improved to 9-3 following the slow start. Four players—Anson Carter (eight), Mike Watt (7), Mike York (five) and Richard Keyes (five)—had at least five goals. Three more—Tony Tuzzolino, Steve Ferranti and Brian Crane—had scored four goals through 12 games. The freshman, led by York's 13, had already contributed 34 points. Alban and backup goalie Mike Brusseau had each recorded a shutout.

Minnesota next provided a brief bump in the road, winning its Showcase showdown with Michigan State on a breakaway in overtime, 6-5. But the Spartans bounced back by beating a fired-up, almost desperate bunch of Wisconsin Badgers on their home ice, 5-4, and by doing something they sorely needed to do upon returning to CCHA play three days later.

They beat Michigan, 4-3, before 6,729 at Munn Arena.

That hadn't happened since Feb. 19, 1994. But after going 0-for-4 against Michigan in 1994-95, including blowing a 2-0 lead in a 5-4 loss in the Great Lakes Invitational Tournament finals, the Spartans weren't about to be denied this time. Carter produced a pair of goals, the second of which wiped out a 2-1 Wolverines' lead. Ferranti scored what proved to be the decisive goal with 5:13 to play, his second consecutive game-winning goal and fourth in eight games. Alban made 27 saves and contributed his first career assist. And the penalty killers shut Michigan out on five power plays, including a two-man advantage in the second period.

Life was good.

The Wolverines earned a measure of revenge a few weeks later in the GLI finals, 3-1, but the Spartans reeled off nine consecutive wins after that. They started that streak by beating Alaska-Fairbanks on three consecutive nights in Alaska (displaying focus and a commitment to winning on a lengthy trip that might have been perceived as a mini-vacation by a lesser team) and took over first place in the CCHA in the process. They played about as efficiently and effectively as the staff thought possible in a 7-3, 3-0 sweep at Illinois-Chicago. They blasted Ferris State (7-2) and Notre Dame (7-1).

Next up was Western, for a critical home-and-home series Feb. 9-10. The Spartans were 20-3 and first in the CCHA. The Broncos were 16-4-3 and second. They were also eyeing a sweep that would tighten the league-championship picture dramatically.

Western appeared capable of producing it, too, following a 7-1 win at home on Friday night. But after falling behind 1-0, the Spartans got consecutive goals from Carter, Taylor Clarke and Tuzzolino, and came away with another game they had to have, 3-2. Finishing in first place, and hanging a banner in the Munn Arena rafters for the first time since 1990, remained well within the Spartans' grasp.

All of that changed the following weekend at The Joe.

In another crucial two-game test, this one against contenders Lake Superior and Michigan, the Spartans' season got away from them.

The problems started when MSU fell behind the Lakers 2-0 on Friday. Normally, that's tantamount to disaster, since the Lakers have excelled since the late 1980s at playing the patient, grinding, cycling, frustrating, take-advantage-of-mistakes-for-your-goals-and-then-hold-a-lead-at-all-cost style the New Jersey Devils rode all the way to the Stanley Cup in 1995. This time, the Spartans responded with four consecutive second-period goals and then hung on (Alban made 15

saves in the third period alone among his season-high 31) for a dramatic, 4-3 victory. Alas, it was a costly one, for senior defenseman Bart Vanstaalduinen had been lost for the season due to a knee injury that would require surgery.

Vanstaalduinen had never made any headlines for his offense (three career goals), but he was well-liked enough by his teammates to have emerged as a team leader behind Carter, and he was exceptionally steady defensively. Losing his services was a major blow.

Had Vanstaalduinen been the only casualty on the blue line, MSU might have been able to overcome it. But State had opened the season shorthanded when sophomore Jon Gaskins developed a blood disorder before the first weekend of play. Although Gaskins made it back by midseason and wound up playing in 17 games, he never could get himself in the type of game-shape or play with the level of confidence and consistency the Spartans needed him to.

"He was by far and away our best defensive defenseman," Mason said of Vanstaalduinen. "Before you lost him, you didn't realize how important he was in that area. You always look at defensemen in terms of how many goals and assists they get and how well they move the puck. You forget how good a guy can be defensively."

Without Vanstaalduinen, and without the Gaskins the Spartans thought they'd have "we were struggling behind the blue line," Mason lamented, "especially in penalty killing and in stability in the close games.

"You get into a position where you really can't stop the other team the way you should, the good teams."

As the defense was falling apart, so was the offense.

Carter, a senior captain, a preseason All-America- and Hobey Baker Award-candidate and the Spartans' heart-and-soul, wasn't right by this time, either. He had been cross-checked from behind and into the goalpost by Western's Kyle Millar during MSU's 3-2 victory on Feb. 10, suffering a gash to the forehead in the process. And although he never came out of the lineup, headaches, dizziness and other discomfort would result whenever Carter engaged in contact thereafter, and contact was a large part of Carter's overall package.

He wasn't the same player down the stretch, registering a mere one goal and two assists in his final 10 games.

"It changed my game," Carter said of the incident. "By no means did I want to come out of the lineup. I still played through it. But it was tough for me because I like to play a physical style. Every chance I get to run someone over, I do. But with my head hurting the way it was, every time I'd hit a guy I'd start getting dizzy, or my helmet would open up the cut again.

"I couldn't crash, I couldn't bang, I couldn't do the things I like to do to get myself involved in a game. Whenever I'd do that, my head would start hurting and I'd end up sitting on the bench wondering, 'when is this ever going to go away?' It was frustrating because I couldn't play the style of hockey that Anson Carter can play."

Without enough depth and experience on defense, with sparkplug Clarke playing down the stretch on a knee that would later require surgery, and with Carter unable to do what he had done for the past three seasons, the Spartans simply weren't the same team.

"All of a sudden there we were asking other people to do it, and I think as a whole we got uptight a bit and we just weren't as good a team," Mason said.

"We took it to the limit, I thought. We still had a chance for the league title, one point away...But the bottom line was we just weren't as good a team. When you get that close, let's face it, you wrack your brain trying to figure out what you could have done to put it over the top; that's part of coaching. But when you get right down to it, reality sets in. Hey, when you don't have the same bullets, you can't fire the same gun."

With a chance to lock up the CCHA regular-season title against Bowling Green at home on March 9, the gun misfired and the Spartans lost, 5-1. They ended the regular season by getting blanked in Ann Arbor, 3-0 (Michigan's first shutout of Michigan State since Feb. 10, 1968). MSU wound up third (with 45 points, along with Western Michigan) for the third consecutive season, one point behind Lake Superior and Michigan.

In the playoffs, the Spartans needed three games to get past Ferris State in a best-of-three CCHA quarterfinal series at Munn, but just one each to check out of the CCHA Final Four (6-2 at the hands of Michigan) and the NCAA West Regional.

And so it eventually ended with a thud. With the clock winding down and the Michigan fans jeering and Carter spending his last shifts as a Spartan running into any Lowell player he could find simply because there was nothing else left to do.

"I knew I didn't have to save any hits because I was worried about being dizzy for the next period, so I said the heck with it," Carter explained. "I started punishing people and abusing people the way I could have been all along if I hadn't been hit from behind."

Although it wasn't the ending he or anyone else expected, Carter's career was a glorious one none the less.

He was a lanky 6-foot-1 and 150 pounds when he accepted a scholarship to attend Michigan State. But by the time he arrived on campus, Carter had added 20 pounds. And by the time he had skated off the Munn ice for the final time, Carter had bulked up another 20 more, scored more goals than all but five of the players who had preceded him in Green and White, and perhaps provided as many individual highlights as any Spartan ever.

When he was right, Carter was that exciting. What's more, he became as complete a player as any coach could ever hope for.

""He turned out to be much more than I expected," Mason said. "Bringing him in we thought he'd be a good player. I saw his skill, but I didn't see his ability, as a kid, in terms of what he could bring to the ice other than skill.

"He brought a lot of defensive capabilities I didn't

know he had. He brought some toughness along the boards I didn't know he had. And his caring way about things, I didn't know he had."

Carter, meanwhile, came to State thinking he'd produce big all along.

"I read a lot of hockey publications, and I can remember looking at one where Coach Mason was talking about our freshman class," Carter revealed. "He said, 'We have some good guys coming in, but we don't think we have anyone that can come in and score 20 goals right off the bat.'

"Quietly, I said to myself, 'I can score 20 goals in this league; there's no doubt.'"

He ended up settling for 19 as a freshman in 1992-93, playing a secondary role while senior Bryan Smolinski popped home 31, helped set up 37 more, earned first-team All-America honors and jumped immediately to the Boston Bruins at season's end.

Once Smolinski left, Carter took over.

He scored 30 goals and 54 points as a sophomore, and was a first-team All-CCHA pick. As a junior, Carter netted 31 goals, totaled 51 points, was named first-team All-CCHA, second-team All-America and was a Hobey Baker finalist.

After considering a jump to the professional ranks (he was a 10th round draft pick of the Quebec Nordiques in 1992), Carter opted to stay at State. Heading into his senior season, he was the nation's leading returning goal scorer and had earned consensus recognition as one of the best players in the country.

And although the numbers—23 goals, 20 assists, 43 points—don't suggest it, Carter got even better during his last go-around as a Spartan.

"I talked it over with my parents, and they reminded me that when I signed my letter-of-intent, I made a four-year commitment to Michigan State," Carter sad. "And I thought this was an opportunity for me to give back to the program by coming back.

"Being a captain, I really didn't come back to put up huge offensive numbers. If I thought I had had something to prove offensively, I would have gone into the American Hockey League. This year,

I tried to hone my skills in other areas of the game, and even more importantly, I tried to bring the team together. I thought I did that pretty well at the beginning of the year."

Carter did so by, "showing the guys I was willing to play defense even when I wasn't scoring," he said. "There were some games where I had chances to score and didn't, and other games where I didn't have chances. But at the same time, that never stopped me from back-checking hard or working my butt off on a five-on-three (penalty killing) situation, or finishing my checks."

Carter also continued trying to fight through all the holding, hooking, slashing, cross-checking and at times tackling opponents had been dishing out in an effort to stop him ever since Smolinski had departed.

"He probably took more abuse than almost anybody I've ever seen," Mason said of Carter. Rarely, however, did Carter ever lose his cool.

"The fact that I didn't retaliate, I think some of the guys learned from that," he said. "I took more abuse than the normal guy on our team, and they could say, 'Look, Anson's getting abused and he's turning his cheek the other way even though he wants to snap and go crazy. He's not above the team, why should I be?'

"Some people told me I should have been a little more selfish. I figured you can think about yourself all you want, but eventually the team is going to have to come through. Look at New Jersey (the Devils won a Stanley Cup in 1995 relying on a no-stars, all-for-one concept), they had a solid team. And all the teams I've ever played on, whether it was baseball, basketball or hockey, we were a team, that was the bottom line.

"You can say all you want about individual stats, but the team comes first. That's what I tried to reiterate this year with the younger guys."

With freshmen defensemen Jeff Kozakowski and Chris Bogas, with freshmen forwards Bryan Adams, Mike Ford, Mark Loeding and York, with sophomore forwards Mike Watt and Richard Keyes and Sean Berens, with Alban...with anyone who was willing to follow, Carter did his best to lead.

Playing it that way didn't earn Carter the Hobey Baker (he wasn't a finalist) or All-America honors (not even second-team). Carter even failed to three-peat as a first-team All-CCHA selection.

Mason was proud of Carter's efforts none the less.

"I'd have to say this was his team," the coach acknowledged.

"He was a great leader in terms of his commitment to the game. He respected the game, he understood the game, and as much (media) attention and publicity as he got here, he was able to handle it pretty darn well and still have the respect of the other players on the team.

"Believe me, that's not easy to do, because he had a lot of attention thrown his way, and deservedly so. I thought he brought the team together and kept them together as best he could.

"With any luck at all, he would have been a first-team All-American this year. The problem was, he does so many things away from the puck, and you don't get credit for that."

It didn't matter. Carter had come to Michigan State in the first place not to make All-America, but "because of the reputation for developing pro players. The track record...the Millers, (Rod) Brind' Amour, Joe Murphy, Bobby Essensa, Chris Luongo...I just thought I'd have a good shot at playing pro hockey if I came here and learned under Coach Mason," he said.

He left as another shining example of what Spartan Hockey prides itself on, and as a budding professional star.

"He's one of the all-time great players I've ever coached in terms of everything he provided to the game," Mason said.

The team Carter leaves behind meanwhile, "is headed in the right direction, there's no question in my mind," Mason insisted. "There are a lot of young players on this team that are continuing to develop and understand

how to play at this level."

They learned in 1995-96 by watching one of Michigan State's best ever. In the process, they won more games (28) than any MSU team since 1989-90 (35), tied the school record for shutouts in a season (four, in 1958-59), played well enough to help push the school-record regular-season sellout streak at Munn to 185 games and counting, and fostered hope that another breakthrough season was on the horizon.

That was a development worth celebrating, no matter how the 1995-96 season ended.

Despite not winning a Central Collegiate Hockey Association title since 1990, Ron Mason saw his team moving in the right direction following the 1995-96 season.

The enthusiasm of a scientist...

CHAPTER 13

Chapter 13

The inspiration, the realization that certain plays could be anticipated and thus taken advantage of; the understanding that, much like physics, certain actions would in fact produce subsequent, predictable reactions came early for Ron Mason. It was as a pee wee that Mason discovered hockey was more than just a scrambly, free-flowing, group-grope for the puck.

"The first coach that I ever had that gave me any kind of system at all, his name was Johnny James," Mason recalled. "He took over our pee wee team, and I'll never forget it.

"I was a center and he said, 'Whenever the puck goes into the corner, you always go in and back your guy up because they'll probably be trying to throw it up the boards.' A little light went on in my head when he said that. So I did it and I did it...and I used to get loose pucks all the time. Then I started thinking, 'This game's easy.'"

Mason was only 10- or 11-years old at the time (he can't remember which) when playing for that pee wee team in his native Seaforth, Ontario. Still, "I was probably destined to be a coach right then and there," he said.

Other lessons would follow. But it wasn't until Mason had made his way to the Montreal Junior Canadiens that he would be exposed to another as important, and to one that would make as lasting an impression.

"The Junior Canadiens and Sammy Pollock," Mason said, shaking his head at the gravity of that situation decades later. "Being with that

The current salesmen and caretakers of Spartan Hockey: Assistant coach Tom Newton (left), head coach Ron Mason (center), and assistant coach David McAuliffe (right).

organization, with him, really taught you the sense of loyalty through work ethic. You really got a sense of how important it was to do your best and how winning was the result of work ethic, and how when you didn't win, you should never have to question how hard you worked and if you did, you were a loser.

"That gave me a hell of a background as far as what frame to coach from. Whether or not I always hated to lose, I don't know. But with the Junior Canadiens, if you didn't hate to lose when you got there, they taught you how to hate to lose."

Mason still hates to lose today. That, in part, is one reason why Mason has been able to win more games than any collegiate mentor in the history of North America.

It wasn't, however, as simple as, 'I hate to lose, therefore I will not.' There were still an infinite number of lessons to be learned. And throughout the years, Mason was always a willing student. He remained as thirsty for the answers as he had been while learning at the feet of "The Master", Pollock (who would go on to lead the Senior Canadiens, the NHL-dynasty Canadiens, as general manager from 1964-65 through 1977-78). Mason remained as hungry for hockey knowledge as he had been while playing for the Peterborough Petes, where Mason had absorbed all he could from Scotty Bowman (who would go on to become the all-time winningest coach in NHL history during stints in St. Louis, Montreal, Buffalo, Pittsburgh

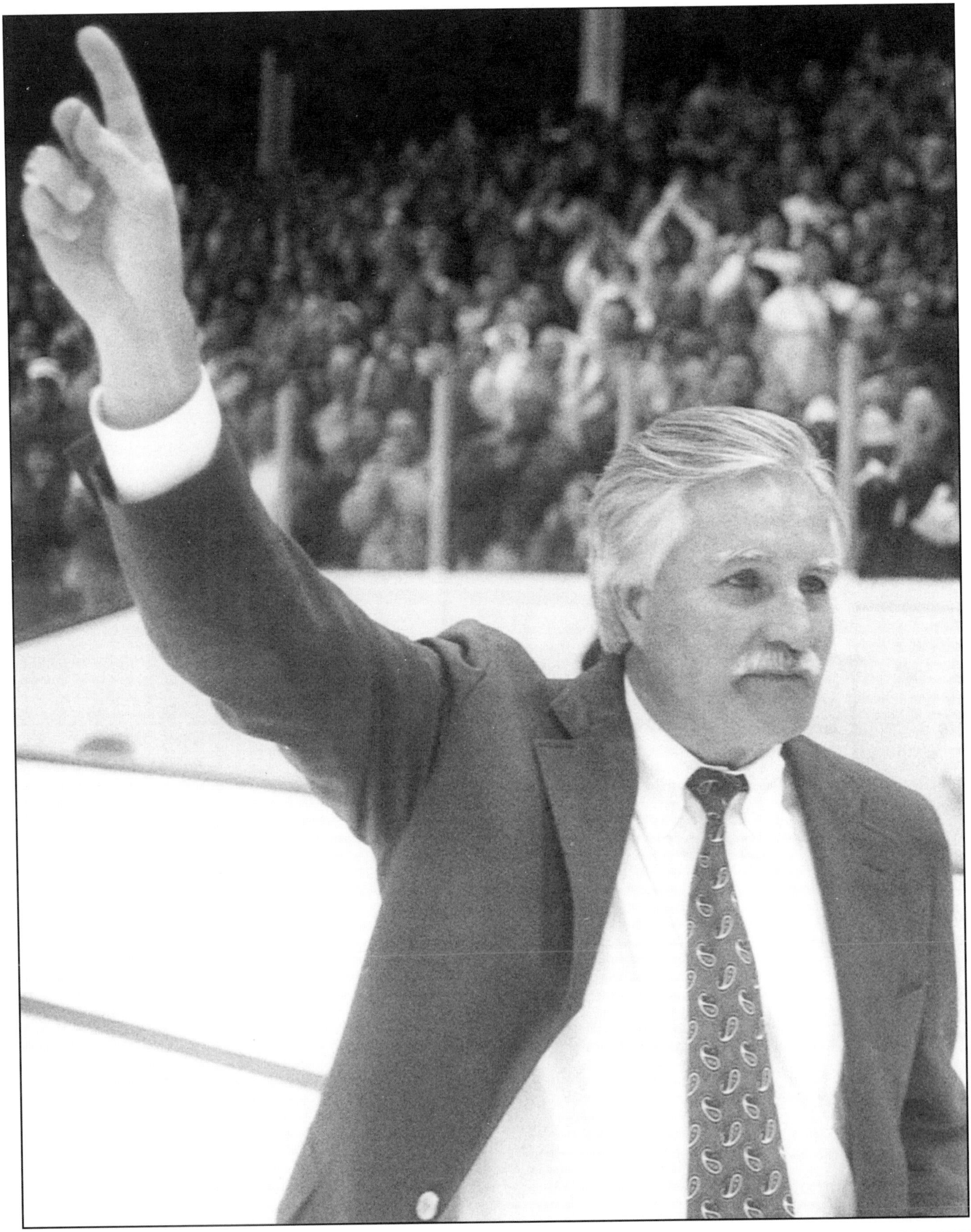

and Detroit). The imprint both men left is evident every time Mason steps behind a bench.

The final influence that ultimately drove Mason into coaching was financial.

When he decided to go to college (at St. Lawrence; Mason would have preferred Michigan State, but Spartans coach Amo Bessone wasn't really interested), rather than remain in the junior ranks, Mason was right then and there pretty much giving up on possibly reaching the NHL. At the time, getting that far by going through college hockey was almost unheard of. Still, Mason was convinced he'd be better off in the long run.

"I might have been good enough to be a cup-of-coffee player in the National League, who the hell knows?" Mason suggested. "But I remember some of the great players I was around at the time...One of them was Ralph Backstrom, and when he signed to play pro for a certain amount of money, I said, 'You know what? My mother makes more money than that teaching school.' I think it was five-grand or something like that. It was crazy. I thought, 'If a great player like that is going to make that kind of money, what the heck am I doing here? There's no way I'll ever come close to that.'

"So I decided to be a school teacher."

Not long after that, class was in session.

Mason's coaching career began in Sault Ste. Marie, Mich., in 1966-67. It was there where he started the Lake Superior program—Lake Superior was at the time a branch campus of Michigan Tech—from scratch. His first team went 15-5. Four of the next six won 20 or more games. His 1971-72 team won the NAIA national championship, and three others finished as runners-up. His seven-year record in The Soo was 129-47-8.

From there it was on to Bowling Green, where Mason soon established the Falcons as a national power. After a 20-19 season in Mason's first year at BG in 1973-74, the Falcons went 23-10-2, 21-9-2, 28-11-0, 31-8-0 and 37-6-2. The five-year run produced three regular-season CCHA championships, three league playoff titles, a trip to the NCAA Final Four in 1977-78 and an NCAA-record 31 victories in 1978-79. Mason's overall record at Bowling Green was 160-63-6.

Still, the grass seemed a bit Greener in East Lansing, Mich., and when Michigan State made him an offer, Mason ultimately found it was one he couldn't refuse. That was back in 1979. And after a slow start (Mason experienced the first two losing seasons of his collegiate career in his first two seasons at MSU), the program at Michigan State was soon elevated to previously uncharted heights.

Beginning in 1981-82 and running through 1996-97:

Mason's Spartans qualified for the NCAA Tournament 14 times in 16 years, including a run of nine straight from 1981-82 to 1989-90 (MSU was the only team to reach the tournament all nine years over that span)...

Mason's Spartans reached the NCAA Final Four five times, capturing the national championship in 1986 and losing in the title game to North Dakota in 1987...

Mason's Spartans won CCHA regular-season championships in 1985, '86, '89 and '90, and league playoff titles in 1982, '83, '84, '85, '87, '89 and '90...

Mason's Spartans won 460 games, lost 187 and tied 42, helping Mason to become the fastest coach to reach the 500- and 600-victory plateaus, and the only coach to record 700-plus career victories...

Victory No.1 came over the VFW Chippewas in 1966. No. 675, the U.S. Colleges record-setter, came over Kent State in the CCHA playoffs in 1993. But whether he has been trying to best the U.S. record of Len Ceglarski (who retired with 674 career wins in 1992), the North American record of Clare Drake (who won 697 games with the University of Alberta; Mason passed him in 1994), or simply get the best from his players on a

---

On March 12, 1993, following a 6-5 victory over Kent State University, Ron Mason became college hockey's all time winningest coach with 675 wins.

given night, Mason hasn't thought much about the significance of his ever-growing victory total (775 at the close of 1995-96, and average of 24.1 a year over 31 years). At least not yet.

"Someday, when I'm in Florida trying to catch that nice, big marlin," Mason said. "When I'm 75 and out of coaching I'll probably say to myself someday, 'Wow, I won a hell of a lot of hockey games.' But when you're still in it ,every year is another year and every game is another game and you just don't have time to sit back and really recollect.

"Don't get me wrong, beating Kent (and passing Ceglarski) was nice. It was nice to have it happen at home, nice to be able to be recognized in front of your fans. But once he retired, you knew it was going to happen eventually. It wasn't like it was a big surprise."

Nor, in a way, has Mason's success over the years been all that stunning. Certainly, no coach starts out in the business thinking "I'm going to set the NCAA and North American records for career victories" (Well, perhaps Shawn Walsh did, but that's another story). Yet when Mason tired of "mental masturbation" while working toward his doctorate degree at the University of Pittsburgh and jumped at the chance to start a program that Lake Superior was offering, he didn't do so without a plan.

Over the years that plan hasn't changed, even as the faces and locations have.

"In this program or at any other program, I've tried to approach it the following way," Mason explained. "You have the university policies and people you have to deal with there, so you have to deal with them in a very honest, professional way. You're part of the faculty, more or less, you're part of the university, so make sure you can relate to the people in the university. If you do and you need help, you'll get it.

"I've also always been a big believer that the community should be part of your job. In other words, be responsible to the community in ways your position allows you to be. Help out with charitable organizations, speak at different events, pro-

mote youth hockey...I've always thought that was important. I did it at Lake Superior, I did it at BG and I've done it here.

"The final aspect of it is how you run your program. Strategy changes all the time; nothing is sacred there. What is sacred is having a system of play and having discipline, those two things."

Mason's system, the details of which are subject to change, always involves having more than one system available, just in case things aren't going well one way and another approach must be tried. As for the discipline aspect of his approach, it's not what you might think.

"I've always been a disciplinarian in terms of making players adjust to team rules, and I'm not talking about team rules like when you go to bed and what you wear. I'm talking about team rules regarding hits, turnovers, takeaways, plus-minus...We always set up some team rules there, and I've always been tough in making our guys play as a team rather than as individuals."

If Mason has an all-encompassing philosophy, it is this: "You have to have talent to win, and you have to have discipline to make the talent work together."

Once that's accomplished, the rest often takes care of itself. Maybe that's why Mason has been able to win in the 1960s, '70s, '80s and '90s. Maybe that's why he's thrived at an obscure outpost (Lake Superior), at a hungry upstart in a lowly-regarded league anxious to force its way alongside the national elite (Bowling Green) and finally, at a once high-profile program that needed to be rebuilt and then meticulously maintained while fending off repeated challenges as one of college hockey's top dogs (Michigan State).

The forechecking schemes change. So does the power-play, the breakout and the use of the neutral zone. The belief that a team must be built from the goal out and must be strong defensively, and that only through discipline will a team be able to maximize its talent are the constants.

"He was clean-shaven and he had short hair then," Northern Michigan coach Rick Comley, who played for Mason at Lake Superior, recalled. "But he was also able to adapt with the times and stay one step ahead."

Later came the moustache, the long hair parted in the middle, the wide lapels and open-collar look. Mason has always had style and has always had a presence about him. But the substance of his convictions, experiences and character is why former players, coaches and associates still enjoy his company whenever a chance to get together arises, and why they still seek his advice and approval.

In that regard, Mason is like "The Godfather" (a nickname given to Mason in recent years by a selected few of those associates and one Mason isn't especially fond of, even though it's

can learn so much whenever you do."

Mason has seemingly always had the ability to get to the bottom of what's happening and why, and a knack for conveying what he's discovered to others.

"When I was about 13 years old, I was at the Huron Hockey School (of which Mason is a part-owner), and Ron told me if I ever wanted to play college hockey, I had a scholarship waiting for me at Bowling Green," said Newell Brown, an assistant coach with the Chicago Blackhawks and a former Spartan center, former MSU assistant coach and the former head coach of the AHL's Adirondack Red Wings. "When I decided I wanted to pursue that avenue, Ron was true to his word. He

Mason's Spartans won their third straight CCHA playoff title in 1984.

meant to imply power and respect; not an association with organized crime).

"I still enjoy sitting down with him and talking hockey," said former Spartan great Kelly Miller, who completed his 11th NHL season in 1995-96. "He's a wealth of knowledge. He has an unbelievable grasp on the game. He can pick a game apart, a forechecking system or a power play...he can see things most people can't see.

"It's just enjoyable to chat with him. You

was at Michigan State by then, but I was going to go wherever he was coaching.

"If he'd have been in Alaska, I'd have gone there. That's how badly I wanted to play for him."

Those that do don't always know what to make of him. And their reactions to him are as varied as their respective backgrounds and abilities. Consider, for example, the perceptions of a couple of 1980s-era Mason players at Michigan State.

Brown's: "We were always comfortable around him. We could knock on his door, walk into the office, sit down, almost put our feet up on his desk...but the respect was always there."

Mitch Messier's: "You never wanted to get called into his office. I think he had the legs shortened on that one chair of his on purpose, so that every time you sat in his office you had to look straight up. You could just see him over the corner of his desk. He'd have those little reading glasses on, he'd just sit there looking down at you...You just felt so small."

And yet Messier reveres Mason as much as Brown.

"Best coach I've ever seen," said Messier, who went on to play in the IHL, the NHL and in Europe after leaving Michigan State.

Why? Because of Mason's knowledge of the game, Messier insists, and because of Mason's uncanny ability to handle people in an unlimited number of situations and circumstances.

"He just holds a power over that entire place," Messier said of Mason's stature in the East Lansing community.

"And as far as handling players, he could always bring out the best in players and he could put you in a position to do well, even if you didn't understand it at the time. My senior year, I had 21 goals and 21 assists after a game against Ferris, and he walks by a few days later and says, 'Hmmmm...Mitch Messier...21 goals, 21 assists, 21 games...Who'd have thought that?...Just the coach,' and then he walks away.

"You didn't always understand, but he was easy to play for, because if he gave you shit, he was also going to give you a chance to stick it up his ass. He wasn't going to sit you down and let you smolder into nothing. If he sat you down or screamed at you between periods, he'd never just bench you. If he screamed at you or benched you, he'd let you think about it, then he'd give you a chance to go out and do something about it."

That's one Mason method of handling players. There are others.

"The coach can't be the team leader and the coach can't be the team cop," Mason insists. "Certain team leaders have to police other players

and take care of their own. If they do, you have the chemistry you need."

Mason has never underrated the importance of nurturing the proper team chemistry over the years.

"One time we were playing at Michigan,'"Messier remembered. "They had been scoring on some weak shots and finally, they got a goal on one from near center ice that Norm (Foster) had tried to jump and catch and ended up redirecting behind him. I think there were about 11 minutes left. So I skate over to the bench —and meanwhile Bobby Essensa has had like a hot dog and two Snickers bars between periods; he was the worst McDonald's-eatin', junk-food junkie you ever saw—and I said, 'Hey Mase, you better get this guy out of the game.' Then I skate over to Bobby and say, 'Start warming up.' Here I am just a player, but in the heat of the moment you say stuff, you know?

"So Bobby looks at me—he has chocolate all over the sides of his face—and Coach C (assistant Terry Christensen) is yelling, 'Hey, don't you say that,' and Donnie (McSween) is saying to me, 'Don't listen to him.' Finally, Mase looks at me, he looks at Donnie, he looks at Coach C and then he looks over at Bobby and says, 'You're going in.' So they pull Norm out, I think it was 6-6 at the time, and they never got a shot the rest of the way and we ended up winning the game.

"Mase was pretty good about stuff like that. You could say stuff in the heat of the moment and he wouldn't hold it against you."

For the record, Mason said he couldn't remember the exact details of that particular situation, but added that he thought in this particular instance, Messier might have been exaggerating.

So did Christensen.

"Guys didn't come to the bench and say 'get this guy out,' or 'get that guy out,'" Christensen insisted. "But it wouldn't surprise me if Mitch came over and said, 'Hey, this guy is having a tough night, do you think we should get him out of there?' And it wouldn't surprise me if Ron, even though he always had a good pulse about what was going on in a game, would use the information given to him

Always a teacher, Mason discusses strategy with his team during a time out.

by his players. They're the ones that are out there, and with any good coach, if a player comes to the bench and has something to say, you listen.

"And it definitely wouldn't surprise me if Bobby Essensa had chocolate all over his face."

Somehow, it always comes back to people. And Mason is as much an expert on human nature as he is the game.

"His common sense has gotten him where he is," said Shawn Walsh, a longtime Mason assistant at Bowling Green and Michigan State before becoming the head coach at Maine. "He's a guy you can lean on and know you're going to get sound advice."

Like any true Godfather.

"Without question, I took his blueprint right to Maine," continued Walsh, who built a nothing Black Bears program into a perennial national-championship contender and captured the 1992-1993 title with a 42-1-2 mark. "It's a knack. It's an ability to relate to people and to organize a plan. Ron has a great sense for the game, a great ability to read the game and players' decisions. But his

ability comes not just in recognizing hockey players, but people, office workers, personnel staff...He was always one that appreciated the Zamboni driver and the trainer, and he knew how important both of those people and their attitudes were to the overall good of the operation. And we always had sound, efficient student managers.

"Little things, that's what it always comes back to. In terms of the physical plant, we were always doing something to improve. The very first thing we did at Michigan State was a paint job underneath Munn Arena. It was all grey. We needed to paint it Green and White. It was a simple thing, but it needed to be done. And I can remember having the press box re-wired a few years later so the coaches could watch power-play replays at the end of each period, which was way ahead of our time in college hockey."

As far as the actual playing of college hockey is concerned, Mason has not yet re-invented the wheel. But nor has he married himself to a strategy or system (with the exception of building from the goal out, which will remain a sound philosophy as long as pucks are dropped) to the point where he has become unwilling to explore alternative concepts, new or old.

"He's a very sound X's & O's guy, but he was always big on keeping it simple," Walsh said. "I would describe him as patient. He always wanted to have a Plan B in reserve during a game. Just in case a certain thing didn't work, he wanted to know, what are you going to turn to? I think deep down he has a conservative streak to him, he likes to hold the liberal side for later in a game if he needs it. But at the same time he was always liberal about things like face-off plays, penalty killing...

"We used to have some great arguments in the office after practices evaluating personnel and schemes. I think he liked it that way. Of course, he knew he had the final say, but he always wanted to hear differing opinions, and then he wanted to hear why. He wanted everything put into the test tube

Mason celebrates yet another tournament title at Joe Louis Arena with captains Dan McFall (left), Kelly Miller (center), and Don McSween (right).

before the final result came out, and he wanted all the information so there would be no surprises once it did.

"Some of my fondest memories are the buzz sessions we used to have during the Huron Hockey School in the summer. Ron would enjoy those tremendously, even thought he had been coaching for over 20 years. We'd have Ron, myself, Ted Sator (a former NHL head coach and an assistant with the Hartford Whalers in 1995-96), Tom Newton (then an assistant at Western Michigan, now Mason's assistant at MSU), Terry Christensen or George Gwozdecky, Barry Smith (an assistant

coach on two Stanley Cup winners in Pittsburgh and one in Detroit) and whoever else happened to be around. Everybody would come to the buzz sessions with a topic and we'd just kick those topics around. Ron enjoyed those as much as anybody.

"Another guy that did was a young goalie coach in junior hockey named Jeff Jackson. He'd never say a word. He'd just sit there and take note after note."

Jackson, a former backup goalie at MSU who never lettered, won national championships while running the program at Lake Superior State in 1991-1992 and 1993-1994 before becoming a national coach and elite development director with USA Hockey in 1996. And he is just one among a host of coaches touched by Mason's influence either through the Huron Hockey School or Mason's tenures at Lake Superior, Bowling Green or Michigan State.

Walsh and Christensen (the head coach of the East Coast Hockey League's Tallahassee Tiger Sharks) are in that fraternity. So are Comley, Brown, Newton, Paul Titanic (University of Toronto), Doug Ross (Alabama-Huntsville), Mark Mazzoleni (formerly of Miami of Ohio), Steve Cady (formerly of Miami of Ohio), Tom Anastos (formerly of Michigan-Dearborn as a head coach and MSU as an assistant), Lyle Phair (a former assistant at Illinois-Chicago), Sator, Mike Keenan (an NHL head coach with the Philadelphia Flyers, New York Rangers and St. Louis Blues), John Markell (Ohio State) and Jim Wiley (who in 1995-96 was named the interim head coach of the San Jose Sharks).

They worked with and learned from Mason on campus, or at Huron, a hockey school Mason became involved with in the late 1960s or early 1970s ("I can't remember which") that first opened in Huron Park, Ontario, and today operates all across North America every summer. The school has thrived thanks to a once almost-revolutionary philosophy: Rely on professional educators with a solid background in hockey to teach the game to kids; not jocks or ex-jocks to simply lend a famous name to an otherwise run-of-the-mill stating of hockey basics.

People such as Mason and Keenan ("He was a no-name back then just like the rest of us") made it work.
Just as Mason did at Lake Superior. And BG. And MSU.

Just as Comley, Walsh and others have running programs of their own.

"As players, they're not learning anything more from me than they learn from any other coach. The big thing is, there's more to the game than they think," Mason said. "As (assistant coaches), they learn there's more to the game than just dropping the puck and practicing."

There's the physical plant, and the off-ice staff, and working within the university hierarchy, and community involvement, and developing a system while remaining flexible enough to adjust it, and instilling discipline, and recruiting, and dealing with the media, the alumni, the NCAA...Develop the ability to handle all of that, do it for 30 years or so, resist the urge to seriously pursue potential offers from the pros (as Mason has occasionally done over the years) and you, too, might win 700-plus games.

"That sheer number...It's just amazing," Walsh said. "When you look at the way college hockey has evolved, from scholarship changes, to the impact of professional hockey, to rules changes, to the style of the game, to face masks, to...We're talking three decades...

"And the thing I still like the most about Ron is the enthusiasm in his voice when you call him up after his team has had a good practice. To me, it's the enthusiasm of a scientist when he knows he's on to something."

With Mason, who turned 57 on Jan. 14, 1997, it's an enthusiasm that's almost impossible not to detect. And whether you're exposed to it from over the television or radio, from across an interview room, from that one chair in his office with the short legs, from the back of a Blue Line Club function ,or on the other end of a telephone from Orono, Maine, or Pittsburgh, Pa., it's an enthusiasm that is nothing if not contagious.

When you hear that type of enthusiasm from Ron Mason, it's hard not to get excited about Spartan Hockey. And it's harder still not to immediately begin looking ahead to the next time you'll be lucky enough to wedge your way into a seat at Munn Arena on a Friday or Saturday night, when the Spartans will take the ice, the band will strike up the MSU Fight Song and "awe inspiring" won't begin to describe the feeling.

It rekindles the great memories
you have of being there...

CHAPTER
14

Chapter 14

The day the 1996-97 college hockey season concluded was in many ways a typical day as far as the program at Michigan State was concerned in the 1990s. For when North Dakota battled and ultimately defeated Boston University for the national championship on Saturday, March 28 at the Bradley Center in Milwaukee, Wisc., Michigan State was merely a spectator. For the seventh time in eight tries in the decade, the Spartans had come up short in their bid to reach the Final Four, falling the previous week to Minnesota in the NCAA West Regional in Grand Rapids and ending a season that had often teased with flashes of spectacular play with a not-quite-what-they-had-in-mind 23-13-4 record.

Yet in other rinks in other towns where pucks were dropped with two points in the NHL standings at stake rather than an NCAA Championship trophy, Michigan State was there. In Pittsburgh, the Penguins hosted the Los Angeles Kings with defensemen Jason Woolley and Neil Wilkinson in the lineup. On Long Island, center-winger Anson Carter and the Boston Bruins battled Bryan Smolinski and the Islanders. In Landover, Md.,

Following a standout freshman season, the Detroit Red Wings made Joe Murphy the first U.S. college hockey player drafted No. 1 overall in the National Hockey League. Murphy's NHL career has taken him from Detroit to Edmonton to Chicago and St. Louis.

Kelly Miller and the Washington Capitals greeted Rod Brind' Amour and the Philadelphia Flyers. In Phoenix, Bob Essensa, Rem Murray and the Edmonton Oilers dropped by to say hello to the Coyotes.

This, too, has been a staple of the game in the decade.

When the 1996-97 season opened in September with the historic World Cup of Hockey tournament, MSU had been the only program represented on both finalists (Smolinski played for Team USA, which staked its claim to world dominance with a two-games-to-one victory over Canada and Brind' Amour). And when the Detroit Red Wings ended their 42-year Stanley Cup drought in June, they denied the Flyers and Brind' Amour, who was a warrior throughout even as Philadelphia was getting swept and finished with 13 playoff goals, tying Colorado's Claude Lemieux for the NHL postseason high. In between, the latest wave of Ron Mason-coached players established themselves at professional hockey's highest level, as Carter, Murray and Steve Guolla

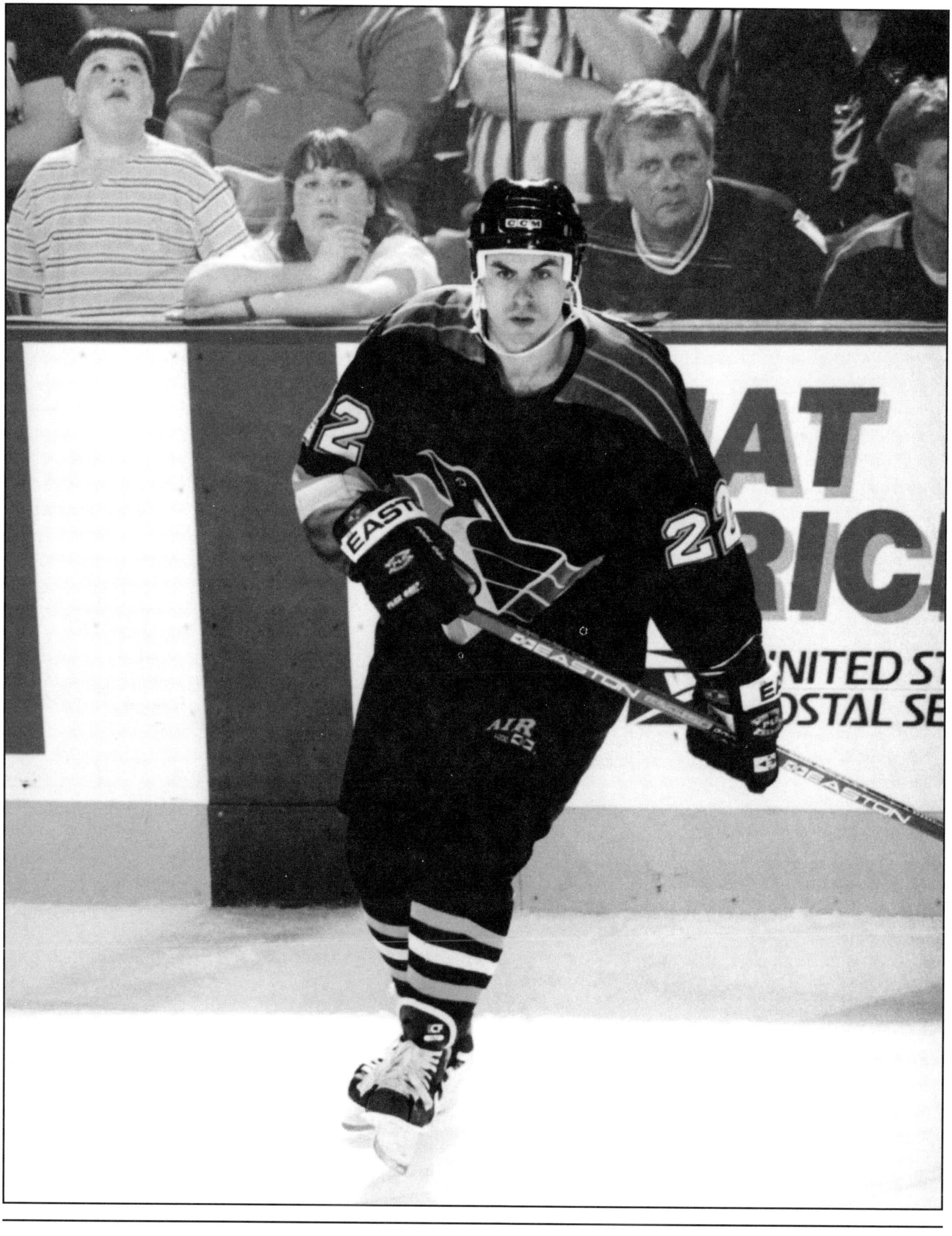
CCM
22
EASTON
22
EASTON
AIR
NITED ST
OSTAL SE
EASTON

(San Jose) made their NHL debuts; Woolley, after four frustrating campaigns in the Washington and Florida organizations, found a niche in Pittsburgh; and Essensa, who had been unjustly scapegoated and banished to the minors following San Jose's monumental playoff upset of Detroit in 1994, made his triumphant return after a couple of years spent wasting away in San Diego, Adirondack, N.Y., and Fort Wayne, Ind.

"The Green and White," Carter observed, "is going strong in the National Hockey League."

Indeed, for on that last Saturday in March when the Fighting Sioux beat BU, there were 14 Michigan State products represented on the daily statistics sheet released by the NHL. Only Wisconsin, with 15, had more.

"There are other teams in college that are powerhouses in college, Michigan for one. But when their players turn pro, what happens to them?" Carter continued. "Coach Mason, he finds pro players. He and his assistants have that eye for talent where some of the guys might not dominate at the college level, but by the time they get to the pros they have what it takes.

"You might not be that type of player when you first get to Michigan State, but by the time you're ready to leave, you're ready to handle anything when it comes to the pros."

That's true in the case of players such as Carter, who spent four seasons in Green, and for those such as Brind'Amour, who played just one season at Michigan State and yet had this to say as his eighth in the NHL was winding down:

"I'm so glad I went there...It was perfect for me."

The NHL obviously agrees.

"The reason our kids do well in the pros is I teach them how to play away from the puck,"

Mason said. "That's something pro coaches respect when they get there. Then they have to show whether they're capable of scoring goals or not, but if they can they'll have a pretty good spot on any team they're on because they're not just about scoring goals.

"Anson Carter knows how to play away from the puck. He can play in a defensive role because he's been taught that. That's what I've heard back from coaches who have coached our kids professionally. When they get them, they're surprised how well they understand the defensive side of the game."

Still, it isn't easy. It isn't as simple for most any recruit as signing on to become a Spartan, putting your time in and then moving on to fame, fortune and the NHL.

This is why Mason coaches perseverance as well as the power play.

Carter knows. A former 10th-round pick of Quebec in 1992, Carter was traded from Colorado to Washington before he had even worn a professional jersey. And at the outset of the 1996-97 season with the Caps, he bounced up and down between the big club and the Caps' American Hockey League affiliate in Portland, Maine, so many times he lost count before finally being set free via a trade to the Boston Bruins.

In Boston, Carter starred, and served notice that much bigger and better things are ahead. Dues, however, were most definitely paid along the way.

"I knew going into the year I was going to spend some time in the minors, whether or not I was good enough to play, because their organization likes to have their top prospects spend at least a year in the minors," Carter explained. "But all the going back and forth, it was tough. It made it tough mentally, because it happened six or seven times and it wasn't a reflection of my play, it was just their way of doing things."

Carter opened the season with the Caps because of injuries, and got to experience an NHL opening night in the home whites and all of its accompanying bells, whistles and glitz.

"The first game was at home against the

After stints with Washington and Florida, Jason Woolley has found a home on the blue line with the Pittsburgh Penguins. Woolley and the other Spartans in the National Hockey League keep close tabs on each other throughout the season.

Photo Courtesy: Pittsburgh Penguins

Chicago Blackhawks...pretty unbelievable, to tell you the truth," Carter said. "I had played in exhibition games, so I didn't think it would be that big a deal, I didn't think I'd be nervous. But I found myself sitting on the bench thinking, 'Wow, there's Chris Chelios, there's Bob Probert, there's Kevin Miller...and here I am playing.'

"The tough part was, I wasn't really playing. I only played four or five shifts that night."

It was like that most nights. The Caps, if they had to dress and play their younger players, were determined to play them only sparingly. Thus Carter, who proved to himself that "I could play at this level" in his third or fourth exhibition game and wound up tied for the team lead in scoring in the preseason, mostly watched. Or headed back to Portland when others got healthy. Or hurriedly returned when injuries struck again.

"One time in the middle of November I was waiting for them to call because I knew they had a lot of injuries. I was sitting at home, watching TV, waiting for the phone to ring...but it didn't ring," Carter said. "All of a sudden it rings at 6 a.m., 'get on a plane and get to Florida.' Here I am with all my winter stuff on; it didn't even register that I was going to Florida, I just went.

"When I got there, this major heat wave strikes me. So I had to go by a golf shirt, shorts, stuff like that because I hadn't brought anything like that with me.

"I played that night after traveling for five or six hours, because when you get called up like that you're not flying charter. I had to go to Boston, then to Pittsburgh and then to Miami, and I had connections delayed.

"I played well, though. I remember I was tired, but I played well, anyway. Everyone even said I had played well. It didn't matter, though. After a couple more days I got sent back down again."

Carter at least found the time to score his first NHL goals between shuttles.

"We're playing Florida and I had just come off the bench on a line change," he said. "Mike Eagles was forechecking and something happened

in the corner, he got tangled up with (Panthers goalie John) Vanbiesbrouck. All of a sudden, I was between the face-off circles and I looked down and the puck was at my feet and there was no one in the net. I one-hopped it in. It wasn't what I had pictured.

"You look in the box score and it says 'Carter 1, unassisted.' I told some of my friends that I had gone coast-to-coast and then top shelf, but they had seen it on the highlights. I had to change my story pretty quick."

Carter had to change his address pretty quickly as well after finally finding out that he had been included as a part of a major, late-season trade between the Capitals and Bruins.

"I'm at a restaurant in Virginia watching a Bullets game with my old college roommate—she lives down there—and we see this blurb go across the screen, 'Caps make big trade, find out more at halftime,'" Carter remembered. "So we race back to her place...and we missed halftime.

"All we heard was the guy saying 'maybe this will finally put them over the edge,' but they didn't mention any names. So I said, I'm going to give (Caps lineman) Jason Allison a call, because he was the only guy whose number I knew by heart.

"So I called him and said 'I heard the Caps made a big trade,' and he said 'yeah, they did.' And I said 'who did they trade, (Peter) Bondra?, (Michal) Pivonka? Who?' And he says 'they traded us.' I thought he was pulling my leg. So I asked him once again 'who did they trade?' And he said 'me, you and Ace (goalie Jim Carey)' I said 'who did they get in return?' He said '(Bill) Ranford, (Adam) Oates and (Rick) Tocchet.'

"I said 'yeah...that is a pretty big trade.'"

Carter wasn't exactly welcomed upon his arrival in Boston.

"It was a media circus every day for a while," he said. "They kept asking me stuff like, 'isn't there a lot of pressure on you? Isn't this another Harry Sinden money-saving deal? I remember one article even said, 'if this Carter kid is so good, how come he spent so much time in the minors?' That really burned me because I knew the kind of player I could be if given an opportunity."

Thankfully, providing an opportunity was what the Bruins had in mind when they traded for Carter. And as a Bruin, Carter played regularly down the stretch with Allison and Tim Sweeney. Carter also played on the power play and killed penalties. And by the time the season had drawn to a close Carter, had scored eight goals and registered five assists for 13 points in his 19 games as a Bruin. His overall rookie numbers included 11 goals, seven assists and 18 points in 38 games, but Carter still wasn't finished.

He followed up his first NHL season by reporting directly to Helsinki, Finland for the annual World Championship tournament. There Carter tied for the team lead with four goals in 11 games and helped lead Canada past Sweden two games to one for the gold medal.

"I told Anson after the tournament, 'I'm not letting you off the hook next season now that I know what you can bring to the table,'" Team Canada and Bruins teammate Don Sweeney told The Hockey News. "Anson was just outstanding."

About the only thing Carter didn't eventually get a handle on as an NHL rookie was how to deal with coming across fellow Spartans now wearing a different sweater on a regular basis.

"Rem Murray tried to get my attention one time when we were playing Edmonton," Carter reported. "But that was back when I was hardly playing with Washington. He was just trying to say hi, but I was so focused on the game because it was one of my rare shifts...we talked afterwards. One time I took a face-off against Smoke (Smolinski) and I said 'what's going on?' I wasn't sure if I should have said that or not.

"I know where our guys are and if a team has them. I know Jason Muzzatti (formerly of Hartford and now a Carolina Hurricanes goalie) and Jason Woolley. I try to talk to them after the games.

"I even fought Brind' Amour one time this year. I was finishing a check and he cross-checked me and I turned around and looked at him and he said 'hey, let's go.' I knew who he was.. and I don't

go looking for fights, but if somebody's gong to drop their gloves and challenge me I'm going to show up.

"It was a pretty good fight, actually. And I wound up dropping him; it was a TKO. The guys in Washington were pretty surprised because that was my first fight in the National Hockey League and he's a pretty big boy, his nickname is 'Rod the Bod' (due to Brind' Amour's devotion to the weight room and body building). I think from that point on I earned a lot of respect from the guys."

Woolley, from a figurative sense, experienced that punch-to-the-head sensation a few times in 1996-97 as well, just as he had since leaving Michigan State following the 1992 Winter Olympics. As it did for Carter, Woolley's season eventually blossomed, but not before he experienced his share of bumps in the road.

"Coming to Pittsburgh allowed me to play in a system that I need to play in, one where I'm most effective," said Woolley, who was dealt to the Pens by Florida along with Stu Barnes in exchange for Chris Wells in mid-November. "I would have been very happy coming here if Mario Lemieux wasn't here and if Jaromir Jagr wasn't here just because I would have finally been able to do my thing.

"But geez, when you look out on the ice and see those guys playing with you, and I played with them most of the year as a unit...I learned so much from these guys, especially Mario...

"Let's put it this way, I'll never forget it."

Prior to his arrival in Pittsburgh, Woolley's career had been mostly forgettable.

He had registered for classes at MSU in January of 1992, but that had mostly been a negotiating ploy. And so when the Olympics ended, Woolley signed on with Washington, which had drafted him on the fourth round in 1989.

"They wanted me to come back because they felt they had a national championship team (the Spartans made it to the Final Four in 1992 but lost to eventual national champion Lake Superior, 4-2, in the semifinals. Had Woolley returned...who knows what might have happened?) But Coach

Mason also wanted me to turn pro. I talked to him quite a bit about it and he had a lot to do with that whole thing," Woolley explained.

What Mason nor anyone else could or would explain was Washington's habit of holding younger players back. Woolley played one game with the Caps and 15 with the AHL's Baltimore Skipjacks in 1991-92. The following year it was 26 in Washington and 29 in Baltimore, then 10 in Washington and 41 with Portland...

"I was treated with such little respect from the time I turned pro until I left that organization," Woolley said. ""I just didn't count. I had always proven myself at the minor-league level. We won a Calder Cup (symbolic of the AHL championship) in Portland. I did everything I could down there..."

It was never enough. Woolley, 6 feet tall and 190 pounds, is more of a finesse defenseman than a physical one. He can skate, he can shoot, he can pass and he can also hold his own in the defensive end. But what he doesn't do is mash people in front of the net, and unfortunately for Woolley some teams simply refuse to look past that.

He was released by Washington and left "relieved to escape all that b.s.," but also with "such a bad taste in my mouth that I wasn't sure if I wanted to play in the NHL anymore."

Woolley settled for playing with the IHL's Detroit Vipers at the start of the 1994-95 season while he tried to sort it all out.

"I came pretty close to saying 'why don't I just sign a three- or four-year deal?'" Woolley acknowledged. "I knew I could make some good money in the IHL and I'd have some security. When you're in that situation, you just don't want to mess with the crap anymore. It's more mentally draining than anything, and that was just killing me."

Luckily for Woolley, he ultimately opted for a deal that would allow him to return to the NHL, an option Woolley would welcome when the Florida Panthers came calling. Or so he thought. Very soon, however, Woolley discovered that the climate in Miami was much the same as it had been in Landover, Md. The Panthers used him sparingly,

or not at all.

By the conclusion of the 1995-96 season, Woolley was little more than a power-play specialist and once again frustrated.

"Not getting the opportunity to earn the respect, and that's not so much from the coaches but from the other players, you have to have the ice time to get that and I just wasn't getting the ice time," he said. "I played three shifts a game if I played.

"I had been so successful at the college and Olympic levels, and I knew I could be successful at the NHL level if I could only get out of the gate. But I had also heard of people getting buried and that worried me. I kind of felt like a horse behind the gate and those doors just wouldn't open.

"I got off to a good start against Boston (in the playoffs) and I kind of got hot, but that all came with ice time, with an opportunity. But when it came to Game 3 against Philadelphia (in the Eastern Conference semifinals), they told me I was sitting again and it was a real shocker."

Woolley was used occasionally against Pittsburgh in the Eastern Conference finals, and even less in the Stanley Cup finals against Colorado.

"And then this year (1996-97) started off just awful," he continued. "I had had a chance to play in 13 playoff games the year before and had had a very good statistical season (34 points in 52 regular-season games, eight more in 13 games in the playoffs) even though there were a lot of games where I just didn't get the ice time. I'd slip in a point here and a point there, and you have to remember that points were hard to come by in Florida. We never scored more than two goals a game. It was like pulling teeth getting points down there.

"But that didn't seem to matter. I never did understand the situation, but I sat the first 16 games. Just sat there and watched. You talk about frustrating...I was right back to square one. I was just hoping somebody would pull me out of it based on my performance the previous year."

The Penguins did.

Suddenly, Woolley was with a team where offense mattered.
Suddenly, Woolley was with a team that would allow him to play his game. The Penguins paired Woolley with fellow offensive defenseman Fredrik Olausson, and played those two behind the line of Lemieux, Jagr and Ron Francis. And although the

Jason Muzzatti was a first round draft pick for the Calgary Flames in 1988. He is among six Spartans to have been selected in the first round of the National Hockey League draft. After several seasons in the Calgary organization, Muzzatti established himself as a top notch netminder with the Hartford Whalers. In the summer of 1997 Hartford traded Muzzatti to the New York Rangers. Photo Courtesy: Calgary Flames

Penguins didn't last long in the postseason (losing in five games to Brind' Amour and the Flyers in Round One), Woolley still managed to become a part of what was clearly one of the most intimidating and imposing five-man units in the league in 1996-97.

Woolley established career highs in games (60), assists (30) and points (36) in his first year with the Pens, and matched his career standard for goals (six).

He also continued following the careers of other ex-Spartans across the NHL, a practice that for Woolley and others became habit the moment they left East Lansing.

"We all take a lot of pride in that," Woolley maintained. "We're all pretty happy for each other, and we all pick up the papers to see how the other guys are doing. I still check on State even when I'm playing here in Pittsburgh. I'm still calling to wish 'em luck in the (NCAA) tournament, and any chance I get to watch them on TV, I like to watch.

"It's very interesting to see that even the people who went to other colleges, they don't have the unity that we have at Michigan State. And the friendships that we keep throughout our NHL careers, I think that's something special.

"The people there are all still so nice, they welcome the pro hockey players back with open arms. And then trainer there, Dave Carrier, he still takes care of us. Guys still call back to him to ask him about injuries.

"The guys (in the NHL) from junior hockey, they can't believe it. I'll be playing against Smolinski or Brind' Amour or whomever, and after the game we'll go out to dinner. And the guys from junior hockey will be saying stuff like 'hey, cut the cord,' or 'give it up,' you know, giving me grief. But I know that they know that there are very few people that have those kind of ties, and that deep down they're kind of jealous.

"It's an awesome feeling, really."

"Awesome" also describes the feeling the 1996-97 Spartans were enjoying after knocking off undefeated Michigan, 5-4, at Munn Arena on Nov. 2. Alas, the feeling wouldn't last. This was an MSU team that had already lost to Eastern lightweights Boston College and Northeastern, and one that would follow up the Michigan win by losing at home to Alaska-Fairbanks.

All season long, the enthusiasm generated by big wins over Michigan (there would be another by a 2-1 count in front of 19,983 at Joe Louis Arena in February), Wisconsin, Colorado College, Lake Superior and Miami would be tempered by almost unconscionable setbacks, including two against lowly Ohio State (one of those was at home, just the Buckeyes' second win ever in Munn Arena).

"We thought this year we'd make the next step," Mason admitted. "I felt this year we really turned the corner in terms of our skill and talent, and that's why we were able to beat the upper-division teams. We had an excellent record against teams above .500 across the country. We beat Michigan twice, we had a winning record against Lake Superior (1-0-2 in league play, although the Lakers embarrassed the Spartans, 5-0, at Joe Louis in the semifinals of the Great Lakes Invitational), we were 3-1 against Miami...That shows me our talent level is definitely improved.

"We lacked experience, though, and ended up getting beat by teams we shouldn't have. That's experience and that's maturity. We didn't have the maturity to make sure we'd win the ones we should have."

The highlight of the season, other than the two wins over the Wolverines, of course, was produced in MSU's final winning effort. Down 3-0 entering the third period in the CCHA semifinals March 14 in Detroit and playing without junior left winger-center Sean Berens, who had been suspended by Mason for violating team rules, the Spartans rallied for three goals to tie Miami, then won the game in overtime.

The low point came eight days later, when the Spartans, fresh from losing the CCHA Playoff Championship to Michigan by a 3-1 count, were drummed out of the NCAA Tournament by Minnesota, 6-3, at Van Andel Arena in Grand Rapids. That loss was Michigan State's seventh straight against Minnesota, and the Spartans' fourth straight in the first round of an NCAA regional.

Still, there was much to be encouraged about, even as the Final Four remained out of reach.

Sophomore center Mike York finished with 18 goals, 29 assists and a team-leading 47 points, and became the first sophomore to top the Spartan scoring chart since Craig Simpson in 1984-85. Junior goaltender Chad Alban allowed three goals or less in 16 of his final 18 starts, turned in a goals against average of 2.72 overall (sixth best in Spartan history) and recorded three shutouts, running his CCHA career record-tying total to six.

The defense allowed just 2.95 goals per game overall, Michigan State's lowest figure since the 2.27 the Spartans coughed up in 1984-85. Six regular defensemen, two reserves and three goaltenders were scheduled to return to attempt to better that mark in 1997-98.

The Spartans finished the regular season with the fourth-best record in the country against teams over .500 (9-5-3), including a 6-5 slate against teams that made the NCAA Tournament.

And the penalty-killing units, despite being riddled for three power-play goals by Minnesota in the season finale, finished with an 87.3 percent success rate.

"Chad's back, the D is back and we'll have three outstanding centers, three centers that are as good as any I've ever had here in York, Berens and Shawn Horcoff, who was great as a freshman," Mason said, looking to the 1997-98 campaign with equal parts enthusiasm and anticipation. "Down the middle and in goal we'll be in great shape.

"Now it all depends on what happens on the wings. If Mike Watt comes back, he's going to be maybe the premier left wing in college hockey."

As spring turned to summer, however, it was unknown whether Watt, a 6-1, 211-pound second-round pick of the Edmonton Oilers in 1994, would return for his senior season or turn pro.

Such are the dilemmas that a program with MSU's pedigree of producing NHL-caliber talent must face.

Watt eventually signed with Edmonton, yet, "we're still going t be a good, solid team," Mason insisted.

"Chad Alban is the best I've ever had, without a doubt, at handling the puck. The other team shoots it in and he gets it and he makes decisions with it. He either passes it and hits the open man or shoots it off the boards into the neutral zone. He's really matured here, he has a chance to be an All-American, he's right there, and he's the kind of kid you have to have in net if you're going to make a run at something.

"Mike York, he'll make the next step. We have a premier player there. And Tyler Harlton is an unbelievable defenseman. He's like a Joby Messier the year Joby was so good (as a first-team All-America selection in 1991-92). You'll see Harlton playing at the next level.

"And Horcoff, he reminds me of Ronnie Francis. He skates a little like Ronnie, he has great work habits and he has unlimited potential."

Perhaps it will be Horcoff that Terry Christensen notices one day when he turns on his television to watch the NHL. Christensen, the head coach of the East Coast Hockey League's Tallahassee Tiger Sharks, was an assistant to Mason at Michigan State from 1980-81 through 1989-90. And like the rest who have left the program for professional hockey, he still keeps tabs on former Spartans populating the NHL.

Perhaps it will be Horcoff after all. Or Peter White, who led the AHL in scoring in 1996-97 as a member of the Philadelphia Phantoms. Or perhaps it will be Watt, or Harlton...

No matter the player, Christensen knows his reaction will be the same.

"There's just such a sense of pride," Christensen said. "And another thing it does, when you turn on the tube and see a guy who played at Michigan State playing in the NHL, when you see him out there performing, it rekindles the great memories that you have of being there."

Memories that, as far as the NHL is concerned, are getting easier and easier to recall all the time for those who have in some way over the years been involved in the awe inspiring, storied history of Spartan Hockey.

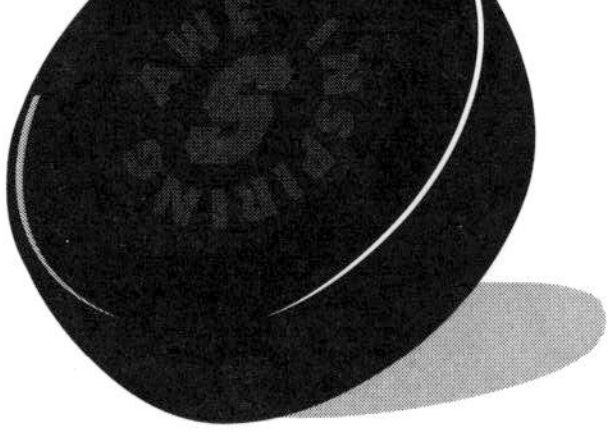
AWE INSPIRING

Memorable Events in Michigan State Spartan Hockey History

● Jan. 11, 1922 ....Michigan State plays its first intercollegiate hockey game, a 5-1 loss to Michigan.

● Feb. 11, 1923....................Michigan State records its first victory, a 6-1 decision over the Lansing Independents.

● Jan. 12, 1950 ....Michigan State plays its first game since 1930, a 6-2 loss to Michigan Tech.

● Nov. 29, 1951 ....Amo Bessone coaches his first game at Michigan State, an 8-2 home win over the Ontario Agricultural College.

● Feb. 6, 1954.....................Michigan State goaltender Ed Schiller makes a Spartan-record 73 saves in a 5-4 loss to Denver.

● Feb. 1956.........................Weldie Olson plays for the United States in the Winter Olympics.

● March 1, 1958..................Michigan State loses at home to Minnesota, 5-1, but completes the first winning season in Spartan history at 12-11.

● March 1959.....................Goalie Joe Selinger is named a first-team All-American.

● March 13-14, 1959 ....Michigan State qualifies for the NCAA Final Four for the first time in school history, defeating Boston College, 4-3, in the semifinals, and losing to North Dakota, 4-3, in overtime, in the national championship game.

● Feb. 1960.........................Weldie Olson and Gene Grazia play for the United States in the Winter Olympics, and Team USA skates away with the gold medal.

● March 1962.....................Goalie John Chandik is named a first-team All-American.

● March 1964.....................Defenseman Carl Lackey is named a first-team All-American.

● March 1965.....................Forward Doug Roberts is named a first-team All-American.

● March 1966.....................Forward Doug Volmar is named a first-team All-American.

● March 18-19, 1966 ....Michigan State defeats Boston University, 2-1, in the semifinals, and then Clarkson, 6-1, in the finals to capture the school's first national championship.

● March 17-18, 1967 ....Michigan State finishes in third place at the Final Four, losing to Boston University, 4-2, in the semifinals, and beating North Dakota, 6-1, in the consolation game.

● Feb. 1968.........................Doug Volmar plays for the United States in the Winter Olympics.

● March 1969.....................Goalie Rick Duffett is named a first-team All-American.

● March 1971.....................Forward Don Thompson is named a first-team All-American.

● March 1972.....................Goalie Jim Watt is named a first-team All-American.

● March 1973.....................Defenseman Bob Boyd is named a first-team All-American.

● Dec. 28, 1973 ....Michigan State wins its first Great Lakes Invitational Tournament championship, beating Michigan Tech, 5-4, in the finals.

● March 1974 ....Defenseman Norm Barnes and forward Steve Colp are named first-team All-Americans.

● Oct. 25, 1974 ....Michigan State opens Munn Arena with a 4-3 loss to Laurentian.

● Nov. 16, 1974 ....Michigan State plays in front of a sellout crowd at Munn Arena (6,255) for the first time during a 6-2 victory over North Dakota. Goalie Ron Clark sets a Spartan record by making 30 saves in the first period.

● March 1975 ....Forward Tom Ross is named a first-team All-American.

● March 1976 ....Forward Tom Ross becomes Michigan State's first two-time first-team All-American.

● March 3, 1979 ....Amo Bessone coaches his final game at Michigan State, a 5-3 win over Michigan.

● Oct. 19, 1979 ....Ron Mason coaches his first game at Michigan State, a 7-6 victory over Western Michigan.

● Feb. 28, 1981 ....Michigan State closes out 22 seasons in the Western Collegiate Hockey Association with a 5-4 overtime victory over Colorado College at home. The Spartans finished 12-22-2 overall and 7-20-1 (last place) in the WCHA.

● Oct. 23, 1981 ....Michigan State opens play in the Central Collegiate Hockey Association with a 4-3 victory over Lake Superior State College at Munn Arena.

● Feb. 13, 1982 ....Michigan State captures its first CCHA playoff championship with a 4-1 victory over Notre Dame at Joe Louis Arena in Detroit.

● March 1982 ....Goalie Ron Scott is named a first-team All-American.

● March 18-19, 1982 ....Michigan State loses, 3-2 and 6-2 at New Hampshire, and drops a two-games, total-goals NCAA first-round series, 9-4.

● Dec. 29, 1982 ....Michigan State defeats Michigan Tech, 5-3, in front of a North American college hockey record crowd of 21,247 at Joe Louis Arena.

● March 1983 ....Goalie Ron Scott becomes Michigan State's second two-time first-team All-American.

● March 12, 1983 ....Michigan State beats Bowling Green, 4-3 in overtime, to win the CCHA playoff championship. Spartans All-America goalie Ron Scott stops Falcons All-America forward Brian Hills on a penalty shot minutes before MSU's game-winning goal in OT.

● March 19-20, 1983 ....Michigan State loses, 6-5, and ties, 3-3, dropping a two-games total-goals NCAA first-round series at Harvard, 9-8.

● Dec. 30, 1983 ....Michigan State wins the Great Lakes Invitational Tournament championship by beating Michigan Tech, 6-2, in front of a North American college hockey record crowd of 21,402 at Joe Louis Arena.

● Dec. 29, 1984 ....Michigan State wins its third consecutive Great Lakes Invitational tournament championship, 7-0 over Michigan Tech, in front of a North American-record crowd of 21,576 at Joe Louis Arena.

● March 17-18, 1984 ....Michigan State finishes fourth at the NCAA Final Four in Lake Placid, N.Y., losing to eventual national champion Bowling Green, 2-1 in the semifinals, and 6-5 to North Dakota in the consolation game.

● March 1985 ....Michigan State places three players on the first-team All-America team for the first time as forwards Kelly Miller and Craig Simpson and defenseman Dan McFall are so honored.

● March 6, 1985 ....Michigan State wins its fourth straight CCHA playoff championship with a 5-1 victory over Lake Superior.

● March 24, 1985 ....Michigan State has its national championship hopes abruptly crushed as Providence pulls off a 4-2 upset and takes a two-games, total-goals series, 6-5, at Munn Arena. The Spartans' record-setting season ends at 38-6 overall, one game short of the Final Four.

● Dec. 27, 1985 ....Michigan State wins its fourth straight Great Lakes Invitational Tournament championship, 2-1 over Michigan Tech.

● March 1986 ....Forward Mike Donnelly is named a first-team All-American.

● March 22, 1986 ....Forward Mike Donnelly sets an NCAA West record for goals by scoring his 55th, 56th and 57th of the season in a 6-4 NCAA Tournament win over Boston College at Munn Arena.

● March 29, 1986 ....Forward Mike Donnelly's 59th goal of the season provides the final margin as Michigan State captures its second national championship with a 6-5 victory over Harvard in the NCAA finals at the Providence Civic Center.

● March 1987 ....Forward Mitch Messier is named a first-team All-American.

● March 7, 1987 ....Michigan State wins its fourth CCHA playoff championship in five years by beating Bowling Green, 4-3, in overtime.

● March 28, 1987 ....Michigan State comes up short in its bid to record back-to-back national championships, losing to North Dakota, 5-3, in the NCAA finals at Joe Louis Arena.

● Feb. 1988 ....Kevin Miller plays for the United States and Geir Hoff plays for Norway in the Winter Olympics.

● March 25-26 1988 ....Michigan State loses 4-2 and 4-3 at Minnesota, blowing a 3-1 third-period lead in the second game and dropping a two-games, total-goals NCAA quarterfinal series, 8-5.

● March 12 1989 ....Michigan State wins its sixth CCHA playoff championship in eight years, 4-1, over Lake Superior.

● March 24-26 1989 ....Michigan State loses 6-3 at Boston College, then storms back to win 7-2 and 5-4 in overtime to capture a best-of-three NCAA quarterfinal series, two games to one, and advance to the Final Four.

● March 1989 ....Forwards Kip Miller and Bobby Reynolds are named first-team All-Americans.

● March 30-April 1 1989 ..Michigan State loses to Harvard, 6-3, in the semifinals at the Final Four in St. Paul, Minn. The Spartans go on to conclude their fourth Final Four appearance over the last six seasons with a 7-4 victory over Maine in the consolation game.

● Feb. 17 1990 ....Michigan State wraps up its second consecutive CCHA regular-season championship and fourth in six years with a 5-2 win at Michigan.

● Feb. 23 1990 ....Michigan State extends its CCHA-record unbeaten streak to 27 games (24-0-3) with a 4-3 victory at Lake Superior.

● March 1990 ....Forward Kip Miller becomes Michigan State's second two-time first-team All-American.

● March 11 1990 ....Michigan State wins its seventh CCHA playoff championship in nine years, 4-3, over Lake Superior.

● March 24-25 1990 ....After beating Boston University, 6-3, in the first game of a best-of-three NCAA quarterfinal series at Munn Arena, Michigan State loses the second game, 5-3, and then blows a 3-1 second-period lead and the series, 5-3, in game three.

● April 1 1990 ....Kip Miller is named the winner of the Hobey Baker Award, college hockey's version of the Heisman Trophy, by the Decathlon Athletic Club of Bloomington, Minn.

● March 1991 ....Defenseman Jason Woolley is named a first-team All-American.

● March 1-2 1991 ....Michigan State loses at Western Michigan, 4-3 and 3-2, in the CCHA quarterfinals. The losses prevent the Spartans from reaching the CCHA Final Four in Detroit for the first time since joining the league in 1981-82, and drop Michigan State to 17-18-5 overall, MSU's first losing season since 1980-81.

● Feb. 1992 ....Jason Woolley plays for Canada in the Winter Olympics.

● March 1992 ....Forward Dwayne Norris and defenseman Joby Messier are named first-team All-Americans.

● March 26-28 1992 ....Michigan State upsets Boston University, 4-2, and Maine, 3-2, to advance to the Final Four.

● April 2 1992 ....Michigan State loses to Lake Superior, 4-2, in the semifinals at the Final Four in Albany, N.Y.

● April 26 1992 ....Ron Mason is awarded the Spencer Penrose Award, given annually by the American Hockey Coaches Association to the Division I Coach of the Year.

● Nov. 21 1992 ....Ron Mason wins his 368th game at Michigan State, 6-2 over Illinois-Chicago, and passes Amo Bessone (367) for first place on the Spartans' all-time list.

● March 1993 ....Forward Bryan Smolinski is named a first-team All-American.

● March 12 1993 ....Ron Mason wins his 675th game overall, 5-2 over Kent, and passes Len Ceglarski for sole possession first place on the all-time U.S. college hockey victories list.

● Jan. 21 1994 ....Ron Mason wins his 400th game at Michigan State, 6-3 at Michigan.

● Feb. 1994 ....Dwayne Norris plays for Canada and Geir Hoff plays for Norway in the Winter Olympics.

● March 18 1994 ....Ron Mason wins his 698th game, 3-2 in overtime over Bowling Green in the CCHA semifinals, and passes Clare Drake for first place on the all-time North American college hockey victories list. The Spartans had trailed 2-0 with under 10 minuts to play, but rallied to force OT by tying the game with 010.9 remaining. Junior Steve Guolla scored all three MSU goals

- March 26 1994 ....Michigan State is eliminated in the first round of the NCAA West Regional at Munn Arena with a 4-3 loss to Massachusetts-Lowell.
- March 24 1995 ....Michigan State is eliminated in the first round of the NCAA West Regional in Madison, Wisc. with a 5-3 loss to Wisconsin.
- March 23 1996 ....Michigan State is eliminated in the first round of the NCAA West Regional at Munn Arena with a 6-2 loss to Massachusetts-Lowell.
- Feb. 15 1997 ....Michigan State extends its regular-season sellouts streak at Munn Arena to 196 and beats Lake Superior, 6-3.
- March 1 1997 ....Goalie Chad Alban ties the CCHA career shutouts record with his sixth in a 0-0 tie with Bowling Green.
- March 14 1997 ....Michigan State rallies from a 3-0 third-period deficit to defeat Miami, Ohio, 4-3 in overtime, in the CCHA semifinals.
- March 22 1997 ....Michigan State is eliminated in the first round of the NCAA West Regional in Grand Rapids with a 6-3 loss to Minnesota.

Spartan Hockey Records

● Career Goals
138 - Tom Ross (1972-76)
132 - Steve Colp (1972-76)
116 - Kip Miller (1986-90)
110 - Mike Donnelly (1982-86)
107 - Bobby Reynolds (1985-89)
106 - Anson Carter (1992-96)
105 - Dwayne Norris (1988-92)
103 - Shawn Heaphy (1987-91)
 98 - Mark Hamway (1979-83)
 96 - Daryl Rice (1972-76)

● Career Assists
186 - Tom Ross (1972-76)
168 - Steve Colp (1972-76)
155 - Peter White (1988-92)
147 - Rem Murray (1991-95)
145 - Kip Miller (1986-90)
140 - Kevin Miller (1984-88)
136 - Bill Shibicky (1983-87)
132 - John Sturges (1972-76)
130 - Steve Suk (1991-95)
129 - Daryl Rice (1972-75)

● Career Points
324 - Tom Ross (1972-76)
300 - Steve Colp (1972-76)
261 - Kip Miller (1986-90)
230 - Peter White (1988-92)
225 - Daryl Rice (1972-76)
222 - Bill Shibicky (1983-87)
218 - Rem Murray (1991-95)
218 - Dwayne Norris (1988-92)
210 - Mitch Messier (1983-87)
209 - John Sturges (1972-76)

● Career Penalty Minutes
466 - Don Gibson (1986-90)
371 - Tony Tuzzolino (1994-97)
323 - Bill Shibicky (1983-87)
308 - Nicolas Perreault (1991-94)
304 - Jim Cummins (1988-91)
299 - Kip Miller (1986-90)
287 - Kohn Sturges (1972-76)
286 - Bob Boyd (1970-73)
284 - Joby Messier (1988-92)
277 - Kevin Miller (1984-88)

● Career Goals-Against Average
(30 games minimum)
2.65 - Bob Essensa (1983-87)
2.88 - Mike Gilmore (1988-92)
2.98 - Mike Buzak (1991-95)
3.00 - Chad Alban (1994-97)
3.08 - Ron Scott (1980-83)
3.09 - Joe Selinger (1956-59)
3.14 - Norm Foster (1983-87)
3.23 - Jason Muzzatti (1987-91)
3.54 - Rick Duffett (1967-71)
3.62 - Gaye Cooley (1965-67)

Season Goals
59 - Mike Donnelly (1985-86)
51 - Tom Ross (1975-76)
48 - Kip Miller (1989-90)
44 - Dwayne Norris (1991-92)
44 - Mitch Messier (1986-87)
43 - Bill Shibicky (1986-87)
43 - Steve Colp (1973-74)
42 - Bobby Reynolds (1987-88)
40 - Steve Colp (1975-76)
38 - Tom Ross (1974-75)

Season Assists
60 - Pat Murray (1989-90)
59 - Tom Ross (1974-75)
56 - Kevin Miller (1986-87)
56 - Norm Barnes (1973-74)
54 - Steve Colp (1975-76)
54 - Tom Ross (1975-76)
54 - Steve Colp (1973-74)
53 - Kip Miller (1989-90)
53 - Craig Simpson (1984-85)
52 - Kevin Miller (1985-86)
52 - Newell Brown (1981-82)
52 - John Sturges (1974-75)

Season Points
105 - Tom Ross (1975-76)
101 - Kip Miller (1989-90)
 97 - Mike Donnelly (1985-86)
 97 - Tom Ross (1974-75)
 97 - Steve Colp (1973-74)
 94 - Steve Colp (1975-76)
 92 - Mitch Messier (1986-87)
 88 - Tom Ross (1973-74)
 84 - Pat Murray (1989-90)
 84 - Craig Simpson (1984-85)

Season Penalty Minutes
167 - Don Gibson (1989-90)
134 - Ron Heaslip (1976-77)
129 - Jeff Harding (1978-88)
124 - Bob Boyd (1972-73)
120 - Tony Tuzzolino (1996-97)
120 - Tony Tuzzolino (1995-96)
118 - Don Gibson (1987-88)
113 - Bruce Rendall (1986-87)
112 - Kevin Miller (1985-86)
110 - Jim Cummins (1990-91)

Season Goals-Against Average
(15 games minimum)
1.64 - Bob Essensa (1984-85)
2.63 - Norm Foster (1984-85)
2.64 - Ron Scott (1982-83)
2.66 - Mike Gilmore (1990-91)
2.67 - Joe Selinger (1958-59)
2.72 - Chad Alban (1996-97)
2.72 - Mike Buzak (1993-94)
2.74 - Norm Foster (1983-84)
2.74 - Rick Duffett (1968-69)
2.79 - Bob Essensa (1983-84)

● **Year by Year Leaders - Goals**
1949-50 - Don Kauppi, Bill McCormick, 6
1950-51 - Bill McCormick, 11
1951-52 - Weldie Olson, 13
1952-53 - Weldie Olson, 18
1953-54 - Weldie Olson, 19
1954-55 - Weldie Olson, 21
1955-56 - Gene Grazia, Ross Parke, 15
1956-57 - Ross Parke, 12
1957-58 - Ross Parke, 19
1958-59 - Terry Moroney, 23
1959-60 - Jack Roberts, 8
1960-61 - Art Thomas, 17
1961-62 - Claude Fournel, 20
1962-63 - Bob Doyle, Dick Johnstone, 15
1963-64 - Doug Roberts, 21
1964-65 - Mike Jacobson, 29
1965-66 - Doug Volmar, 26
1966-67 - Tom Mikkola, Doug Volmar, 21
1967-68 - Nino Christofoli, 16
1968-69 - Ken Anstey, Bill Watt, 13
1969-70 - Gilles Gagnon,
         Don Thompson, 14
1970-71 - Gilles Gagnon, 27
1971-72 - Don Thompson, 32
1972-73 - Steve Colp, 35
1973-74 - Steve Colp, 43
1974-75 - Tom Ross, 38
1975-76 - Tom Ross, 51
1976-77 - Russ Welch, 22
1977-78 - Leo Lynett, 18
1978-79 - Joe Omiccioli, 20
1979-80 - Leo Lynett, 27
1980-81 - Mark Hamway, 18
1981-82 - Mark Hamway, 34
1982-83 - Mark Hamway, 30
1983-84 - Kelly Miller, 28
1984-85 - Craig Simpson, 31
1985-86 - Mike Donnelly, 59
1986-87 - Mitch Messier, 44
1987-88 - Bobby Reynolds, 42
1988-89 - Bobby Reynolds, 36
1989-90 - Kip Miller, 48
1990-91 - Shawn Heaphy, 30
1991-92 - Dwayne Norris, 44

1992-93 - Bryan Smolinski, 31
1993-94 - Anson Carter, 30
1994-95 - Anson Carter, 34
1995-96 - Anson Carter, 23
1996-97 - Mike Watt, 24

● **Year by Year Leaders - Assists**
1949-50 - Bob Gorman, 7
1950-51 - Neil Bristol, Dick Lord,
         Bob Revou, 9
1951-52 - Jack Mayes, 18
1952-53 - Steve Raz, 18
1953-54 - Weldie Olson, 22
1954-55 - Jim Ward, 28
1955-56 - Ross Parke, 21
1956-57 - Ross Parke, 13
1957-58 - Joe Polano, 23
1958-59 - Dick Hamilton, 26
1959-60 - Andre LaCoste, 8
1960-61 - Real Turcotte, 28
1961-62 - Real Turcotte, 25
1962-63 - Dick Johnstone, 14
1963-64 - Mac Orme, 25
1964-65 - Doug Roberts, 33
1965-66 - Doug Volmar, 28
1966-67 - Sandy McAndrew,
         Tom Mikkola, 25
1967-68 - Ken Anstey, 19
1968-69 - Ken Anstey, 20
1969-70 - Don Thompson, 18
1970-71 - Don Thompson, 38
1971-72 - Don Thompson, 35,
1972-73 - Bob Boyd, 41
1973-74 - Norm Barnes, 56
1974-75 - Tom Ross, 59
1975-76 - Tom Ross, Steve Colp, 54
1976-77 - Jim Cunningham, 35
1977-78 - Russ Welch, 23
1978-79 - Russ Welch, 30
1979-80 - Russ Welch, 37
1980-81 - Gary Haight, 17
1981-82 - Newell Brown, 51
1982-83 - Newell Brown,
         Mark Hamway, 29
1983-84 - Craig Simpson, 43

1984-85 - Craig Simpson, 53
1985-86 - Kevin Miller, 52
1986-87 - Kevin Miller, 56
1987-88 - Steve Beadle, 37
1988-89 - Kip Miller, 45
1989-90 - Pat Murray, 60
1990-91 - Jason Woolley, 44
1991-92 - Peter White, 51
1992-93 - Bryan Smolinski, 37
1993-94 - Steve Guolla, 46
1994-95 - Rem Murray, 36
1995-96 - Mike York, 27
1996-97 - Mike York, 29

● Year by Year Leaders - Points
1949-50 - Don Kauppi, 11
1950-51 - Bill McCormick, 18
1951-52 - Jack Mayes, 29
1952-53 - Jack Mayes, 30
1953-54 - Weldie Olson, 41
1954-55 - Jim Ward, 43
1955-56 - Ross Parke, 36
1956-57 - Ross Parke, 25
1957-58 - Ross Parke, 36
1958-59 - Joe Polano, 41
1959-60 - Jack Roberts, 14
1960-61 - Real Turcotte, 43
1961-62 - Claude Fourne, 35
1962-63 - Dick Johnstone, 29
1963-64 - Mac Orme, 40
1964-65 - Doug Roberts, 61
1965-66 - Doug Volmar, 54
1966-67 - Tom Mikkola, 46
1967-68 - Ken Anstey, 30
1968-69 - Ken Anstey, 33
1969-70 - Don Thompson, 32
1970-71 - Don Thompson, 57
1971-72 - Don Thompson, 67
1972-73 - Steve Colp, 60
1973-74 - Steve Colp, 97
1974-75 - Tom Ross, 97
1975-76 - Tom Ross, 105
1976-77 - Russ Welch, 44
1977-78 - Russ Welch, 40
1978-79 - Russ Welch, 46

1979-80 - Leo Lynett, 61
1980-81 - Mark Hamway, 33
1981-82 - Newell Brown, 73
1982-83 - Mark Hamway, 59
1983-84 - Craig Simpson, 57
1984-85 - Craig Simpson, 84
1985-86 - Mike Donnelly, 97
1986-87 - Mitch Messier, 92
1987-88 - Bobby Reynolds, 67
1988-89 - Bobby Reynolds, Kip Miller, 77
1989-90 - Kip Miller, 101
1990-91 - Jason Wolley, 59
1991-92 - Dwayne Norris, 83
1992-93 - Bryan Smolinski, 68
1993-94 - Steve Guolla, 69
1994-95 - Rem Murray, 56
1995-96 - Anson Carter, 43
1996-97 - Mike York, 47

● Year by Year Leaders - Penalty Minutes
1949-50 - Jim Doyle, 20
1950-51 - Dick Lord, 48
1951-52 - Dick Lord, 59
1952-53 - Derio Nicoli, 60
1953-54 - Derio Nicoli, 65
1954-55 - Derio Nicoli, 73
1955-56 - Butch Miller, 56
1956-57 - Ed Pollesel, 63
1957-58 - Fred Devuono, 50
1958-59 - Ed Pollesel, 70
1959-60 - Ed Ozybko, 48
1960-61 - Marty Quirk, 50
1961-62 - Jim Jacobson, 44
1962-63 - Jim Jacobson, 79
1963-64 - Jim Jacobson, 79
1964-65 - Bob Brawley, 59
1965-66 - Tom Purdo, 57
1966-67 - Doug Volmar, 100
1967-68 - Dick Bois, 56
1968-69 - Bill Watt, 45
1969-70 - Bill Watt, 72
1970-71 - Bob Boyd, 88
1971-72 - Rick Olson, 85
1972-73 - Bob Boyd, 124

1973-74 - Norm Barnes, 107
1974-75 - John Sturges, 93
1975-76 - John Sturges, 80
1976-77 - Ron Heaslip, 134
1977-78 - Jeff Barr, 85
1978-79 - Ted Huesing, 68
1979-80 - Ken Leiter, 96
1980-81 - Gary Haight, 64
1981-82 - Gary Haight, 75
1982-83 - Newell Brown, 70
1983-84 - Harvey Smyl, 92
1984-85 - Harvey Smyl, 100
1985-86 - Kevin Miller, 112
1986-87 - Bruce Rendall, 113
1987-88 - Jeff Harding, 129
1988-89 - Don Gibson, 107
1989-90 - Don Gibson, 106
1990-91 - Jim Cummins, 101
1991-92 - Joby Messier, 85
1992-93 - Bryan Smolinski, 91
1993-94 - Nicolas Perreault, 109
1994-95 - Tony Tuzzolino, 81
1995-96 - Tony Tuzzolino, 120
1996-97 - Tony Tuzzolino, 120

● **Year by Year Leaders -**
  Goals-Against Average
  (10 games minimum)
1949-50 - Delmar Reid, 11.20
1950-51 - Delmar Reid, 5.80
1951-52 - Delmar Reid, 5.73
1952-53 - Gerald Bergin, 5.28
1953-54 - Ed Schiller, 3.73
1954-55 - Ed Schiller, 4.58
1955-56 - Ed Schiller, 4.28
1956-57 - Joe Selinger, 3.40
1957-58 - Joe Selinger, 3.27
1958-59 - Joe Selinger, 2.67
1959-60 - Eldon VanSpybrook, 5.24
1960-61 - John Chandik, 3.53
1961-62 - John Chandik, 3.79
1962-63 - John Chandik, 4.30
1963-64 - Harry Woolf, 4.33
1964-65 - Alex Terpay, 2.54
1965-66 - Gaye Cooley, 3.11

1966-67 - Gaye Cooley, 4.00
1967-68 - Rick Duffett, 3.40
1968-69 - Rick Duffett, 2.74
1969-70 - Rick Duffett, 4.10
1970-71 - Jim Watt, 4.08
1971-72 - Jim Watt, 3.55
1972-73 - Ron Clark, 3.96
1973-74 - Gary Carr, 4.43
1974-75 - Ron Clark, 4.31
1975-76 - Dave Versical, 4.32
1976-77 - Dave Versical, 5.43
1977-78 - Mark Mazzoleni, 5.36
1978-79 - Doug Belland, 5.07
1979-80 - Mark Mazzoleni, 5.81
1980-81 - Ron Scott, 3.89
1981-82 - Ron Scott, 2.85
1982-83 - Ron Scott, 2.64
1983-84 - Norm Foster, 2.74
1984-85 - Bob Essensa, 1.64
1985-86 - Bob Essensa, 3.33
1986-87 - Bob Essensa, 2.78
1987-88 - Jason Muzzatti, 3.41
1988-89 - Jason Muzzatti, 3.03
1989-90 - Mike Gilmore, 2.73
1990-91 - Mike Gilmore, 2.66
1991-92 - Mike Gilmore, 3.07
1992-93 - Mike Buzak, 2.93
1993-94 - Mike Buzak, 2.72
1994-95 - Chad Alban, 2.73
1995-96 - Chad Alban, 3.07
1996-97 - Chad Alban, 2.72

Team Records

SEASON

Most Wins - 38 (1984-85)
Most Losses - 27 (1977-78)
Most Ties - 8 (1990-91)
Most Points - 76 (1984-85)
Most Games Played - 47 (1988-89)
Highest Winning Percentage - .864 (38-6-0, 1984-85)
Highest Winning Pct., Home - .913 (20-1-2, 1985-86)
Highest Winning Pct., Road - .864 (19-3-0, 1984-85)
Lowest Winning Percentage - .000 (0-14-0, 1950)
Lowest Winning Pct., Home - .000 (0-8-0, 1950)
Lowest Winning Pct., Road - .000 (0-6-0, 1950)
Most Goals - 277 (1988-89)
Most Assists - 439 (1988-89)
Most Total Points - 716 (1988-89)
Most Penalties - 524 (1987-88)
Most Penalty Minutes - 1,109 (1988-89)
Most Power-Play Goals - 91 (1988-89)
Most Short-Handed Goals - 24 (1983-84)
Most Saves - 1,555 (1975-76)
Most Shutouts - 4 (1958-59; 1995-96)
Most Overtime Games - 11 (1991-92; 1986-87)
Largest Goal Differential - 162 (1984-85)
Longest Unbeaten Streak -
    22 (Dec. 29, 1984-Feb. 15, 1985)
Longest Winning Streak -
    22 (Dec. 29, 1984-Feb. 15, 1985)
Longest Winning Streak, Home -
    16 (Jan. 6, 1984-Nov. 23, 1984)
Longest Unbeaten Streak, Home -
    20 (Jan. 4, 1986-Nov. 1, 1986)
Longest Winning Streak, Road -
    12 (Oct. 15, 1988-Dec. 15, 1988)
Longest CCHA Unbeaten Streak -
    27 (Oct. 27, 1989-Feb. 23, 1990)
Most 20 - Goal Scorers - 7
    (Rod Brind'Amour, Danton Cole, Shawn Heaphy,
    Kip Miller, Pat Murray, Bobby Reynolds and
    Peter White) (1988-89)
Most Game Misconduct Penalties-11 (1990-91)

SERIES

Most Goals - 26, vs. Ohio (Feb. 17-18, 1961)
Most Assists - 48, vs. Ohio (Feb. 17-18, 1961)
Most Points - 74, vs. Ohio (Feb. 17-18, 1961)
Most Penalties - 37, vs. Ohio State (Oct. 10-11, 1986)
Most Penalty Minutes -
    91, vs. Ferris State (Dec. 15-16, 1988)
Most Saves -
    123, vs. Denver (Feb. 5-6, 1954)
Largest Margin of Goals -
    24, vs. Ohio (MSU 25-1; Dec. 4-5, 1964)

GAME

Most Goals - 18, vs. Ohio State (Dec. 7, 1957)
Most Assists - 28, vs. Bowling Green (Feb. 8, 1985)
Most Points - 43, vs. Bowling Green (Feb. 8, 1985)
Most Penalties -
    23, vs. Miami (Jan. 9, 1988), Ohio State
    (Oct. 10, 1986) and Ferris State (Jan. 18, 1985)
Most Penalty Minutes -
    60, vs. Northeastern (Oct. 15, 1983)
Largest Margin of Victory -
    18, vs. Ohio State (MSU 18-0, Dec. 7, 1957)
Most Game Misconduct Penalties -
    6, vs. Michigan (Feb. 16, 1991)
Fewest Saves -
    6, vs. Miami (Oct. 24, 1986)
    7, vs. Boston University (Nov. 18, 1988)
    8, vs. Alaska Fairbanks (Jan. 8, 1985)
    9, vs. Michigan (Jan. 26, 1985)

PERIOD

Most Goals - 8, vs. Ohio State (Dec. 7, 1957 - 3rd)
Most Assists - 14, vs. Ferris State (March 3, 1990 - 2nd)
Most Points - 21, vs. Ferris State (March 3, 1990 - 2nd)
Most Penalties - 14, vs. Michigan (Feb. 16, 1991 - 1st)
Most Penalty Minutes -
    53, vs. Ferris State (Dec. 16, 1988 - 2nd)
Most Saves -
    30, vs. North Dakota (Nov. 16, 1974 - 1st)
Largest Margin of Goals -
    8, vs. Ohio State (Dec. 7, 1957 - 3rd)

Spartan Honor Roll

HOBEY BAKER MEMORIAL AWARD

1990 Kip Miller

FIRST-TEAM ALL-AMERICA SELECTIONS

Selected by Amencan Hockey Coaches Association

1959 Joe Selinger, G
1962 John Chandik, G
1964 Carl Lackey, D
1965 Doug Roberts, F
1966 Doug Volmar, F
1969 Rick Duffett, G
1971 Don Thompson, F
1972 Jim Watt, G
1973 Bob Boyd, D
1974 Norm Barnes, D
     Steve Colp, F
1975 Tom Ross, F
1976 Tom Ross, F
1982 Ron Scott, G
1983 Ron Scott, G
1985 Dan McFall, D
     Kelly Miller, F
     Craig Simpson, F
1986 Mike Donnelly, F
1987 Mitch Messier, F
1989 Kip Miller, F
     Bobby Reynolds, F
1990 Kip Miller, F
1991 Jason Woolley, D
1992 Joby Messier, D
     Dwayne Norris, F
1993 Bryan Smolinski, F

SECOND-TEAM ALL-AMERICA SELECTIONS

Selected by American Hockey Coaches Association

1984 Dan McFall, D
1985 Gary Haight, D
1986 Don McSween, D
1987 Don McSween, D
1990 Jason Muzzatti, G
1994 Steve Guolla, F
1995 Anson Carter, F

BAUER COLLEGE HOCKEY PLAYER OF THE YEAR

1986 Mike Domnelly
1990 Kip Miller

CCHA PLAYER OF THE YEAR

1990 Kip Miller
1992 Dwayne Norris

CCHA ROOKIE OF THE YEAR

1984 Bill Shibicky
1986 Joe Murphy
1989 Rod Brind'Amour

CCHA COACH OF THE YEAR

1985 Ron Mason
1989 Ron Mason
1990 Ron Mason

NCAA Championship Summary

Year	Champion	Runner-Up	Third Place	Fourth Place	Site
1948	Michigan	Dartmouth	Boston College/Colorado College		Colorado Springs, Colo.
1949	Boston College	Dartmouth	Michigan	Colorado College	Colorado Springs, Colo.
1950	Colorado College	Boston University	Michigan	Boston College	Colorado Springs, Colo.
1951	Michigan	Brown	Boston University	Colorado College	Colorado Springs, Colo.
1952	Michigan	Colorado College	Yale	St. Lawrence	Colorado Springs, Colo.
1953	Michigan	Minnesota	Rensselaer	Boston University	Colorado Springs, Colo.
1954	Rensselaer	Minnesota	Michigan	Boston College	Colorado Springs, Colo.
1955	Michigan	Colorado College	Harvard	St. Lawrence	Colorado Springs, Colo.
1956	Michigan	Michigan Tech	St. Lawrence	Boston College	Colorado Springs, Colo.
1957	Colorado College	Michigan	Clarkson	Harvard	Colorado Springs, Colo.
1958	Denver	North Dakota	Clarkson	Harvard	Minneapolis, Minn.
1959	North Dakota	**MICHIGAN STATE**	Boston College	St. Lawrence	Troy, N.Y.
1960	Denver	Michigan Tech	Boston University	St. Lawrence	Boston, Mass.
1961	Denver	St. Lawrence	Minnesota	Rensselaer	Denver, Colo.
1962	Michigan Tech	Clarkson	Michigan	St. Lawrence	Hamilton, N.Y.
1963	North Dakota	Denver	Clarkson	Boston College	Boston, Mass.
1964	Michigan	Denver	Rensselaer	Providence	Denver, Colo.
1965	Michigan Tech	Boston College	North Dakota	Brown	Providence, R.I.
1966	**MICHIGAN STATE**	Clarkson	Denver	Boston University	Minneapolis, Minn.
1967	Cornell	Boston University	**MICHIGAN STATE**	North Dakota	Syracuse, N.Y.
1968	Denver	North Dakota	Cornell	Boston College	Duluth, Minn.
1969	Denver	Cornell	Harvard	Michigan Tech	Colorado Springs, Colo.
1970	Cornell	Clarkson	Wisconsin	Michigan Tech	Lake Placid, N.Y.
1971	Boston University	Minnesota	Denver	Harvard	Syracuse, N.Y.
1972	Boston University	Cornell	Wisconsin	Denver	Boston, Mass.
1973	Wisconsin	Denver	Boston College	Cornell	Boston, Mass.
1974	Minnesota	Michigan Tech	Boston University	Harvard	Boston, Mass.
1975	Michigan Tech	Minnesota	Boston University	Harvard	St. Louis, Mo.
1976	Minnesota	Michigan Tech	Brown	Boston University	Denver, Colo.
1977	Wisconsin	Michigan	Boston University	New Hampshire	Detroit, Mich.
1978	Boston University	Boston College	Bowling Green	Wisconsin	Providence, R.I.
1979	Minnesota	North Dakota	Dartmouth	New Hampshire	Detroit, Mich.
1980	North Dakota	Northern Michigan	Dartmouth	Cornell	Providence, R.I.
1981	Wisconsin	Minnesota	Michigan Tech	Northern Michigan	Duluth, Minn.
1982	North Dakota	Wisconsin	Northeastern	New Hampshire	Providence, R.I.
1983	Wisconsin	Harvard	Providence	Minnesota	Grand Forks, N.D.
1984	Bowling Green	Minnesota-Duluth	North Dakota	**MICHIGAN STATE**	Lake Placid, N.Y.
1985	Rensselaer	Providence	Minnesota-Duluth	Boston College	Detroit, Mich.
1986	**MICHIGAN STATE**	Harvard	Minnesota	Denver	Providence, R.I.
1987	North Dakota	**MICHIGAN STATE**	Minnesota	Harvard	Detroit, Mich.
1988	Lake Superior	St. Lawrence	Maine	Minnesota	Lake Placid, N.Y.
1989	Harvard	Minnesota	**MICHIGAN STATE**/Maine		St. Paul, Minn.
1990	Wisconsin	Colgate	Boston College/Boston University		Detroit, Mich.
1991	Northern Michigan	Boston University	Clarkson/Maine		St. Paul, Minn.
1992	Lake Superior	Wisconsin	**MICHIGAN STATE**/Michigan		Albany, N.Y.
1993	Maine	Lake Superior	Boston University/Michigan		Milwaukee, Wis.
1994	Lake Superior	Boston University	Harvard/Minnesota		St. Paul, Minn.
1995	Boston University	Maine	Michigan/Wisconsin		Providence, R.I.
1996	Michigan	Colorado College	Vermont/Boston University		Cincinnati, Ohio
1997	North Dakota	Boston University	Michigan/Colorado College		Milwaukee, Wis.

*No Consolation games played in 1948, and from 1990 to present

Coaches Register

Coach	Years	Seasons Coached	G	W	L	T	PCT.
No established coach	1922-23	2	9	2	7	0	.222
John Kobs	1925-30	6	27	8	18	1	.315
HaroldPaulsen	1950-51	2	31	6	25	0	.194
Amo Bessone	1951-79	28	814	367	427	20	.463
Ron Mason	1979-present	18	763	486	233	44	.666
TOTALS	**1922-96**	**56**	**1644**	**879**	**710**	**65**	**.554**

DON'T MISS SPARTAN HOCKEY at THE JOE

IT'S SMART HOCKEY

98

SCHEDULE OF GAMES

33rd Great Lakes Invitational
Saturday, December 27 @ 6:30pm
Sunday, December 28 @ TBD
"Smart Hockey" Doubleheader
Saturday, February 21 @ 7:00pm
CCHA Championship
Friday, March 20 @ 5:00pm and 8:30pm
Saturday, March 21 @ 7:30pm

COLLEGE HOCKEY AT "THE JOE"

Order your seats NOW! (313) 396-7575

Proud to Support Spartan Hockey

From savings accounts to low-cost loans, MSU Federal Credit Union can help with your financial *goals*.

MSUFCU serves MSU faculty, staff, students, alumni and their families. Call member services at 333-2424.

MICHIGAN STATE UNIVERSITY
FEDERAL CREDIT UNION
–the financial institution of the MSU community–

Main Office • 600 E. Crescent Rd. • (517) 353-2280
800-MSU-4-YOU • http://www.msufcu.org
523 East Grand River • (517) 353-5565
1925 West Grand River • (517) 353-0886 NCUA

Spartan Letterwinners

Name; Years Lettered; Position; Jersey Number; Hometown; (Goals-Assists-Points or Goals-Against Average, Saves); Penalties/Minutes

A

Adamo, Vincent; '95-96-97; Mgr.; Rochester

Adams, Bryan; '96-97; F; #16; Fort St. James, B.C.; (10-15-25); 22/63

Addley, Jeffery; '74-75-76-77; F; #19; Wayne, N.J.; (16-15-31); 18/36

Alban, Chad; '95-96-97; G; #29; Kalamazoo; (2.88, 1,937 savw); 10/31

Albers, Matt; '92-93-94; C; #25; Ann Arbor; (83-11); 38n7

Altobelli, Aldo; '57-58; G; #20; West Springfield, Mass.; (1.50; 31 saves)

Anastos, Thomas; '82-83-84-85; P; #20; Dearbom; (70-73-143); 48/102

Anstey, Kenneth; '67-68-69; F; #11; Sudbury, Ont.; (33-49-82); 17/34

Arkeilpane, David; ' 86-87; F; #26; Amherst, N.Y.; (12-12-24); 19/38

Armstrong, Robert; ' 58-59-60; D; #3; Chatham, Ont.; (1-7-8); 40/83

Atack, James; '59-60-61; F; #8; Niagara Falls, Ont.; (8-15-23); 7/14

B

Bacon, Jeff; '79; F; #6; Mississauga, Ont.; (2-35); 13/29

Balai, Joseph T.; '56; F;#17; Marquette; (4-0-4); 4/8

Baldwin, Patrick; '61-62-63; F; #19; Detroit; (1913-32); 11/22

Barker, Arthur; '56; D; #2; Calgary, Alta; (1-12); 5/10

Bames, Norrnan; '72-73-74; D; #3; Rexdale, Ont.; (22-98-120); 120/249

Barr, Jeffery; '76-77-78-79; D; #23; Bloomington, Minn.; (3-24-27); 121/266

Barrett, Robert; '81-82; Mgr.; Grosse Pointe Woods

Barry, Robert; '52-53; D; #3; Boston, Mass.; (23-5): 1/2

Bartels, Walter; ' 88-89-90-91; F; #25; Plymouth; (19-33-52); 20/40

Beadle, Steve; '87-88-89-90; D; #4; Lansing; (42122-164); 66/134

Beaty, Daniel; '82-83; F; #19; Bloomington, Minn.; (8-17-25); 17/34

Beck, Brad; '83-84-55-86; D; #4; Vancouver, B.C.; (15-55-70); 92/209

Belland, Douglas; '79-80; G; #I; Sudbury, Ont.; (5.66; 984 saves)

Berens, Sean; '95-96-97; F; #18; Palatine, Ill.; (48-S5-103); 43/94

Bergin, Gerald; ' 52-53; G; #I; Detroit; (5.00; 550 saves)

Betterly, Patrick; '75-76,'78; D; #6; Detroit; (2568-93); 42/99

Blair, William; '50-51; D;#6; Atlantic, N.J.; (1110-21); 9/18

Blostein, Jay; '75-76-77; Mgr.; Metuchen, N.J.

Bogas, Christopher; '96-97; D; #4; Cleveland Heights, Ohio; (8-24-32); Sl/113

Bois, Richard; '66-67-68; D; #3; Espanola, Ont.; (8-20-28); 71/148

Bolton, Darl; '73-74-75-76; C; #21; Copper Cliff, Ont.; (10-15-25); 15/30

Bolton, George; '51, '53, '56; F; #12; Grosse Pointe; (6-4-10); 6/12

Bonnacci, Anthony; '57; D; #17; Sault Ste. Marie; (3-1-4); 5/10

Boucher, Thomas; '58, '60-61; F; #7; Sudbury, Ont.; (3-5-8); 2/4

Bowen, Thomas; '73-74; G; #I; Birmingham; (4.41; 415 saves)

Bowman, Gary; '58; D; #14; Detroit; (0-0-0); 1/2

Boyd, Robert; '71-72-73; D; #5; Rexdale, Ont.; (21-90-111); 126/286

Brawley, Robert; '65-66-67; D; #2; Sault Ste. Marie; (5-24-29); 64/131

Breck, Samuel; '51; Mgr.; Detroit

Brind'Amour, Rod; '89; F; #21; CampbellRiver, B.C.; (27-32-59); 27/63

Bnstol, Comelius; '50-51; F; #7; Greenwich, Conn.; (8-13-21); 7/14

Brothers, Kenneth; '77; F; #20; St. Clair Shores; (3-3-6); 3/6

Brooks, Raynard; '51-52-53; F; #15/16; Chatham, N.Y.; (8-19-27); 18/44

Brusseau, Michael; '96-97; G; #39; Detroit; (3.67, 135 saves); 3/17

Brown, Newell; '81-82-83-84; F; #8; Comwall, Ont.; (75-127-202); 100/208

Brown, Steve; ' 84-85-86-87; Mgr.; Brooklyn

Buck, Conrad; '51-52; F; #5; Lexington,

Mass.; (12-6-18); 8/16

Bullock, Robert; '81; F; #14; Newark, Del.; (00-0), 5/10

Burkett, Michael; '91-92-93-94; F; #9; Toronto, Ont.; (19-29-48); 61/130

Buzak, Michael; '92-93-94-95; G; #32; Edmonton, Alta.; (2.98; 2,836 saves); 6/12

C

Cahill, Kelly; '74-75-76; D; #5; Grand Rapids, Minn.; (2-21-23); 59/118

Calder, Mark; '71-72-73-74; F; #16; Toronto, Ont.; (84-80-164); 41/93

Calvert, William; '50-51; F; *; Ville St. Laurent, Que.; (0-5-5); 3/6

Cammett, Bryan; '77; F; #17; Grosse Pointe Farms; (0-0-0),0/0

Calnpanini, Henry; '53-54-55; F/D; #5; West Springfield, Mass.; (1-8-9); 28/65

Campbell, Joseph; '76-77-78; F; #7; East Lansing; (27-42-69); 29/58

Campbell, Robert; '71 -72; F; #22; East Lansing; (0-0-0); 0/0

Carlson, Gustaf; '60; D; #5; Waltham, Mass.; (00-0); 0/0

Carr, Gary; '74; G; #I; Rexdale, Ont.; (4.43; 989 saves),0/0

Carter, Anson; '93-94-95-96; C; #22; Scarborough, Ont.; (106-72-178); 67/132

Chandik, John; '61-62-63; G; #I; Port Colborne, Ont.; (3.80; 1,780 saves), 0/0

Charest, Georges; '69; D; #6; Lewiston, Maine; (0-0-0); 0/0

Chaurest, Michel; '70-71-72-73; F; #11; Montreal, Que.; (64-58-122); 76/168

Checco, Albert; '60-61;F;#18; Hibbing, Minn.; (1-5-6); 1/2

Christofferson, Keith; '57-58; F; #9; Maidstone, Sask.; (7-5-12); 9/18

Christofferson, Melvin; '58-59-60; D; #6, Maidstone, Sask.; (4-7-11); 28/56

Ciungan, Gregory; '74-75; D; #23; Ecorse; (110-11); 3/6

Clark, Ron; '72-73-74-75; G; #I; Fredericton, N.B.; (4.25; 2,430 saves)

Clarke, Taylor; '95-96; F; #26; Rochester Hills; (21-18-39); 46/95

Clement, Sean; '85-86-87-88; D; #22; Nepean, Ont.; (14-43-57); 113/226

Clifford, Brian; '93-94-95-96; F; #14; Williamsville, N.Y.; (24-17-41); 28/56

Clifford, James; '78-79-80-81; D/F; #2; Amherst, N.Y.; (3-17-20); 70/151

Cole, Danton; '86-87-88-89; F; #7; Lansing; (6994-163); 57/122

Colp, Steven; '73-74-75-76; F; #7; Toronto, Ont.; (132-168-300); 72/158

Cooley, Gaye; '66-67; G; #23; North Bay, Ont.; (3.62; 1,344 saves)

Cooper, Lawrence; '54-55; F; *; Calgary, Alta.; (0-9-9); 1/2

Coppo, Michael; '64-6546; F; #7; Hancock; (4447-91); 23/54

Coughlin, Kevin; '76-77-78; F; #14, South Boston, Mass.; (23-41-64); 51/108

Counter, Douglas; '76-77-78; D; #22; New Market, Ont.; (3-32-35); 13/26

Coyne, John; '71-72-73; Mgr.; Pompton Plains, N.J.

Crane, Brian; '94-95-96-97; F; #21; Grosse Pointe; (21-21-42); 45/121

Cregg, Richard; '73; F; #9; Kirkland Lake, Ont.; (0-0-0); 0/0

Cristofoli, Nino; '66-67-68; F; #14; Trail, B.C.; (29-23-52); 28/67

Cummins, Jim; '89-90-91; F;#27; Dearborn; (2022-42); 112/304

Cunningham, James; '77; F; #15; St. Paul, Minn.; (11-25-36); 33/66

Curry, Edgar; '51; Mgr.; Bar River, Ont.

D

Daley, Daniel; '61-62-63; D; #6; Arlington, Mass.; (1-1-2); 10/20

Davey, Neil; '84; D; #3; Edmonton, Alta.; (1-56); 25/50

Dean, Scott; '93; F; #12; Lake Forest, Ill.; (2-35); 15/30

DeBenedet, Nelson; '67-68-69; D/F; #4; Copper Cliff, Ont.; (14-17-31); 38/79

DeCenzo, Mark; '75-76-77-78; F; #11; Grand Rapids, Minn.; (14-27-41); 17/34

Delellis, Joseph; '61; D; *; Leamington, Ont.; (00-0); 0/0

DeMarco, Frank; '70-71-72-73; F; #9; Sudbury, Ont.; (29-16-45); 11/22

DeMarco, Gerald; '69-70-71; F; #15; Sudbury, Ont.; (29-26-55); 24/51

DeMarco, Michael; '69-70-71; D; #3; Sudbury, Ont.; (8-38-46); 33/66

DeMarco, Robert; '67-68-69; D; #5;

Sudbury, Ont.; (4-31-35); 13/26

DeVuono, Alfred; '57-58-59; F; #7; Sault Ste. Marie; (29-14-43); 40/88

DiPace, Darryl; '78-79; F;#12; Mt. Clemens; (2424-48); 31/62

Distel, David; '80; D; #17; Southfield; (1-2-3); 13/26

Donnelly, Michael; '83-84-85-86; LW;#14; Livonia; (110-86-196); 76/161

Doyle, James; '50-51; D; #3; ThiefRiverFalls, Minn.; (2-7-9); 17/34

Doyle, Robert; '61-62-63; F.; #17/7; Montreal, Que.; (42-41-83); 22/44

Dredge, Bradley; '78; F; #28; Southfield; (2-13); 4/8

Drews, Uve; '71-72-73-74; D;#4; Atikokan, Ont.; (1-8-9); 18/36

Druckman, Marc; '50; *; *; Detroit; (0-0-0); 0/0

DuBois, Stanley; '54-55-56; F; #20; Detroit; (24-6); 2/4

Drzffett, Richard; '68-69-70-71;G; #25; Kirkland, Ont.; (3.54; 1,809 saves)

Duffett, Wayne; '66-67-68; F; #15; Kirkland, Ont.; (19-18-37); 23/46

E

Eisley, Jeff; ' 81 -82-83-84; D; #22; Detroit; (2380-103); 96/199

Elliot, Anthony; '62-63-64; F; #9; Blenheim, Ont.; (20-16-36); 20/40

Ellion, Charlie; '92; D; #26; Sault Ste. Marie; (00-0); 1/2

Enrico, William; '67-68-69; F; #18; Duluth, Minn.; (7-7-14); 11/25

Essensa, Robert; '84-85-86-87; G; #33; Toronto, Ont.; (2.68; 1,737 saves)

F

Fales, Thomas; '70-71-72; Mgr.; Dearbom Hts.

Fallat, Robert; ' 66-67-68; F; #7; Espanola, Ont.; (24-30-54); 44/115

Faunt, William; '65-66-67; F; #8; Sault Ste. Marie; (21-33-54); 11/22

Faust, Ralph; '66-67; Mgr.; Chicago, Ill.

Feamster, Peter; '77; D; #5; Detroit; (0-3-3); 8/ 16

Fernandez, Richard; '83-85-86; LW; #28; Dearborn; (11-8-19); 19/38

Ferranti, Steven; '94-95-96-97; F; #15; Sterling Heights; (31-50-81); 29/69

Fifield, WHliam; '70; F; #19; Agincourt, Ont.; (1110-21); 2/4

Finegan, Daniel; '69-70-71; D; #4;

Islington, Ont.; (1-6-7); 32/64

Finn, Frank; ' 79-80-81 -82; F; #18; Livonia; (3556-91); 50/127

Finneran, William; '50-51-52; D; #17/14; Wilmette, Ill.; (1-7-8); 4/8

Fisher, Gerald; '65-66-67; G; #I; Detroit; (4.05; I ,074 saves)

Flanders, Walt; '50; F; *; Grosse Pointe; (1-0-1); 2/4

Flegel, Gord; '82-83-84-85; C;#9; Regina, Sask.; (71-92-163); 38/88

Fleming, Ryan; '93-94-95-96; D; #28; Mead, Wash.; (5-26-31); 12/24

Folkening, Ryan; '93; F; #27; Williamston; (0-22); 7/14

Foote, Jack; '60; D; #3; Windsor, Ont.; (0-0-0); 3/6

Ford, Jack; '63-64-65; D;#5; Blenheim, Ont.; (318-21); 14/36

Ford, Michael; '96-97; F; #23; Vernon, B.C.; (4-4-8); 8/16

Forrest, Stuart; '65; F; #7; Birmingham; (0-0-0); 0/0

Foster, Norman; '84-85-86-87; G; #41; Vancouver, B.C.; (3.14; 2,407 saves)

Foumel, Claude; '60-61 -62-63; F; #16; Montreal, Que.;(37-28-65); 25/50

French, Douglas; '66-67-68; D; #6; Espanola, Ont.; (5-13-18); 69/152

Friedman, Alan; '60-61-62; Mgr.; Queens, N.Y.

G

Gaffney, Norman; '69-70; F; #24; Port Huron; (0-0-0); 1/2

Gagne, Rob; '90-91; Mgr.; Detroit

Gagnon, Gilles; '70-71-72-73; F; #10; Montreal, Que.; (67-87-154); 24/48

Gagnon, Marc; '78; F; #24; *; (0-3-3); 7/14

Gandini, David; '78-79; F; #9; Warren; (14-2135); 9/26

Garbarz, Doug; '91-92; D; #28; Dearbom; (1-67); 30/60

Gardiner, Todd; '81-82-83; F; #23; Livonia; (92-11); 8/16

Garvey, John; '72-73-74; F; #19; Framingham, Mass.; (2-6-8); 10/28

Gaskins, Jon; '95-96-97; D; #2; Pekin, Ill.; (211-13); 17/34

Gemmel, Curtisl '96-97; F; #8; Calgary, Alta.; (5-1-6); 7A4

Gemmel, Taylor; '96; G; #35; Calgary, Alta.; (0.00; 3 saves); 0/0

Gibson, Donald; '87-88-89-90; D; #2; Hartney, Man.; (22-47-69); 218/466

Gieche, Adelbert; '50; D; *;

GrossePointe; (0-11); 6/12

Gilmore, Mike; '89-90-91-92; G; #30; Farmington Hills; (2.91; 1,475 saves)

Gipp, John; '53-54-55; F/D; #18; Calumet; (1021-31); 24/48

Goble, Gary; '63-64-65; F; #18/17; St. Catherines, Ont.; (6-25-31); 13/26

Golden, Richard; '60; F; #19; Holyoke, Mass.; (0-0-0); 0/0

Gorman, Robert; '50-51; F; #11; Cleveland, Ohio; (5-10-15); 9/18

Gottwald, Paul; '79-80; F; #10; Troy; (12-22-34); 10/20

Grazia, Eugene; '55-56-57-58; F; #10; Springfield, Mass.; (24-20-44); 11/22

Greene, David; '57-78; Mgr.; Hamden, Conn.

Gresl, Michael; '97; G; #1; AmherstJunction, Wis.; (438; 25 saves); 0/0

Guolla, Steve; '92-93-94-95; F; #11; Scarborough, Ont.; (62-125-187); 23/46

Gustafson, Leif; ' 88; F; #28; East Lansing; (I - I 2); 0/0

Guzall, Ray; '88-89-90-91-92-93-94; Mgr.; Warren

H

Haight, Gary; '81 -82-83, '85; D; #24; Edmonds, Wash.; (27-100-127); 113/237

Hamilton, Brad; ' 86-87-88-89; D; #3; Thornhill, Ont.; (22-81-103); 112/248

Hamilton, Richard; '57-58-59; F; #10; Sarnia, Ont.; (20-47-67); 11/25

Hamway, Mark; '80-81-82-83; F; #27, Detroit; (98-103-201); 50/101

Hancock, John; '68-69-70; Mgr.; Grosse Isle

Hansen, Robert; '51,'53; F; *; Grosse Pointe; (31-4); 2/4

Harding, Jeff; '88; F; #24; Agincourt, Ont.; (1720-37); 62/129

Hargreaves, Richard; '63-64-65; F; #9/10; Winnipeg, Man.; (23-22-45); 52/112

Harlton, Tyler; '95-96-97; D; #6; Pense, Sask.; (4-19-23); 83/181

Harpell, Gary; '79-80-81-82; F; #16; Green Bay, Wis.; (20-40-60); 48/99

Harper, Kelly; '91-92-93-94; F; #23; Scarborough, Ont.; (30-51-81); 34/69

Harris, Robert; '75-76-77; F; #9; Scarborough, Ont.; (36-36-72); 40/80

Hathaway, Leland; '67-68; F; #16; Cranston, R.I.; (7-11-18); 6/12

Hawn, Louis; '53; Mgr.; Trenton

Heaphy, Donald; '64-65-66; D; #4; Copper Cliff, Ont.; (15-24-39); 45/101

Heaphy, Shawn; '88-89-90-91; F; #12; Sudbury, Ont.; (103-91-194); 111/239

Heaslip, Ron; '76-77; D/F; #24; Dundas, Ont.; (12-28-40); 88/229

Hendrickson, David; '54-55-56; F; #17; Eveleth, Minn.; (16-17-33); IV24

Hendrickson, Gustave; '60-61-62; D; #3; Eveleth, Minn.; (7-6-13); 14/28

Hiatt, Daniel; '81; F;#3; Seattle, Wash.; (0-0-0); 1/2

Hinkley, Robert; '50; *; *; Cadillac; (0-0-0); 0/0

Hirth, Mark; '89; F; #8; Ann Arbor; (7-4-11); 6/ 12

Hodgins, Brad; '97; D; #7; Duncan, B.C.; (313-16); 27/73

Hoff, Geir; '86-87; F; #10; Oslo, Norway; (6-2026); 30/68

Hogan, Dennis; '70-71 -72; F; #23; Sudbury, Ont.; (3-1-4); 6/12

Horcoff, Shawn; '97; C; #10; Castlegar, B.C.; (10-13-23); 10/20

Horsch, Mitch; '78-79; D; #25; Hastings, Minn.; (1-9-10); 19/46

Hotchkiss, Harley; '50; F; *; Straffordville, Ont.; (2-2-4); 1/2

Hourigan, William; ' 74; F/D; #18; Detroit; (4-610); 8/16

Houtteman, Lee, '80; F; #24; St. Clair Shores; (0-1-1); 3/6

Houtteman, Richard; '69,'71; F; #18; St. Clair Shores; (3-1-4); 8/16

Howell, Carl; '65; G; #1; Muskegon; (1.8; 77 saves)

Hruby, Paul; ' 57-58-59; F; #18; Chicago,Ill.; (02-2); 0/0

Huesing, Theodore; '77-78-79-80; D; #3; Detroit; (25-76-101); 74/180

J

Jackson, Karl; '54-55-56; F; #17; Mohawk; (43-7); 3/6

Jacobson, James; '62-63-64; D; #8/3; Marquette; (13-28-41); 82/202

Jacobson, Michael; '65-66-67; F; #10; Copper Cliff, Ont.; (56-39-95); 48/96

Jakinovich, Lawrence; '71-72; F; #19; Detroit; (6-3-9); 4/8

James, Kenneth; '55-56-57; F; *; Samia, Ont.; (42-6); 8/16

Jasson, Robert; '56-57-58; D, #4; Winnipeg, Man.; (12-22-34);

29/58

Jelacie, Tony; '78; F; #27; Brainerd, Minn.; (3-58); 2/4

Johnson, Jack; '75-76-77; D; #2; Bloomfield Hills; (8-14-22); 34/68

Johnson, James; '75-76-77-78; F; #16; Bloomfield Hills; (23-31-54); 43/86

Johnson, Robert; '68-69-70; G; #1; Farmington; (4.32; 1,051 saves)

Johnstone, Walter; '61-62-63; F; #12; Copper Cliff, Ont.; (31-55-86); 21/42

Juntikka, John; '67-68-69; D; #18/23; Houghton; (0-4-4); 0/0

K

Kauppi, Donald; '50; F; *; Gardner, Mass.; (6-511); 5/10

Kelly, David; '74-75-76-77; F; #10; Toronto, Ont.; (31-40-71); 63/126

Kempf, Robert; '60-61; D;#5; Duluth,Minn.;(07-7); 14/28

Keyes, Richard; ' 95-96-97; F; #55; Kalamazoo; (36-38-74); 90/214

King, Gordon; '52-53-54-55; F; #9; Little Current, Ont.; (28-30-58); 31/62

Klasinski, Paul; '77-78-79; F; #21; Stevens Point, Wis.; (23-26-49); 62/149

Kozakowski, Jeff; '96-97; D; #27; Garden City; (9-28-37); 33/80

Krentz, Dale; '83-84-85;F;#15; Steinbach, Man.; (47-74-121); 43/110

Kruse, Eric; '92-93-94; G; #1; Ann Arbor; (3.98; 301 saves)

L

Lackey, Carl; '62-63-64; D; #2; Sault Ste. Marie; (12-38-50); 27/57

Lackey, Thomas; '61-62-63; F; #14; Sault Ste. Marie; (32-24-56); 10/20

LaCoste, Andre; '59-60-61; F; #10; Sudbury, Ont.; (26-38-64); 9/18

Lakian, Craig; '79-80-81-82; F; #15; West Bloomfield; (18-30-48); 33/66

Laking, Alan; '70-71-72; F; #12; Garson, Ont.; (4-5-9); 2/4

Lamarche, Andre; '81-82-83; D; #21; Drummondville, Que.; (1-4-5); 13/34

Lambros, James; '92; D; #6; Sault Ste. Marie; (00-0); 0/0

Lanschwager, Kurt; '78-79-80; Mgr.; Frankenmuth

LaPointe, James; '73; G; #1; Ann

Arbor; (5.00; 20 saves)

Lassila, Gordon; '56; D; #5; Mohawk; (1-3-4); 9/24

Lawrence, James; '63-64-65; F; #14/19; Blenheim, Ont.; (10-12-22); 17/42

Leiter, Ken; '80-81-82-83; D; #5; Detroit; (1264-76); 115/241

Lewin, Dennis; '63-6s65; Mgr.;ForestHills, N.Y.

Lewis, Dwight; ' 70-71; D/F; #23; Salisbury, N.B.; (3-3-6); 4/8

Loeding, Mark; '96-97; F; #25; Trenton; (136-19); 37/82

Lord, Richard; '51-52-53; F;#10; Montreal, Que.; (18-17-35); 73/173

Lubanski, Edward; '77; F; #28; Oak Park; (2-13); 7/14

Luongo, Christopher; '86-87-88-89; D; #6; Fraser; (12-57-69); 75/159

Lycett, James; '87-88; F; #18; Trenton; (0-2-2); 5/11

Lynett, Leo; '78-79-80-81; F; #19; Williamsville, N.Y.; (64-78-142); 21/42

M

Maas, Greg; '76; G; #30; Fraser; (6.85; 100 saves)

MacDonald, Glen; '57-58-59; F. #15, Regina, Sask.; (7-10-17); 9/18

Mack, Leslie; '51; Mgr.; Detroit

MacKenzie, William; '56-57-58-59; F; #11; Calgary, Alta.; (18-12-30); 4/8

Maki, Alfred; '51; D; *; Hancock; (0-1-1); 2/4

Marshall, Christopher; '88; F; #26; Quincy, Mass.; (0-2-2); 14J27

Martin, Michael; '63; Mgr.; East Lansing

Martin, Robert; '80-81-82-83; F; #11; Candiac, Que.; (50-40-90); 51/105

Mayes, John; '52-53-54-55; F; #10; London, Ont.; (44-48-92); 31/62

Mazzoleni, Mark; '77-78-79-80; G; #31; Green Bay, Wis.; (5.41; 2,094 saves)

McAndrew, Brian, '65-66-67; F; #12; Copper Cliff, Ont.; (44-68-112); 40/106

McAuliffe, David; '90; D; #19; East Lansing; (01-1); 0/0

McCauley, Wes; '90-91-92-93; D; #21; Georgetown, Ont.; (8-25-33); 48/100

McCormick, William; '50-51-52; F; #8; Ft. Dodge, Iowa; (26-13-39); 12/30

McCue, Kenneth; '73-74; Mgr.; Springfield, Ill.

McDonald, Timothy; '75-76-77-78;

D/F; #4; Grand Rapids, Minn.; (16-59-75); 60/129

McFall, Daniel; '82-83-84-85; D; #6; Buffalo; N.Y.; (36-76-112); 69/138

McLaughlin, Marty; '76-77-78; F; #18; Trenton; (13-15-28); 14/28

McReynolds, Brian; '86-87-88; F; #27; Penetanguishene, Ont.; (40-73-113); 90/196

McSween, Donald; '84-85-86-87; D; #5; Plymouth; (28-101-129); 66/132

Menoni, Glenn; '73-74; F; #26; Chicago, Ill.; (22-4); 4/8

Messier, Joby; '89-90-91-92; D; #22; Regina, Sask.; (21-48-69); 122/284

Messier, Mitchell; '84-85-86-87; F; #12; Regina, Sask.; (86-124-210); 95/194

Michelutti, Robert; '70-71-72; F; #8; Sudbury, Ont.; (11 -27-38); 19/38

Mikkola, Thomas; '65-66-67; F; #20; Copper Cliff, Ont.; (48-72-120); 16/43

Miller, Dean; '78-79; F; #17; East Lansing; (410-14); 2/4

Miller, Elwood; '56,'59; D; #3; Regina, Sask.; (3-3-6); 42/95

Miller, Kelly; ' 82-83-84-85; F; #10; Lansing; (8282-164); 31/66

Miller, Kevin; ' 85-86-87-88; F; #8; Lansing; (61 140-201); 133/277

Miller, Kip; '87-88-89-90; F;#9; Lansing; (116145-261); 137/299

Miller, Lyle; '64; F; #18; Regina, Sask.; (I -3-4); 7/14

Moroney, Brendon; '73-74-75-76; F; #8; Sudbury, Ont.; (62-45-107); 87/174

Moroney, Terry; '58-59-60; F; #7; Sudbury, Ont.; (52-28-80); 22/60

Mulcahy, Matthew; '64-65-66; F; #7/16; Dearbom; (7-5-12); 15/33

Murfey, Christopher; '72-73-74; D; #2; Oak Park; (19-51-70); 38n6

Murphy, Joe; '86; F; #9; Vancouver, B.C.; (2437-61); 25/50

Murray, Patrick; '88-89-90; F; #16; Dublin, Ont.; (59-124-183); 55/127

Murray, Rem; '92-93-94-95; F; #8; Dublin, Ont.; (71-147-218); 35/81

Musat, Nicholaus; '62-63-64; D; #7/4; Detroit; (1-11-12); 47/97

Muscari, John; '77-78; Mgr.; Springfield, Pa.

Mustonen, Thomas; '59-60-61; F; #9; Detroit; (111-12); 47/97

Muzzatti, Jason; '88-89-90-91; G; #29; Woodbridge, Ont.; (3.23; 2,928 saves)

N

Nawojczyk, Ronald; '77-78; Mgr.; Piscataway, N.J.

Nemer, Guy; '80; Mgr.; Southfield

Nicoli, Derio; '52-53-54-55; D/F; #3; Copper Cliff, Ont.; (21-36-57); 108/247

Norrnan, Robert; '58-59-60; D; #2; Simcoe, Ont.; (4-15-19); 62/124

Norris, Dwayne; '89-90-91-92; F; #14; St. John's, Newf.; (105-113-218); 77/192

Northey, Richard; '51-52-53; D/F; #4; Virginia, Minn.; (7-13-20); 15/30

Norton, Steve; '91 -92-93-94; D; #4; Mississauga, Ont.; (3-22-25); 87/174

Nowland, Tom; '85; G;#l; Ann Arbor; (3.70; 55 saves)

Nowotarski, Jark; '75-76; Mgr.; Detroit

Nystrom, Carl; '54; D; *; Marquette; (0-0-0); 0/0

O

O'Connor, Daniel; '69; D; #2; Montreal, Que.; (0-3-3); 12/24

O'Connor, Mictael; *; Mgr.; Taylor

O'Keefe, Kevin; '97; F; #12; Barrington, Ill.; (3-8-11); 3/6

Olmstead, Dennis; '72-73-74-75; F; #14; East Lansing; (14-19-33); 23/54

Olson, Michael; '68-69-70; F; #20; Peoria, Ill.; (1-0-1); 1/2

Olson, Richard; '70-71-72; D; #21; Peoria, Ill.; (2-11-13); 67/145

Olson, Weldon; '52-53-54-55; F;#14; Marquette; (71-54-125); 49/112

Omiccioli, Joseph; '79-80-81-82; F; #7; Timmons, Ont.; (29-37-66); 18/36

Orme, Malcolm; '62-63-64-65; F; #20; Kirkland Lake, Ont.; (21-33-54); 26/55

Ostrofsky, Jason; '95-96-97; Mgr.; Midland

O'Toole, Michael; ' 87-88-89; F; #23; Don Mills, Ont.; (17-24-41); 77/178

Oulahen, Steven; ' 74; F; #22; Leamington, Ont.; (0-0-0); 1/2

Ozybko, Edward; '59-60-61; D/F; #4/5; Guelph, Ont.; (2-11-13); 41/103

P

Panks, Gary; '61; F; #20; Sault Ste. Marie; (0-1I); o/o

Paraskevin, Kenneth; '78-79-80-81;F; #20; Detroit; (43-36-79); 80/170

Parke, Ross; '56-57-58; F; #12; Winnipeg, Man.; (39-46-85);

19/41

Parker, Jeff; ' 84-85-86; F; #1 l; White Bear Lake, Minn.; (33-45-78); 123/255

Passerini, Harold; '52; F; *; West Springfield, Mass.; (8-5-13); 15/33

Pattullo, Robert; '68-69-70; F; #16; Dearborn; (18-19-37); 10/23

Pavelich, Paul; '72-73-74-75; D; #20; Allen Park; (2-20-22); 75/152

Perreault, Nicolas; '91-92-93-94; D; #2; Loretteville, Que.; (26-34-60); 148/308

Peterson, Carl; '57; F/D; #21; Plymouth; (0-0-0); 0/0

Peterson, Donald; '55-56; Mgr.; *

Phair, Lyle; '82-83-84-85; #17; Pilot Mound, Man.; (82-77-159); 119/257

Phillips, Charles; '67-68-69; F;#17; CopperCliff, Ont.; (10-9-19); 9/18

Pitawanakwat, Jeff; '90-91; F; #7; Wikwemikong, Ont.; (4-5-9); 21/42

Polano, Joseph; '57-58-59; F; #8; Sudbury, Ont.; (27-51-78); 19/46

Pollesel, Bruno; ' 57-58-59; D; #5; Copper Cliff, Ont.; (6-11-17); 53/117

Pollesel, Edward; '57-58-59; D; #6; Copper Cliff, Ont.; (13-27-40); 84/181

Polomsky, John; '54-55-56; D; #3; Cleveland, Ohio; (6-6-12); 34/71

Pomerleau, Bertrand; ' 54-55-56; F; #7; Lewiston, Maine; (7-7-14); 5/10

Price, Herbert; '70-71; D; #6; Farmington; (4-13-17); 52/116

Purdo, Thomas; '65-66; D;#5; Detroit; (3-15-18); 39/81

Q

Quirk, Martin; '61 -62-63; F.; #10; Montreal, Que.; (11-20-31); 36/72

R

Rasmussen, Gary; '71-72-73; Mgr.; Royal Oak

Raz, Steven; '52-53-54-55; F; #16; Lethbridge, Alta.; (20-28-48); 46/124

Reid, Delmar; ' 50-51 -52; G/F; #I; East Lansing; (7.02; 1,260 saves)

Rendall, Bruce; '86-87-88; F;#17; ThunderBay, Ont.; (35-34-69); 123/251

Revou, Robert; '51-52-53; F; #12; Lexington, Mass.; (11-15-26); 4/8

Reynolds, Robert; '86-87-88-89; F;#15;Fenton; (107-89-196);

98/196

Rice, Daryl; '73-74-75-76; F; #17; Richmond Hill, Ont.; (96-129-225); 102/204

Rizzo, Dee; '82-83-86; F/D; #25; Pittsburgh, Pa; (2-17-19); 34n6

Roberts, David; '70-71-72; D; #2; Detroit; (1033-43); 57/127

Roberts, Doug; '63-64-65; F; #8; Detroit; (5653-109); 44/122

Roberts, Jack; '58-59-60; F; #11; Detroit; (1713-30); 11/25

Ross, Tom; '73-74-75-76; F; #12; Dearborn; (138-186-324); 47/94

Roth, Ronald; '65-66; D; #18; St. Paul, Minn.; (0-1-1); 2/4

Roy, Robert; '53-54-55; Mgr; Hancock

Rucks, Arron; '79; F; #14; Santa Ana Calif.; (1017-27); 11/25

Russell, Kerry; '88-89-90-91; F;#ll; Kamloops, B.C.; (56-86-142); 95/198

Russo, Patrick; '68-69-70; F; #8/5; Sault Ste. Marie; (21-26-47); 21/45

S

Sauve, Joseph; '54-55; D; #6; Regina, Sask.; (37-10); 29/85

Schiller, Edward; '54-55-56; G; #I; Winnipeg, Man.; (4.26; 2,097 saves)

Schuster, John; '65-66-67; F; #21; Wyandone; (02-2); 0/0

Scialli, Vincent; '67-68; Mgr.; Birmingham

Schneider, Michael; '81-82-83-84; Mgr.; St. Clair Shores

Scott, Ron; '81-82-83; G; #31; Guelph, Ont.; (3.08; 2,884 saves)

Selinger, Joseph; '57-58-59; G; #I; Regina, Sask.; (3.09; 1,973 saves)

Sergeant, Dale; ' 54; F; *; Rochester, Minn.; (0-00); 0/0

Shackelford, John; '53; G; #18; Grosse Pointe; (3.75; 216 saves)

Shalawylo, Bill; '91-92-93; F; #33; Warren; (1113-24); 19/38

Shepherd, Craig; ' 88, ' 90; F; #20; Edina, Minn.; (6-2-8); 22/44

Shibicky, William; '84-85-86-87; F; #16; Burnaby, B.C.; (86-136-222); 159/323

Short, Jack; '73-74; Mgr.; Orchard Lake

Shutt, William; '79-80-81; D; #4; Mississauga, Ont.; (1-15-16); 47/108

Sibbald, John; '52; F; #12; Sault Ste. Marie; (32-5); 1/2

Siegel, Donald; '77; F; #27; Muskegon; (1-4-5); 5/10

Silka, Frank; '60-61-62; D; #4; Detroit;

(9-2635); 23/46

Simpson, Craig; '84-85; C; #27; London, Ont.; (45-96-141); 34/71

Sipola William; '70-71-72-73; F;#8/18; Vlrginia, Minn.; (26-27-53); 18/36

Slack, Michael; '76; F; #27; D'Anjou, Que.; (11-2); 3/6

Slater, Cbris; '94-95-96; D;#44; Mattawan; (1148-59); 37r74

Smith, Chris; '93-94-95-96; D; #7; Canton; (2138-59); 80/160

Smith, Thomas; '75; D; #25; Springfield, Mass.; (1-3-4); 20/48

Smith, William; '66-67; Mgr.; Ypsilanti

Smolinski, Bryan; '90-91-92-93; F; #15; Genoa Obio; (80-101-181); 97/219

Smyl, Harvey; ' 83-84-85; F; #7; St. Paul, Alta.; (26-37-63); 110/258

Sokoll, Randolph; '69-70-71; F; #14; Detroit; (4541-86); 31/62

Springer, Ronald; '68-69; D; #22; St. Clair Shores; (1-0-1); 5/10

Stewart, Jamie; '88-89-90; G;#37; Langley, B.C.; (4.07; 436 saves)

Stewart, Michael; '90-91-92; D; #3; Indus, Alta.; (6-21-27); 45/109

St. Jean, Donald; '72; F; #20; Sudbury, Ont.; (914-23); 7/14

Stoltzner, Michael; '78-79-80-81; F; #9; Arlington Hts., lll.; (19-33-52); 29/66

Sturges, John; '73-74-75-76; F; #15; Scarborough, Ont.; (77-132-209); 123/287

Suarez, Joseph; '50-51; D; #2; Dearborn; (1-34); 12/32

Suk, Steve; '92-93-94-95; C; #16; Riverwoods, 111.; (39-130-169); 52/104

Sullivan, Chris; '93-94-95; D; #5; Hull, Mass.; (3-7-10); 27/55

Sutton, Daniel; '78-79-80-81; D; #26; Rexdale, Ont.; (12-39-51); 78/164

Sveden, Ronald; '54-55; G; *; Needham, Mass.; (3.65; 342 saves)

Swanson, Alan; '68-69-70; D/F; #1 l; Marquette; (13-18-31); 26/52

Sylvester, Dean; '95; F; #12; Hanson, Mass.; (1515-30); 11/38

Sylvia, Richard; '53; D; #4; Belmont, Mass.; (00-0); 0/0

Sztykiel, John; '76-77; G; #30; East Lansing; (7.43; 120 saves)

T

Taylor, David; '81-82-83-84; D; #29; Charlottetown, P.E.I.; (12-55-67); 59/137

Terpay, Alex; '64-65; G; #I; Tonawanda, N.Y.; (4.00; 332 saves)

Thomas, Arthur; '61-62-63; F; #11; Dearborn; (33-30-63); 2/4

Thomas, John; '52-53-54; F; #14; Winnipeg, Man.; (8-18-26); 25/50

Thomas, Nigel; '80-81-82-83; F; #12; Victoria B.C.; (14-15-29); 17/34

Thompson, Donald; '70-71-72; F; #7; Toronto, Ont.; (65-91-156); 53/125

Thompson, Michael; '90-91-92; F; #18; Scarborough, Ont.; (6-9-15); 12/24

Tilley, Thomas; '85-86-87-88; D; #21; Trenton, Ont.; (25-62-87); 98/198

Tosto, Rick; '86; F; #19; Dearbom Heights; (4-8-12); 5/10

Trocinski, Robert; '81-82; G; #30; Rochester; (4.00; 299 saves)

Turcotte, Real; '60-61-62-63; F; #15; Montreal, Que.; (32-60-92); 15/38

Tumer, Bart; '91-92-93-94; F; #19; Beaverton, Ore. (22-28-50); 62/133

Tuzzolino, Anthony; '94-95-96-97; F; #33; East Amherst, N.Y.; (39-58-97); 154/371

V

Van Meter, Clifford; '58; Mgr.; Detroit

VanSpybrook, Eldon; '58, '60; G; #I; Wallaceburg, Ont.; (5.41; 790 saves)

Vanstaalduinen, Bart; '93-94-95-96; D; #24; Indus, Alta.; (3-28-31); 71/142

Vedejs, Dainis; '64-65; D; #17; Grand Rapids; (0-1-1); 2/4

Versical, David; '76-77-78; G; #I; Grosse Pointe Shores; (5.12; 3,108 saves)

Volmar, Douglas; '65-66-67; F; #9; Cleveland Heights, Ohio; (74-49-123); 70/178

W

Waks, Charles; ' 54-55; F; *; Winnipeg, Man.; (310-13); 3/6

Ward, James; '52-53-54-55; F; #15; Portland, Ore.; (37-51-88); 28/59

Ware, Mike; '93; F; #17; Toronto,

Ont.; (1-1-2); 11/22

Watt, James; '70-71-72; G; #I; Duluth, Minn.; (3.82; 1,897 saves)

Watt, John Michael; '95-96-97; F; #19; Seaforth, Ont.; (53-45-98); 109/233

Watt, William; '68-69-70; F; #9; Duluth, Minn.; (25-37-62); 58/136

Weaver, Michael; '97; D; #5; Bramalea, Ont.; (0-7-7); 19/46

Welch, Russell; '77-78-79-80; F; #8; Hastings, Minn.; (78-122-200); 60/154

Wemer, Edward; '54; F; *; Wellesley, Mass.; (12-8); 4/8

Wherley, James; '61; G; #21; Intemational Falls, Minn.; (5.57; 271 saves)

White, Peter; '89-90-91-92; F; #17; Montreal, Que.; (75-155-230); 41/83

Wiegand, Josh; '94; F; #20; Northville; (4-3-7); 21/42

Wiggin, Conrad; '79; D; #22; Etobicoke, Ont.; (2-8-10); 25/53

Wilkinson, Bradley; '78; D; #5; Ann Arbor; (01-1); 2/4

Wilkinson, Neil; ' 87; D; #11; Selkirk, Man.; (34-7); 9/18

Williams, Mark; '63; D; #5; Duluth, Minn.; (23-5); 11/22

Wolfe, David; '52; Mgr.; Glen Cove, N.Y.

Woodward, Rob; '90-91-92-93; F; #20; Deeffield, 111.; (48-47-95); 79/170

Woolf, Harry; '62-63-64; G; #I; Brookline, Mass.; (5.00; 666 saves)

Woolley, Jason; '89-90-91; D; #5; North York, Ont.; (37-107-144); 38-76

Worden, Scott; '91-92-93-94; F; #10; Port Huron; (9-20-29); 62/124

y

York, Michael; '96-97; F; #61; Waterford; (30-56-86); 27/62

z

Zacks, Kenneth; '59-60-61; Mgr.; Hamden, Conn.

Congratulations to all Spartan Hockey Players and Coaches for all the Wonderful Memories.

MICHIGAN STATE
UNIVERSITY
ALUMNI
ASSOCIATION

Your Michigan State University

Alumni Association